The mental he...

www.triggerpul...

The**inspirational**series™

Overcoming adversity and thriving

Another Peak

Everest is Not the Only Summit

BY ALEX STANIFORTH

We are proud to introduce The**inspirational**series™. Part of the Trigger family of innovative mental health books, The**inspirational**series™ tells the stories of the people who have battled and beaten mental health issues. For more information visit: www.triggerpublishing.com

THE AUTHOR

Alex Staniforth is an inspirational speaker, adventurer, endurance athlete and mental health advocate from Cheshire. He survived the 2015 Nepal earthquake during his second attempt to climb Mount Everest and reached 7,125m on the sixth highest peak in the world, Cho Oyu. In 2017, he became the fastest person ever to climb all 100 UK county tops, fundraising for mental health and raising awareness of depression and eating disorders in men. He is also an ambassador for YHA England & Wales, PHASE Worldwide, and won the Pride of Britain Granada Reports Fundraiser of the Year, has raised over £85,000 for charities so far, and was shortlisted for the Cycling Weekly 'Best Charitable Initiative' award 2018. Alex is committed to helping others with their mental health by finding purpose and resilience through outdoor challenges.

First published in Great Britain 2019 by Trigger

Trigger is a trading style of Shaw Callaghan Ltd & Shaw Callaghan 23 USA, INC.

The Foundation Centre

Navigation House, 48 Millgate, Newark

Nottinghamshire NG24 4TS UK

www.triggerpublishing.com

Copyright © Alex Staniforth 2019

All rights reserved. No part of this publication may be reproduced,
stored in a retrieval system, or transmitted in any form or by any means,
electronic, mechanical, photocopying, recording or otherwise, without prior
permission in writing from the publisher

British Library Cataloguing in Publication Data

A CIP catalogue record for this book is available upon request
from the British Library

ISBN: 978-1-78956-077-0

This book is also available in the following e-Book and Audio formats:

MOBI: 978-1-78956-080-0
EPUB: 978-1-78956-078-7
PDF: 978-1-78956-079-4
AUDIO: 978-1-78956-081-7

Alex Staniforth has asserted his right under the Copyright,
Design and Patents Act 1988 to be identified as the author of this work

Cover design and typeset by Fusion Graphic Design Ltd

Printed and bound in Great Britain by Clays Ltd, Elcograf S.p.A

Paper from responsible sources

www.triggerpublishing.com

Thank you for purchasing this book.
You are making an incredible difference.

Proceeds from all Trigger books go directly to
The Shaw Mind Foundation, a global charity that focuses
entirely on mental health. To find out more about
The Shaw Mind Foundation visit,
www.shawmindfoundation.org

MISSION STATEMENT

Our goal is to make help and support available for every
single person in society, from all walks of life.
We will never stop offering hope. These are our promises.

Trigger and The Shaw Mind Foundation

A NOTE FROM THE SERIES EDITOR

The Inspirational range from Trigger brings you genuine stories about our authors' experiences with mental health problems.

Some of the stories in our Inspirational range will move you to tears. Some will make you laugh. Some will make you feel angry, or surprised, or uplifted. Hopefully they will all change the way you see mental health problems.

These are stories we can all relate to and engage with. Stories of people experiencing mental health difficulties and finding their own ways to overcome them with dignity, humour, perseverance and spirit.

In *Another Peak*, Alex opens up an important conversation around how we define ourselves and what we do once those definitions fall away. He leads us through his journey, battling both physical and mental strains, through which he comes to understand that perhaps he doesn't always have to be looking to the horizon for the new. In a world where we constantly feel like we have to strive for that next 'something', sometimes, the better path is being present in the now.

This is our Inspirational range. These are our stories. We hope you enjoy them. And most of all, we hope that they will educate and inspire you. That's what this range is all about.

Lauren Callaghan,
Co-founder and Lead Consultant Psychologist at Trigger

For Lakpa Thundu Sherpa, a humble man with a giant heart, who always looked for those less fortunate.

For Richard Marsh, who lived adventurously and gave his time so freely to help others.

And for everyone fighting the mountains in their own minds. No matter how steep the slope gets, the view on the top is worth the climb. Keep going.

Disclaimer: Some names and identifying details have been changed to protect the privacy of individuals.

Trigger Warning: This book contains references to eating disorders.

Trigger encourages diversity and different viewpoints, and is dedicated to telling genuine stories of people's experiences of mental health issues. However, all views, thoughts, and opinions expressed in this book are the author's own, and are not necessarily representative of Trigger as an organisation.

FOREWORD

by Elise Downing

'I would never go hiking back home,' said Jess as we sat outside a backcountry hut on New Zealand's South Island. We had met the evening before, both hiking the Abel Tasman Coast Track. Jess had quit her corporate job in London the previous year and was on a backpacking trip around Australasia. This was one of several hikes she'd done on her travels but, despite living just a few hours' drive from the Peak District, the Lake District, the South West Coast Path, the many mountains and trails of Wales and Scotland, she had never explored at all back home. Sitting there outside that hut, even with all the sandfly bites and blisters, she was glowing but it had taken a trip to the other side of the world to get her outside with her walking boots on.

I don't think that's an uncommon story.

A weekend getting rained on at the top of a mountain in Derbyshire somehow just doesn't seem to earn you the same kudos as the exact same experience further afield does. And when you visit, say, New Zealand, ticking off a hike is a concrete item on the To Do List in a way that it isn't in the UK. The fundamentals are all the same though: beautiful views, incredible trails, tired legs, soggy sandwiches, camaraderie on the trail, the best beer of your life at the end. Perhaps the story of Great British adventuring just needs retelling. Perhaps it needs a facelift.

Adventure shouldn't be reserved for holidays and exotic places. By adventure I don't just mean big endurance challenges; I mean getting outside, seeing something new, feeling the fresh air on your face, the satisfaction of doing something hard, the peace of mind that comes with it.

When Alex set out to climb all of the UK's 100 county tops and cycle between them, he set in motion the wheels of something significant. He wanted an adventure and a challenge, sure, but Alex also wanted to open up the conversation around mental health, especially in young men, and to raise money for Young Minds. Of course he could have inspired people by continuing to rack up what are undoubtedly phenomenal achievements in the Himalayas, but by bringing his challenges close to home, Alex opened the door as wide as it could go. He invited people to come together, to see their own country in all its glory and to talk about the mountains, both metaphorical and literal.

When I embarked on my own British adventure in 2015, running 5,000 miles around the coast of mainland UK, I had friends who had explored around the world and told tales of hospitality and kindness beyond what I could imagine. They talked of being invited to stay in the homes of strangers, of eating with families, of being joined for miles and miles on bike tours by people they'd known for just hours. *That's lovely*, I thought, *but that'll never happen to me here on home-turf*. I prepared myself for a long and lonely year in a damp tent, eating cold porridge. But what I found, and what I know Alex found too, was that right here on our doorsteps, you can experience the same kindness. It's living and breathing in every community, in every town, and it makes the world seem a little less scary, a little more friendly.

And God knows we need that. We need more happy people. More fresh air and tired legs and hot cups of tea, and cold beers, and views, and sunshine, and people to talk to about the things we're finding hard. It's a vast oversimplification, of course, to say that time outside alone is a cure-all for mental health issues. Many, many people suffer from very real mental health illnesses which need more than just awareness; they need scientific research, medical advances and proper, qualified support.

But if spending time in the great outdoors is a tool that can make just one person suffer a little less, then that's a story worth telling. And if that same person can use the outdoors as a backdrop for a challenge which raises money to support those desperately needed services then it's a story that becomes even more worth telling – as Alex's story most definitely is.

INTRODUCTION

As the old adage has it: After every peak there is a valley.

Life is not all blue skies and beaches. And it's only when we accept this, that life gets so much easier to enjoy. When the black clouds roll out and the good days roll in, it's a potent reminder that things can, and do, get better. This unpredictability helps keep life interesting, and when I discovered that I could ride the waves of life's ups and downs, that understanding took me all the way to Everest ...

Finding purpose in life isn't usually the top priority for a 20-year-old man. But by that age, I had already been fortunate to have seen and experienced things that many people could only dream of. (True to the same old peaks and valleys adage, I'd seen and experienced some things that inspired nightmares too.)

I think it all started at school. Most kids want to fit in at school. Not me. I was terrified of fitting in and sought out approval in different ways. Childhood epilepsy got in the way of the sort of carefree lifestyle a 10-year-old normally enjoys, while going to high school with a humiliating stammer stood me out a mile more. The relentless bullying I suffered didn't exactly acclimatise me either. I believed I was born to fail.

Fortunately, I discovered that life didn't have to be this way. Somehow, I worked out that the course of my life was in my hands. At 13, I caught the bug for big challenges: it started with a tandem paragliding flight, and then a holiday to the Lake District in 2010 introduced me to hillwalking for the first time. This single experience was responsible for planting the dream of climbing Mount Everest in my invincible young mind. It was an epiphany of finally feeling good enough, and rising above my own self-doubts. Life was getting better, and I began working my way towards achieving my dream of climbing Everest. It occurred to me that simply working hard enough made most things possible. By 16, I had completed the National Three Peaks Challenge – climbing the highest peaks of Scotland, England and Wales in about 24 hours. At 17 came Mont Blanc, the highest peak in the Alps, raising over £6,000 for charity in the process.

After sixth form, I abandoned university applications in favour of a course at the University of Life! Outdoor challenges had become my outlet for proving myself right – and the bullies wrong. But the after-effects of bullying cut deep. Riddled with self-doubt, a simple teenage break-up sent me spiralling into depression.

That's when I discovered the transformative power of running; throwing all my negative energy into running, I began to run the blues away. Exercise was more than a challenge, it was a pillar of everyday life, a human need, no less important than sleep. Losing myself beneath the canopies and the patter of pounding trails inspired observations so vivid that my mind even surprised itself. Running linked everything together in a world where everyone was connected, but nothing was connecting.

Peaks and valleys again ... A simple road running injury stopped me taking part in any outdoor sporting activities for most of a year. While I had the benefit of experience on my side when depression returned, I couldn't run it off this time. The forced withdrawal reminded me how dependent on the natural highs of exercise I had become. The ball was taken out of my court for the first time in years. It hit me hard. Without the adrenaline of running to sustain me, I found my control in food instead. While injured, focusing on nutrition and improving my diet would supposedly make me a better runner when the injury healed. But this seemingly positive and proactive step would turn out to be the unhealthiest thing I could ever do. Hours of research created a fascination with diet and a list of "bad" foods that athletes should avoid – a small sacrifice to help them reach their ambitions. And so, I embarked on a draconian regime of disciplined eating, experimenting with 24-hour fasting, and cutting out the sweet foods I loved all at once. Like any fad diet, these unrealistic boundaries eventually slipped, and I gave in to the urges.

Once I had "failed" then there was little reason to stop. The all-or-nothing mindset could rarely settle for one cookie or slice of cake – one usually ended in the entire box, and wolfing down anything that people wouldn't miss. Ice cream, chocolate, biscuits, crisps, desserts, or anything that met the vague "bad" criteria went down in overwhelming proportions. Even porridge covered in sugar would suffice. These mammoth bingeing sessions brought a rush, a kick, a sense of relief; a different kind of fix. The high was short-lived; followed by intense guilt, panic, and self-loathing. There was only one option ...

One evening, I forced myself to throw up in the grass outside. It was disgusting – but exhilarating. Being able to have my cake and eat it came as a revelation: a game-changer. But soon enough, I realised that it was not such a glamorous solution after all. I soon discovered that "it" had a name: bulimia nervosa.

I had recovered back to fitness and attempted a climb of Baruntse, a 7,129m peak in the Himalayas, reaching 6,600m before the acute mountain sickness forced me down. All the while, I continued climbing the exhausting mountain of bulimia day by day, at the mercy of my emotions as life balanced from one extreme to the other.

I was just 18 when I went back to Nepal in 2014. One day away from Everest Base Camp, tragedy struck. An avalanche in

13

the Khumbu Icefall killed 16 climbing Sherpas. The dream was over. But if anything, the disaster on Everest only strengthened my resolve to do more, achieve more, and raise more money for charity. And it felt as if Everest was still waiting for me.

In 2015, at the age of 19, I attempted to climb Everest again. Only a matter of fate had us leaving our tents at Base Camp and creeping through the twinkling ice of the Khumbu Icefall to Camp One when an earthquake hit Nepal and the same tents were martyred to the mountain, along with 22 others who perished in the freak avalanche that followed. We had drawn the long straw; the valley of silence left us blissfully oblivious to the destruction below at Base Camp, where our home on the mountain resembled a plane crash. Losing three of our team-mates left a heavy conscience, and it shook my life beliefs to the core. All I knew was that I owed it to Pasang Temba, Kumar and Tenzing to make my life count on their behalf; I just wasn't sure how I was going to do that yet.

To begin with, I helped form a Walk For Nepal event, which raised over £35,000 for a Nepalese charity over three years. But I knew I still had more to contribute ...

Back home in my home village of Kelsall in Cheshire I found new peace with the world. On radiant midsummer nights on the bike, hearing birdsong above the hedgerows, feeling the warmth filling my bones, and seeing the sun set behind Sandstone Ridge all helped remind me how beautiful the world could be. And I knew I had to keep trying – if I kept throwing good stuff at the wall, it would surely start to stick soon enough.

It still left the question of how anybody could rescue their dream from drowning in the conventional path of life. Our dreams could be replaced – lives could not – and I had been lucky to return home safely. But the journey to achieve the Mount Everest goal had dictated my daily life for so long. Everything was pitted against the question: will this help me reach the goal? I had raised over £30,000 in corporate sponsorship to fund a place on an expedition while I'd been doing my A Levels. Not that I had ever taken academia too seriously, but this all-or-nothing approach was far from sustainable – I couldn't be at fever pitch all the time – and it left an intense fear of idleness. I hadn't survived the avalanche to sit around aimlessly watching TV. Being a busy idiot and hopping from one challenge to another had saved me from facing up to something. When things stopped, I felt like I had nowhere left to run.

So I kept forcing myself out of the door, and when the seasons changed, I carried on running under the sickly glow of streetlights in winter blackness, always looking for a sense of purpose. Running gave me strength and determination, reminding me what I could achieve. As the months went by, I started to believe the difficulties of the injury were in the past. But my sense of purpose was still in recovery.

For a while, my purpose was simplified to numbers on the sports watch, or nothing at all. Bracing the wind, breathing hard, negating the twists and turns; the world seemed to speed up and slow down at the same time until I found my place within it, and the surge of feel-good chemicals somehow made things right. Raising my heart rate lifted my mood, if only for a while, and I just learnt to make the most of it while it lasted. Depression tagged along, barking at my heels, no matter how fast I ran. *What more do you want?* screamed inside my head. Maybe it wasn't about escaping the thoughts at all, but letting them pass.

Everyone might have assumed that I was living the dream: I had discovered a career as a professional speaker, writer, and brand ambassador, sharing my adventure experiences with business teams and schools. Empowering others – and myself – was the most rewarding job in the world. And a more comfortable life sometimes felt more appealing, though once I had experienced the world from such otherworldly places, it was difficult to find the same enthusiasm for everyday things.

Stammering and public speaking were an unlikely duo. I had lived most of my life unable to express myself the way I wanted, continually apologising, and terrified of appearing rude when I couldn't respond to a passing "hello" in the street. My stammer still turned up to social events; I could stand on stage and talk fluently to hundreds of people, then struggle to ask for a bus ticket on the way home. The willingness to stand up anyway and embrace this vulnerability garnered extra respect from the audience. When giving talks, someone once joked that at least the stammer made me more memorable.

It had taken months to be able to speak openly about the Everest experience that was still raw in my mind. As I began speaking to 90 eager children at a school one morning, the stammer began to pull me further down. The children sniggered innocently. Afterwards I was hounded by a mob asking for a signature on scraps of paper, homework, and Pokémon cards.

Businesses were less forgiving, and in a boardroom one afternoon, the stammer had seen straight through this false enthusiasm and returned with a vendetta. It was dire enough that even the laptop shut down halfway through; almost sparing itself the embarrassment. I wanted to get out; I didn't really want to be anywhere.

I ran the final 16 miles home. Most people might look forward to getting home from work and putting their feet up, but the reality for me was like opening a door into the same room. Until I could re-discover the same motivation that got me to Everest twice before, I knew I had to find a new incentive. Before I knew it, this mindless protest had become two cream doughnuts, a multi-pack of cookies, a family-sized chocolate bar, two chocolate muffins, and a festive coffee drink with enough sugar to fuel a car. There was nowhere to purge. Panic set in. With my suit stuffed into my rucksack and swapped for running shoes, I had transformed from confident international adventurer to depressed Forrest Gump.

But each mile I ran was a mile further from these thoughts. Concentration was essential on the trails to prevent coming a cropper on the obscured tree roots, especially considering my ability to trip over a smooth pavement. No matter how fast I ran, life slowed down to a pace that made sense, where I could finally appreciate the little things, from chirping birds to the satisfying crunch of leaves underfoot. In the comforting grasp of nature, it was bewildering that I had to stuff my face to motivate myself to be there.

Sixteen miles later I landed on the stairs at home with a clearer head than the one I'd left with. The usual endorphin rush struggled to get past the blood and mud congealed around my ankles. It felt like a moment of decision, but as autumn 2015 slipped away, the days and weeks continued to blur together with no real agenda.

I felt like I was pulling away; hurtling down the hill with no brakes. Simple phone calls became too much for me, emails had to do. I cancelled meetings for the first time, and opted out of my sponsor's Christmas party. I started avoiding all social events – buffets were too risky. I thought that training for a half marathon would hold me accountable, but even this ended in protest – I gave up eight miles in and walked off home. Some days, taking a few steps forwards was the best I could do. Perhaps it's only when we slip all the way to the bottom that things get real.

It seemed I needed something stronger. The idea of taking anti-depressants to solve something deeper had never sat well. We needed purpose; not pills. But I was exhausted. My GP prescribed sertraline, which gave me a temporary boost; a leg up to help myself when the summit was out of view.

Three weeks later, I returned to another half marathon with a different game strategy – to run further than eight miles. Niggling thoughts tried to knock me off, but I ended up knocking five minutes off my personal best and winning the under-21 age group instead.

Something was still missing, and it was looking straight at me from the photo on my bedroom wall – Everest.

For a while it had been pulled down and dumped in the spare room. Taking a year off from Everest was undoubtedly the right decision to put the demons of Everest 2015 to bed. But 2017 just felt too far away. The longer I went without a challenge, the more my anxiety believed that things would fall apart. After Everest, I couldn't shake off the thought that disaster could be around every corner; nothing would have surprised me any more.

When life got on top of us, natural instincts became impulses and led to rash decisions. I joined an expedition to climb Cho Oyu, the sixth highest peak in the world, in Tibet, the following autumn. Climbing it would give me the best odds of climbing above the 8,000-metre zone and returning to Everest with the biggest possible chance of success.

But it seemed that both the eating disorder and the depression would be accompanying me to Tibet. There would always be Another Peak waiting for me. Another chance to stand up and show the world what I was made of. The only way I knew to beat the clouds, in mind or in the mountains, was to get outside and climb above them.

PART ONE

CHAPTER 1

FALSE SUMMITS

"You climb to reach the summit, but once there, discover that all roads lead down" – STANISLAW LEM

The team convened at Heathrow Airport. There were five of us in total: Arthur, Kam, Charlene, me, and our unflappable leader, Rolfe Oostra.

Arthur was pretty laidback for his 50-plus years. I sensed this was only going to serve him well and learnt that he had already climbed Manaslu, the world's eighth-highest peak. I found myself slightly intimidated by his broad ex-rugby player physique compared to my slim runner's build. Kam was a boisterous Indian lady in her mid-thirties with an impressive climbing CV that belied her girlish manner. As a civil servant, Charlene was more reserved, but her mellow nature made her easy to get along with. Rolfe, had quite a rugged appearance, no doubt a consequence of the extreme corners of the planet he'd climbed, and guided people to. He exuded a natural energy which brought the whole team together. I felt glad to be under his eye.

We spent an eventful couple of days in Kathmandu, the capital of Nepal, taking part in some much-needed team building. Rolfe was clearly pleased at the growing dynamic between us all and I was relieved to hear him declare, 'This is going to be one hell of a trip!' Considering we were about to spend seven weeks in an environment that would rip any conflicts into the open, this boded well.

Physically and mentally, I felt that I had started in the right place.

*

We entered Tibet.

The communist rule of China felt intimidating: the in-flight magazine had described all foreigners as "aliens". The movement of power became quickly obvious as we began driving towards Lhasa. Large signs emblazoned with propaganda welcomed us to the region, or "China's Tibet". Other than this, there was nothing in English and it felt like we could have been anywhere.

A concrete jungle of high-rise buildings, grand monuments, and orderly streets rose before us, a pristine showroom tour of the parts of China they wanted us to see. The Chinese were clearly keen to make an impression on us, and though everything looked beautiful, it all seemed fake, as if we were on a movie set or peering at a postcard.

Tourists had to follow a fixed itinerary from the Chinese Tibetan Mountaineering Association (CTMA) and were accompanied by a dedicated driver and tour guide continuously. We were bundled into a hotel room in Lhasa. There were dazzling chandeliers hanging above water fountains and intricate artwork on the walls. The internet was heavily censored, but we managed to find a way through by using a VPN to get our social media fix. Even our meals were pre-arranged as our tour guide, Dawa, escorted us down a side street and through a back door into a restaurant. Naturally, he hung around the entire time. The watchful eye of

Big Brother was never very far away, and I couldn't stop imagining that saying the wrong thing would have us dragged by the collar out of a side door.

*

Our team was joined by six others sharing the Himalayan Guides permit and logistics. I was pleasantly surprised to see Daniel Wallace, a good friend from both Everest expeditions. His leader, Rob Casserley, would join us later. The four others were a Swiss cardiologist, Thomas, a burly Austrian called Stefan, plus two German women – Billi and Susanne. Billi was an expedition veteran with the wiry and weathered look, well known among the Himalayan mountaineering fraternity. Susanne was a veteran of the boardroom instead, her German persuasion softened by a friendly, motherly glow.

Unlike trekking in Nepal, we were set to travel almost entirely by road across the vast Tibetan plateau at an average of 4,500 metres, altitude to help us acclimatise. The road was called The Friendship Highway, which felt appropriate: being crammed into a minibus for nearly a week would either prove to be a great bonding exercise or would end up with fists being thrown.

A strict speed limit in Tibet made progress frustratingly slow. The mountain road burrowed into valleys of raging milky rivers and imposing hills. The arid desert surrounding us was often called the "Third Pole" for good reason, now bearing the scars of construction projects as China seemed intent on plastering the entire place with concrete. It all had me itching for trekking poles, rope bridges, and the lush green valleys of Nepal. The plateau seemed to defy all life, except for fly-ridden roadside eateries and the occasional mud-walled bungalows with flat roofs, prayer flags on their turrets.

We stopped next in the city of Shigatse, where the concrete jungle and neon lights returned. The acclimatisation stage was supposed to be gentle, and it left little else to do for the remainder of the day than wander and browse the shops.

The daily life was fascinating, and we fascinated the locals. Some of the team battled the language barrier to try and buy mobile phones, while I was engaged in a simple quest to find a McDonald's, plus any kind of Western snack among packs of pickled chicken feet and other weird delicacies in the grocery stores.

*

Our next acclimatisation stop in Tingri carried its own repertoire of horror stories, from sleeping on hay in farmers' huts to severe bouts of food poisoning. It was even once affectionately named by Lonely Planet as a "giant toilet".

Trucks and wagons passed through this half-mile outpost of decaying stone fronts, rusting railings, and hacked meat carcasses hanging on stands to dry or rot.

New buildings and hotels popped up along the way, not really blending in with how everything else looked, like they hadn't made a final decision on the way they wanted the city to present itself. Our hotel turned out to be far better than I'd expected. The dining room had a cosy interior of panelled chests and patterned curtains.

But though the world around me was vibrant and intriguing, I couldn't help the voice in the back of my head, reiterating my biggest concern: food.

Since being diagnosed with an eating disorder, I found myself increasingly wary of the pressures it put on everyday life in normal circumstances. And out here, circumstances were far from normal. At home, I was planned and prepared, but here, I couldn't help but feel almost sick with worry, and was overwhelmed by the food on offer. Fresh vegetables, stir-fried chicken and nuts, a whole variety of soup, and heaps of plain rice were always on standby. Greasy omelettes and bland doughy dumplings made for a carb and protein-rich breakfast, with a bit of jam to sweeten the deal.

I found myself looking forward to meal times and often went for third helpings, wandering off afterwards to find dessert in any form I could get. No one gave my third helpings a second glance. I reasoned with myself that the extra calories would come in handy when we climbed, to retain my muscle mass at such high altitudes. We needed to pack in the calories to help us through the ordeal we knew was coming for us.

It was nothing like the binge eating I'd experienced in the past, but bulimia always expected better. It buzzed furiously at my lack of discipline, especially when it kept reminding me that spending all day sat in a minibus didn't exactly constitute a calorie-sapping workout.

For the next week or so, there was very little to do but listen to music and read, or just gaze out of the window. It should have been an opportunity to just relax and enjoy being in the moment, but without having anything to keep me really busy, my mind kept going back to the bulimia, over and over again.

My bulimia was a tyrant. A barking Sergeant Major type. Always dissatisfied; always critical. I hated its voice in my head. It was fickle too, always creating reasons to eat too much, then playing it cool and leaving my conscious mind to excuse its behaviour. It was hard to tell who was speaking at times.

On this drive to climb an 8000-metre peak, silently battling with myself, I was also reading a binge eating self-help book called *Brain Over Binge* by Kathryn Hansen. Her words spoke to me like nothing else had before. Speaking about her own experience, she showed me that I wasn't alone in the way that I was thinking. The book introduced a five-step process for overcoming binge eating and bulimia that began by re-wiring the same neural pathways in the brain that had created the problem in the first place. It described the functions of the higher human brain and the animal brain in bulimia, the ego-dystonic relationship between both of them that explained why I felt so guilty for the behaviour, yet kept on doing it. Despite what people may have thought, there was much more to it than just simple willpower. By treating binge urges as neurological clutter rather than emotions, the way I usually did, the urges to binge became easier to resist. These urges were like muscle mass – use it or lose it – and the more I didn't act on them, the more I'd retrain the pathways. One final stage of the book used the power of excitement to fuel the recovery mission by celebrating the small wins of resisting the urges, gaining power, and quite literally creating a positive, physical effect on the brain.

Reading the book gave me hope that I might have a new way to put my brain over the binge, and put this big personal mountain behind me.

I had never really bothered with self-help books before this one. I'd wrongly assumed that I knew everything, that the torment of my mind would never end, and that recovery would always be a fragile matter of taking one day at a time. I had been referred for cognitive behavioural therapy (CBT) on the NHS and even paid for a private eating disorder therapist, although spending money only deepened my resentment towards the condition. (Of course, therapy in the form of expeditions cost heaps more.)

But now I was desperate enough to try anything and realised I had foolishly been expecting things to miraculously change without changing my approach. I had never really fully committed to all the angles required to make lasting change.

While being away from my home routine gave me a great opportunity for change, I knew there was no point in trying to instil these new strategies with the stresses that an expedition would have on my personal resources. I couldn't afford to let myself get carried away with it, but the slightest possibility of being able to wrest back some control was exhilarating.

One evening, I tagged along with Dan for one of his regular wanders to catch the sunset and escape the smalltalk of the dining room. There were few roads out of Tingri but this one teased around a corner until the ground fell into nothing and we set our sights on the mountain for the first time.

Cho Oyu and the north face of Everest rose clear in front of us. The blanket of darkness wasn't enough to cover their glory, the tips of them burning like coal. Dan and I eyed up our task, feeling insignificant faced with such a huge task before us.

Somehow, it just felt right.

CHAPTER 2

A brief off-road excursion brought us to Chinese Base Camp, little more than a truck-stop where the expeditions convened at 4,900 metres to acclimatise for a couple of nights. We stepped onto the dirt of the lifeless plateau, which stretched across to the edges of the Himalayas. We instantly began snapping away. Henry admonished us; we had forgotten his warning that photos were forbidden here in strict communist China. Climbers on past expeditions had actually had bullets fired at them in warning for disobeying this rule.

Our first night under canvas brought us food like that from home in the hands of our legendary expedition cook, Bhim.

We took an acclimatisation hike up the boulder-strewn hillside above camp the following morning and, as usual, I was the first to suffer with the effects of the high altitude. It was hardly surprising. I knew that this fatigue was all part of readying our bodies for what would follow. I reminded myself that it wasn't just an overnight process, that there was no use getting frustrated at the basic facts of physiology outside my circle of control.

But I couldn't help feeling that this was more about me than the situation. From Sports Day at school to the Himalayas, I had always been last. I had learnt to use that to my advantage; it helped drive me to succeed, to compete against myself, and find the fire to rise up and finish in the face of it all.

I felt much better when we left the next day for Advanced Base Camp. Despite his looming figure, Stefan followed quietly at the rear, moving deliberately slowly to keep his heart rate as low as possible to help his body adapt to the stress. This theory sounded good enough to me, but my efforts of self-preservation left Henry assuming I was having a bad day. This wasn't too far off the truth as we neared 5,300 metres, and my headache worsened.

Our first stop was an intermediate camp with pretty basic facilities. We called it "Noodle Camp." This barren roadside patch of grey moraine had nothing but our tents, herds of yak tied together, and a dainty shack that served as a boozer for the local staff. The rest of our Sherpa team were waiting for us with handshakes and hugs. I vividly remember their laughing and cheering as we had dabbed flour on each other's faces for the Puja blessing at Everest Base Camp the year before, and then their solemnity after the devastation that followed and challenged their beliefs.

I hadn't seen any of them since, and we embraced, silently acknowledging the events that had bonded us together. In Padawa, Dorjee, Lhakpa Thundu, Jhyabu, and Pasang, we had the strongest support team we could hope for, with 55 summits of Everest totted up between these five superhumans.

*

At breakfast, I had about as much get-up-and-go as a dead slug. Through a splitting headache, I forced myself to pack for the hike to Advanced Base Camp in bursts of effort, before slouching over a stone to wilt in the morning sun. The commotion of packing up tents continued around me. Dan came over urging me onwards. But the doubts this time weren't psychological. Rolfe came over with his trusty oximeter – a small device to test blood oxygen and resting heart rate to indicate how well the body was acclimatising. He clasped it to my finger. Seconds later, concern crossed his face.

'Shit! Man, that's low!'

My oxygen saturation was just 54%, which explained a lot. Anything below 90% back home would mean a hospital admission. Up here, at this altitude, we were looking at anything between 70 and 80 as the norm.

Rolfe consulted with Henry and returned, his usual vigour switched to seriousness: 'You're going back down.'

It was decided that I would descend for more acclimatisation. Rolfe was honest in saying that I'd be four days behind the others and compromised if the weather window came early. He shook my hand before I left, and I couldn't shake the feeling that he somehow knew this was it for me.

Feeling unwell himself, Henry had volunteered to accompany me, while the others happily walked off to Advanced Base Camp. Luckily it didn't take too long for the pick-up truck to arrive and take us back to the tents at Chinese Base Camp, where the rapid drop in altitude made a sudden difference to my wellbeing.

We unpacked into our tents where I sprawled out to recover. With my head still pulsing, I started taking Diamox, a drug to help with altitude sickness. Henry thrust biscuits and water through the tent door, rationing the limited supplies we had, and regularly called out from his tent to ask how I felt. When I struggled to answer, he quickly appeared in the doorway concerned. He asked me to do the Finger to Nose test – a simple co-ordination test for the deadly serious condition high-altitude cerebral edema (HACE). I passed the test and tried to reassure him that it wasn't HACE causing my loss of speech – it was my stammer. Henry let out a bellowing laugh.

'I just bloody hope you improve man!' he said.

Otherwise, I'd be in a truck down to Tingri and going home.

*

We went for tea in a rustic stone hut, stifled by smoke and barely tall enough to walk in. A decaying cabinet in the corner was stocked with Chinese fizzy drinks that had gone flat a decade earlier, with a battered stove and dirt clinging to the walls. The Nomadic Tibetan family spoke not a word of English, tapping prices into a calculator with blank expressions. Less than 10 days into the expedition, I hadn't anticipated being in this hut on the verge of medical evacuation, eating Pot Noodles of unknown contents.

It could have been worse.

On the bench opposite was a climber being examined by a doctor. He was pale and coughing with a sludgy crackle – it was clear from his prognosis that he had high-altitude pulmonary edema (HAPE). The American doctor introduced himself as Dallas. This climber wasn't even part of his team, but the climber's team had left him here, sick as a dog, and Dallas felt obliged to take responsibility for his life.

Henry turned to me at the sight of him: 'We're not joking!'

Back in the tent, I spent the afternoon buried in thoughts. All I could picture was failure.

I had the extra baggage of two Everest disasters to prove this theory in my mind. I just knew that I was going home and started to imagine my life returning without a success. My mind started playing out future conversations of how I would break this news to family and friends ... how I would have to learn to accept it within myself.

The disappointment of my supporters looked painfully vivid – especially considering it hadn't even happened yet. I even went as far as pre-planning the arguments and excuses I'd need on my return. I couldn't help but think that I'd have to reinvent myself, reinvent my career, and suddenly, everything seemed pointless.

It felt even more galling when I remembered that the limiting factor was not my own effort but my biggest asset – my body – letting me down, time and time again.

*

'Shall we eat at the teahouse?' Henry called.

Choices were easier with Henry: you told him when, or he told you. But I enjoyed his company and the chance to chat one-to-one. Every moment seemed to coax a story from decades ago.

'Me and Kame have been here for 40 years – me 12 times – so I'm not sure how, but we'll work it out!' he laughed, telling stories of another climber who had similar altitude problems on Cho Oyu, who also happened to be a retired Olympic athlete.

'Have you ever considered taking up sailing?' he added, after a moment's pause.

*

Testing my oxygen levels again, Henry was relieved to see the saturation had increased to a healthier 70-something percent. I continued to recover and quickly regained my appetite. As my body settled, the anxieties quietened too.

In the back of my mind, I knew Henry had to get back to Advanced Base Camp soon to get everything in order, and I was anxious that it would be easier for them to send me home prematurely, when I simply needed more time.

After a better sleep, I was relieved to see Rob Casserley arrive the following day with his cardiologist wife, Marie-Kristelle. Both Rob and MK, as we'd come to know her, had been on the team for both Everest expeditions and had become firm friends of mine. It seemed like I had a habit of meeting them in calamities. They checked me over as we convened for tea in the hut. Rob adopted more roles than doctor and leader – he was a mentor and someone I massively respected.

Rob picked up on my negative mindset straightaway. Getting stuck in a negative outlook meant that I was destined to fail, especially in an expedition where so much was weighted against us. I had become obsessed with the oximeter readings, constantly checking to see where I was. I'd liked to think that it was myself versus the mountain but now a golf-ball-sized gadget had more control than I did. Cho Oyu might have been a chance to start afresh, but experience told me it was better than to come to these high mountains without any sense of entitlement.

*

I shared a Jeep with Rob and MK the next morning up to Noodle Camp. They pressed on with Henry and it was decided that I would stay for an extra night to make a second but slower attempt to acclimatise.

Spending the afternoon bored out of my mind in the musty shack left me vulnerable to over-thinking. I switched to diaries and wished I could understand the Tibetan man who lived there instead of negotiating for noodles by sign language. Fortunately, Henry had sent Lakpa Thundu, one of the Sherpas, down to meet me with a tent.

Thundu was an unassuming man of slight stature and the strength of a lion behind his squeaky laugh. He was concerned for me and continually tried to drown me with flasks of tea. I retreated to my tent soon after the sun had set and turned the moraine a khaki grey.

Later, Thundu peered inside, shimmying to stay warm, holding a pack of Hobnob biscuits haggled from one of the nearby expeditions. The Sherpa instinct to go this extra mile never failed to amaze me. He was hesitant to share the tent with me; typically, he put his own needs second. He eventually agreed and clambered inside, proudly showing off the sleeping bag given to him by Sir Ranulph Fiennes as a token for guiding him to the summit of Everest years earlier. I crawled into mine, knowing I needed a good sleep if I was to continue, and accepted there was nothing to do but wait until the morning.

CHAPTER 3

Daylight was slow to warm the tent, though Thundu soon brightened the morning with a pot of tea.

'How are you feeling?' he enquired.

After a long sleep, I felt good to go and crawled outside. Thundu shook ice off the tent and refused any help with packing, insisting I save my energy for the day ahead.

From this far-back plateau, Cho Oyu lurked in icy shadows, silent except for the jingling of yak bells and the occasional rattle of a truck. I looked up with a smile, feeling strong in both body and mind as we began trekking to Advanced Base Camp. I kept my feet and mind grounded, and cast my eyes to the foot of the mountain. This was my second chance. I knew I might not get a third.

Passing the time trekking and chatting with Thundu was a privilege. His stories were inspiring. I thoroughly enjoyed listening as he spoke proudly of his two young boys, and his wife Bandi. He mimicked how she always told him not to climb, and though we laughed about it, we both knew the reality of what she was saying. But he knew he had to. This was their way of life.

I asked him what he might do if he wasn't climbing. He just shrugged. His mother was a farmer and still lived in his home village of Pangboche. His father had left them when he was three and, as a result, they couldn't afford schooling. This had brought him here today.

Thundu was so highly regarded as a climbing Sherpa that many climbers would simply not step foot on a mountain without him by their side. My own achievements paled into insignificance compared to his, yet I had made a career in sharing these stories. The sad reality was that most Westerners would only relate to hearing it from one of their own: Thundu's many achievements could only ever seem notable when achieved by someone in the Western world.

*

Thundu was always reluctant to take any of my food. He eventually gave in, after my pestering, and we shared a Twix chocolate bar. He assured me that Base Camp was only 40 minutes away. Sherpa predictions could be anything from 30 minutes to four hours off the truth, but I trusted Thundu.

The afternoon fog left us short-sighted, with each corner of the trail bringing false hopes, until specks of orange, yellow, and blue eventually started to appear where dozens of expedition teams had claimed their own corners of the rocky valley. We knew our team was having a Puja today – to ask for safe passage from the mountain gods. Thundu was especially anxious to be there, hurrying ahead as I scrambled over a rise and down into camp, trying to think of something poignant to say. Rob came running over with a pat on the back, relieved to see the confidence back in my smile. The rest of the team greeted us with hugs and asked how I felt. We had missed most of the ceremony and I superstitiously hoped that wouldn't mean anything sinister as I helped myself to the leftover cookies, Losar pastries, and prawn crackers.

I spent the afternoon settling into our mountain home with individual tents scattered between the boulder field, booby-trapped with guy ropes and sheets of ice. Our toilet was a crater in the rocks covered by a tent for public decency. Horror stories of dropped mobile phones made sure all my pockets were kept firmly zipped. The shower tent was little bigger than a telephone box. I wouldn't get a proper shower for weeks, but I didn't care. None of this was new to me, except the solitude.

Everest Base Camp had been a constant hive of activity with people coming and going at all times. Helicopters were banned in Tibet completely and there were far fewer expeditions. Nobody would make the effort to visit somewhere so remote without good reason, leaving us to our seclusion.

Base Camp life was tough yet beautifully simple. The sun became our timepiece. Once it dropped, the mountain fell from Indian summer to Alaskan winter in a matter of minutes, sending us running to our tents. Our daily routine was dictated mostly by our cook Bhim and his assistants clanging pans loudly to signal dinner was ready. Like feeding time at the zoo, we all flocked into the large dining tent.

Rolfe started to hatch a plan. Charlene had also been slow to acclimatise, so we would both take more acclimatisation time with two extra days to rest, get organised, and sort our gear. This would mean that we'd be three nights behind the others, and making one big rotation wasn't ideal, but it would give us a chance at least.

*

There was no morning alarm. A warming glow filled the tent like a cosy Sunday snooze, but this was all illusion: Cho Oyu's wake-up call was a bucket of iced water. The white pyramid stood in otherworldly proportion, hoisted up by icy ridges and sliced by rock bands. Another bulging peak of immaculate snow-ridges competed for attention across the glacier and the Rolwaling Himal in the sky behind ensured no space was wasted.

I'd missed waking up in the Himalayas.

Camp was already full of life as the team hurried around packing kit at the last minute and I watched them head off on their first trip up the slopes leaving camp to fall silent again. In the meantime, I happily took advantage of the opportunity to explore the camp undisturbed. Our sirdar, Kame, was kept busy managing logistics as the five climbing Sherpas ferried supplies up and down the hill, with 800 kilos of gear to move on the mountain before the climbing got underway.

I joined Bhim and Kame for tea in the kitchen tent. We lived such different lives, but I've always felt anyone can find common ground over a cup of tea. We had lots to talk about, though I was careful about bringing up the trauma of the disaster on Everest the year before, especially when climbers had rocked up a year later acting as though nothing had happened. Bhim had sustained a broken arm in the avalanche at Everest Base Camp. He'd shrugged it off as simply "very bad".

Entirely as expected, they had all picked themselves up and carried on as normal, as the Nepalese always did.

*

Charlene was good company, with a serious but methodical approach to the mountains. She was quickly enlisted as a photographer to take the obligatory sponsor photos with banners. We had little else to do besides making video diaries, playing music, reading, and washing clothes before the sun disappeared and froze them solid.

Sitting still didn't come naturally to me, though it was hard not to sit on the rocks and ponder our existence for a while. Trying to make sense of this landscape was exhausting. Rocks appeared to defy gravity as they clung to the high wall that shadowed us. Across from Base Camp was the snow-frosted crest of the Nangpa La, a beauty spot now turned into a resting place for Tibetan pilgrims.

*

Our peace was disturbed when the rest of the team returned with news of a huge explosion at Camp One where an oxygen bottle had exploded.

Rolfe was reliably first in the dining tent for his java fix before the trays of fried toast, pancakes, and porridge arrived. Shortly after 10.00am, we began a long hike through a corridor of 7,000-metre peaks. The sound of talking and rhythmic tapping of walking poles on rocks continued for hours as we waited for Lake Camp to appear.

*

Climbing over 6,000 metres' altitude never got any easier as I flopped into my tent at Lake Camp. 'Guten Tag!' Rolfe cheered, handing over a canister of gas to help us get through two nights here.

Lake Camp was a precarious spot in the shadows of this mountain crater where booming avalanches had kept the team awake a couple of nights earlier. Ant-like figures trudged up the scree slope opposite Camp One. Everyone at Base Camp had spoken fearfully about the "Killer Hill", earning it a variety of vulgar names, and I assumed this must be it. The trip so far had been a crash course in making assumptions that turned out better than expected, so it was best to wait and experience it firsthand – there was no other way up.

At nightfall, the simple comfort of clinging to a hot water bottle was like a big hug from Grandma. Drinking so much inevitably meant midnight toilet stops as my experiences with the pee bottle rarely ended well. Dashing outside for a pee had never been better: looking up to a beautiful expanse of constellations, ribbons of stars draped like glitter in the luminous darkness. It felt a little lonely without the Base Camp banter, lying in a seven by five-foot space shared with nothing but a few kitbags and gear scattered around.

*

To the sound of a hissing stove, I lay looking through the porch at the peaks across from the glacier. The last time I had been so idle – the previous winter – I'd been in the grip of depression, with plenty to do but very little interest or motivation to do it. Anxiety only wanted to run away, while depression had effectively broken my legs. I was a passenger in the paradox as they played tug and war with my mind and body. Now it was all reversed: there was little to do but I was filled with energy. I instinctively looked for things to fill the nothingness with something meaningful.

I was glad to finally get moving.

Rolfe, Charlene, and I left for our first foray to Camp One. I could only manage a few steps before my heart rate spiked and demanded me to stop. Looking too far ahead was unavoidable with Cho Oyu looming, but I forced myself to look for the rest of the team instead, who would be making their way down to thinner air. Human-shaped outlines soon bobbed into the blue horizon. I was excited to see them and show off my newly adopted positive mindset, especially to Rob and Dan. There were smiles and jokes as we passed, willing each other on. A fixed rope added extra security once the track met a slushy snowline and the ravine on one side fell steeper.

Camp One was perched on a broad saddle at the base of a ridge at 6,400 metres' altitude, though the afternoon cloud had closed in and left this high village feeling strangely claustrophobic. The Sherpas had done the leg work of getting our tents up. The others had left nothing inside but sweet wrappers, stubbed matches, and the gas stoves which would be our lifeline.

*

We sheltered inside our yellow bolt-holes. Boredom was enforced by the need to rest and recover, and the jump in altitude that took effort just to sit upright. Being idle was much easier when there was a good reason for it. The stove bubbled away for most of the afternoon to rehydrate and delay the headache from the jump in altitude. Hours passed in the mundane process of watching ice crystals and the air bubbles disappear into liquid, counting the minutes until it was acceptable to have dinner.

I could never get bored of watching the sunset from the porch of a tent though, no matter how many times I saw it. It was comforting to know that even the mountain giants went to sleep; their white edges melted into violet skies. It was the perfect catalyst for the lucid dreams that most high-altitude mountaineers experienced.

CHAPTER 4

Rolfe popped his head through with the dreaded oximeter in the morning. Again, my blood oxygen saturations were worryingly low. This time, I felt as fine as I might expect to feel at 6,400 metres' altitude – higher than the summit of Kilimanjaro. But the thought of something more serious sent me into a panic.

Henry had warned that getting HACE would mean an 'injection in the backside and getting the hell out of there'. Only now, we were at least a full day from the nearest road. There was nowhere to run to. I couldn't step out of danger, like the classrooms and hospital waiting rooms of my childhood. I couldn't take any deeper breaths, calm myself, take control. There was no choice but to confront it rationally. I tried to draw some comfort from the extreme worst-case scenario ...

If it happened, at least I'd die doing what I loved.

But if adventure didn't kill me, bulimia might. It was no myth that purging carried a risk of sudden death. And there were times when the worst possible scenario was a welcome thought, except when I was lying in bed with a pulsing headache, dehydrated, and a racing heart, wiped of electrolytes.

*

Arthur and Kam appeared the next morning and Arthur crawled inside my tent. We would be sharing as expected. High-altitude mountaineering wasn't the place to get picky about personal space. Luckily, he didn't take up much room. Even so, it took some co-ordination to get in and out of the tent without kicking each other in the face.

Acclimatisation days were spent resting, playing cards, and drinking copious amounts of tea. We were glad to get into action once the call finally came. Our high-altitude boots were laced up and we set off for the series of smooth humps of the northwest ridge. A narrow gutter had frozen into the snow and was safeguarded by fixed ropes. The ridge widened into a white thumb of fresh snow broken only by a thin trail towards the lips of ice wall ahead. I looked back as the world dropped away with bands of grey and white snaking through the valley.

The afternoon winds had me scuffling for the warm layers buried in the base of the bag – Rolfe gave me a deserved telling off for forgetting where we were. Getting up the ice wall was more awkward fumbling with a jumar, a locking metal device for ascending ropes, than a technical climb. It took a few minutes of excitement until Rolfe had belayed us over the top at nearly 6,800 metres.

Conditions weren't good to say the least, with high winds and snowfall. Rolfe announced this would be our high point and Camp Two was out of reach today. It would still be useful acclimatisation and we abseiled back down with quiet relief. Nervously, I looked over my shoulder at the ice wall, wondering where I would run to if I heard the booming roar of an avalanche again.

We spent another night at Camp One before making a welcome return to Advanced Base Camp to recover for the real deal.

*

Back at Base Camp, cabin fever started to set in.

Now we were waiting for the weather gods to play ball, and control was taken out of our court. I had full faith in Henry, Rolfe, and Kame to make things happen. There were meetings with other expeditions to avoid everyone rushing up at the hill in one swoop and falling over each other. Mostly it was to get the lesser-experienced teams safely out of our way.

We watched the mountain every day in hope. That sense of hope wobbled slightly when we woke to see avalanche debris scattered down the snow fields above Camp Two. The uncertainty left us in the "grey zone" where we had time to worry ourselves silly. All we could do was try to keep ourselves busy.

The oximeter was passed around and my score was repeatedly one of the lowest. I asked Rob for advice. I was worried this little device was about to end my summit bid prematurely. Rob grabbed the oximeter impatiently and ordered me to copy his rapid burst of deep breaths. The device reading suddenly jumped into the nineties and made his point clear.

Time passed. We re-organised the tent for the one hundredth time but had to accept that the mountain dust covering everything inside wasn't going to disappear. There was the usual Base Camp camaraderie, and a scrap of cardboard was salvaged to create a leader-board for our popular "Shithead" card game. The Sherpas often joined us and were greatly amused at earning the acclaim of Shithead.

Being the group baby by over 10 years meant I was often the butt of gentle piss-taking when conversation dried up, but I took it on the chin. On Everest, this dynamic had made life even more difficult than it already was, with people dismissing me as the gap year student on a loan from Mummy and Daddy. This time, I felt like a respected member of the team rather than an intern dragged along on the lunch break.

Being so close together coaxed everyone's true personalities out into the open and I enjoyed getting to know the team properly. Stefan was continually coerced into saying 'I'll be back' with his booming Austrian accent while Thomas was likened to Trevor Horn of eighties' band, The Buggles. Kam was like the big sister of the group with an apparent inability to blow her

41

nose. This habit got so annoying that I would walk for hours with headphones to hide the constant sniffling, hoping nobody would notice they weren't connected to anything.

Seven nationalities around one table made for interesting conversations and occasional clashes of opinions. Arthur was usually outspoken but wellmeaning, and Himalayan veteran, Billi, shared high-altitude tales with Rolfe. This wannabe G8 summit covered debates on everything from Brexit to entrepreneurial ideas and the meaning of life. It was often easier to sit back and pour another cup of hot chocolate from the tubs on the table, simply listening rather than getting involved. Staying in the dining tent was far better than trying to read a book by headtorch with cold hands, so I stayed in there often.

Later, we gained access to a satellite internet router from a nearby team that provided us with a weak Wi-Fi connection, bringing the tent to silence as everyone stared at their phones. It was thrilling being able to see how people in the outside world were responding to the soundbites of the trip. Until now, my friends Chris and Ste had been managing my social media channels with satellite phone texts relayed through Mum.

It was this element of story-telling that I loved best. Being on expeditions gave me the opportunity to share these unique experiences and perspectives with people who might never be able to experience it for themselves.

Once the clouds rolled in, the Wi-Fi disappeared and cut us off once again. The mood at Base Camp dropped. For a while, we had forgotten home and hearth – or at least put it to the backs of our minds – but now all that we had left behind came back into focus. We couldn't help but feel that we were dispensable, the world was carrying on perfectly fine without us.

I think we all relished the chance to escape the constant demands of daily life. But it also made me realise just how much I cherished my family and friends, and each time I spoke to them, I treated it as though it might be the last time.

Things obviously felt different after that, a little bit off. Perhaps speaking to our loved ones had heightened our anxiety of what was still to come. It affected me too. I waited until the card games lost interest and the tent was deserted, mirroring the kitchen at home in my silent midnight binges. I felt my heart racing excitedly, even faster than it already had at this altitude. Once undisturbed, I began guzzling down a handful of chocolate bars and energy flapjacks from the free-for-all snack stash. When I finished, I was guilt-stricken and lost touch of my conscientious self.

I knew being sick was out of the question. And I couldn't run like I did at home, often guided by the spot beam of a headtorch along pitch-black country lanes as I desperately tried to run off the sugar-coma of late-night bingeing episodes.

I felt desperate to explain to myself why the bulimia had followed me here, why I was suddenly more preoccupied by food and fantasising over chocolate-chip cookies than the 8,000-metre peak looming at the foot of camp. It seemed pointless, unnecessary.

The binge urges had come suddenly and unpredictably, as usual. They could have easily been lingering for days or weeks, simply waiting for the opportunity to grab my attention. While depression gave little reason to stop bingeing, this self-sabotage returned even during rosier times, and suggested something else was at play.

There were none of the obvious triggers. *Brain Over Binge* suggested that it wasn't emotional at all, but faulty wiring in the brain. I had learnt from the book that the urge to binge would pass within seconds and minutes, and that each time I managed to detach from the urges, they grew weaker. Rational thinking said that waiting at Base Camp was undeniably a difficult environment for any eating disorder: idleness, an excess of food, no running, and the continual comparison to other people's eating habits. They were all excuses that needed to be disconnected from the problem – urges to binge. I stopped trying to figure out my slip-ups, and stopped trying to label them as emotional failings. Instead, I tried to look on them as the result of a very simple human mistake, of listening to a few misfiring neurons in my brain.

Coming to this mountain wasn't going to miraculously save me.

*

The next day, we moved straight for Camp One and spent a night recuperating before going higher to Camp Two. Producing the kit list ready for our summit bid seemed almost too good to believe.

The team of five Sherpas was already burdened by huge loads of oxygen bottles and tents which meant our own rucksacks were filled to our ears. We spent hours deliberating over every gram of gear inside. We left a day behind the Germans and spread out across the glacier at our own paces. We rested briefly beside the path trying to muster some enthusiasm to tackle Killer Hill again.

The next day was make or break. I'd be climbing higher than I ever had before. Porridge sachets in a mug kept things as familiar as they could be. The extra acclimatisation should have made the steep ridge from Camp One easier, except a stomach bug had joined us too. It sapped my remaining strength.

After the ice wall, the going got even tougher and I was too knackered to notice more seracs looming above. By his own admission, Arthur had barely trained for the trip beyond a daily few miles of cycling to work and strength training. He was one of those people who had an irritating natural strength at altitude, fuelled by a solid mindset and self-assurance that made him a poster boy for the 90% mental, 10% physical approach. Moving slowly and often arriving last in camp was his approach, a strategy that had clearly worked for him climbing Manaslu, so I made sure to keep his trademark cowboy hat in close sight. I was conscious of the stereotype that young male climbers often went too fast, so I was surprised to arrive first at Camp Two considering I had deliberately held the reins back.

Once again, it was Thundu who appeared first to take the burden of my rucksack. He strolled effortlessly back towards the line of tents and pointed inside one where my Everest teammate Dan was waiting, having arrived the day before.

We were now sleeping at over 7,000 metres' altitude, higher than anywhere outside of Asia. Everything took forever up in this rarefied air. The most insignificant tasks became overwhelming: pulling on fresh socks was exhausting and resisting temptation to flop backwards into my sleeping bag again was a monumental achievement. Needing the toilet had never been such an inconvenience.

Rob's medical expertise saved the day as always with medicine to settle the stomach drama and prevent a high-altitude shit storm. Everyone was in the same boat – things hadn't looked promising for Charlene either, who had made slow progress from Camp One. I was pleasantly surprised to hear her bootsteps arriving in camp at all. The two of us had effectively been the underdogs of the group and shared the pain with one another. Despite arriving hours late with the patient guidance of Rolfe, I admired how she had pulled a steely determination from the thin air and was back on top form.

I desperately wanted to say the same for myself.

After trying every trick in the book for motivation, I still couldn't muster the same effect. I felt rotten, drained, and nauseous in a way I couldn't describe.

*

The others stirred and left in the middle of the night. I wished Dan all the best. He was going through the motions and didn't say much in response.

I knew that any mistakes made now would destroy me; we didn't recover at 7,000 metres, we only deteriorated.

Besides Mum, I only texted two other people: my friend Jeff Smith and a mentor, Steve Fives. Mum only ever asked whether I was okay for the umpteenth time, her maternal worry palpable, and Jeff and Steve would give me the advice I needed, even if it wasn't what I wanted at the time.

For the summit push, I had been paired with Dorjee Gyalgen, who was by no means a poor deal as the right-hand man for the record-breaking Himalayan climber, Kenton Cool, on his expeditions. This decision was made collectively between the Sherpas, considering all the logistical factors, with the authority of Kame making the final call from Base Camp. I had no idea at the time that Thundu had asked to be paired with me, but the choice had already been made. This was the immensity of the man. He was always looking out for those less fortunate, looking forwards to the challenge when others looked for a way out.

CHAPTER 5

Hauling myself upwards, I clawed weakly at our snow stash in the porch, frozen hard like marble. The pan was filled, and with a fiddle of matches, the stove was lit. Once the snow melted and simmered in bubbles, I would be leaving for the summit of an 8,000 metre peak.

I hoped the bubbles never broke the water's surface.

It should have been a moment of dreams. Nothing stood in my way this time. But my fantasies had conned my emotions completely.

There was no time to sit and watch the pan. I had 40 minutes to down a litre of water, force breakfast in, and pull the gear on. I told myself that the hardest part was done – I had committed – but my inner fire had already gone up in smoke.

Anxious contemplation stole time until the water roared to life. I filled bottles to warm me inside out for the hours ahead. I nibbled Hobnob biscuits like a mouse. Milky boil-in-the-bag granola dribbled down my chin and two cups of tea sat uncertain in my stomach ... at least, until I threw it all up. Again and again, I wretched. The tent walls no longer dripped with thawing frost but with breakfast. My tent-mate Dan was not best pleased.

Anxiety was a disguise artist, but the last time I had felt this way was the morning when we left Everest Base Camp for Camp

One the year earlier, six hours before an avalanche obliterated the lot.

'I think I'll be back soon,' I muttered to Dan. He lay vacant and offered little word of encouragement, exhausted from his own summit and pained by snow-blindness from the night before. There was nothing he could say – he knew too well what I was about to endure.

Wrestling my crampons to the spaceman boots in the porch took a frustrated effort while a gathering of dizzying lights waited. I crawled out towards them in a disorientated mess. Dorjee came and thrust the oxygen canister to my back, fiddling with the valves while the extra kilograms nearly buckled me back to the floor.

An oxygen mask came to my face and whooshed to life. Never had breathing been so comforting. Five years had passed since I had sucked air in these artificial gasps; last time it was 30 feet below the Aegean Sea in Turkey. Now it was at over 23,000 feet and minus-20 degrees.

The lights were gone already. Gone, up, and away. Hood pulled up and mitts fastened. Dorjee ushered me forwards. 'Okay?' he called. I nodded blankly, squinting into the headtorch beam, his studded ears twinkling back. Our summit bid was on.

We followed forwards, chasing the lights towards the rock band and hauling the heavy Millet boots forwards. Each step dragged heavy and laboured as my legs hollowed. Walking in a straight line immediately turned to an odd shuffle of crunching and stumbling all over. Something was wrong. Such a lack of co-ordination could be the onset of something worse, even deadly.

'It's not going to happen,' I slurred, finding it hard to even talk.

Dorjee asked me to repeat myself. 'You okay?' he asked, his voice still tired from summiting just one day earlier.

I shook my head.

Dorjee hurried ahead and called after Rolfe. I stood alone, staring dead into the blackness, when the lights turned down at me like spotlights. I had no perception of distance, nor where I was, but Rolfe was in shouting reach:

'Hey, Alex! Do you have a headache?'

'No ... I can't walk straight!' I cried back.

'Okay mate ... Go back down!'

Someone else had made the call for me and I was in no mind to disagree. There was less than 1,000 metres of rock, snow, and ice above. Rolfe, Charlene, and Padawa would soon be standing on top of it. But nothing was calling me to join them.

Dorjee took me back to the safety of my tent and the lights went out. With oxygen on tap, I crashed to sleep. In the early hours, I woke again with frozen feet. Shit. I had been too lethargic to bother getting back in my sleeping bag, and it took an anxious effort to warm them again before I lost toes as well as dreams.

*

Within 10 minutes, my summit bid was over. Years had been stolen by one moment. Like an athlete falling at the first hurdle – the years of preparation ruined – it was all over, and that was it. I was going down again, in more ways than one. And the question remained: *what the hell was I doing here in the first place?*

CHAPTER 6

'Oh God,' Rob sighed as I keeled forwards.

He reached for his radio and the support of Henry over 1,000 metres below as I puked again. I remember nothing but withering on my knees, martyred by the slopes. Rob asked for a Sherpa to assist and spare me the burden of the rucksack. But no Sherpa was coming. Camp Two was being dismantled and everyone was fully loaded for the long journey back to Advanced Base Camp.

*

Dan was equally battered as we staggered down like a pair of drunkards, regularly hitting the deck.

'Come on, Dan,' Rob urged, as he fell to a heap again, demanding to take a breather. I'd rarely heard Rob sound so anxious.

Above the slope were ugly seracs with deep cracks glued together only by blue ice. I knew we had to keep moving before that glue no longer worked. We joined the false security of Camp 1.5 where the others had congregated outside a lonely yellow tent. Our crux was a few metres ahead. A Romanian climber was waiting to descend first but the ropes had jammed. Oblivious to the increasing threat of warmth releasing the seracs above, he didn't seem in too much of a hurry and happily spoke about his country with pride. We'd be visiting Romania in the afterlife at this rate of progress. Clutching my knees to try and ground myself, I said nothing.

After an hour or so, it was my turn. I grasped hard. One mistake here and I would hurtle down like a zip wire. Stefan had selflessly waited halfway to help each of us operate the jumars and stayed close as we arm-wrapped down the rope into Camp One.

I slumped to the ground beside our tents.

*

The remnants of Camp One were grabbed from the tents and loaded into our rucksacks until gear dangled off every strap, removing any choice other than to continue moving down. Lying around complaining wouldn't get us off this mountain.

Strength crept back as we lost altitude and oxygen leaked into my blood until the hellish scree slope spat us onto the glacier for the final time. The tracks of this dirty rock expanse were misleading at the best of times.

Half a Snickers bar was the only thing I'd been able to keep down for nearly 18 hours.

Stefan crept ahead in this race of rabbit versus roadkill. Visualisation of relief drove me through it all.

*

Sunburnt lips froze to the icy can. Coca Cola had never tasted so good.

In the darkness, we toasted to nothing but our safe return. Silence remained for the clatter of stones as the porter hurried onwards to the trailing summiteers. The sugar rush gave us a final boost until the sleepy yellow lights of Base Camp emerged. There would be no victory walk into camp but no less joy.

The relief of being back safe took over completely. I had spent hours visualising the moment of glory – what I'd do first, what I craved and longed for – none of it seemed to matter anymore.

Kame stood outside our mess tent with a welcome nod of approval. Inside, it was primed for our arrival: heater roaring, fresh cups, and gallons of boiling water.

But even water turned my stomach.

One by one, the team arrived back. The Sherpas were even later, hauling everything off the mountain in our wake. Dinner came and my appetite seemed to return too. Bhim came in proudly displaying a celebratory cake impressively glazed with "Well Done!" The altitude had knocked everyone sick, but I was going to eat my cake and have it too. Being tucked in the sleeping bag once more signalled some relief. My strained heart pounded so hard into the floor that I barely slept.

*

The next day was bittersweet once it dawned on us that the only thing left to look forward to was getting back home. We had all played a role in the process that got 10 of 12 on the summit, which was a great success by Himalayan standards.

It was difficult not to feel like the kid who didn't get an invite to the birthday party as they deservedly swapped summit photos and stories from up high. I was pleased for them but now I felt that we had nothing in common.

I had always imagined that summitting would have me skipping like a lamb, rejoicing at life feeling complete, so I was surprised they looked somewhat underwhelmed; deflated even. Maybe the achievement would sink in once they got home.

*

While the rest of the team licked their wounds from summit day, I was determined to make the most of the opportunity to wake and fall asleep in the mountains rather than skulking in a corner. A tower of rock protruded from the boulder field above Base Camp, held up by prayer flags that dangled like spiders' legs. I had been eyeing the spot for weeks and now there was nothing to lose.

An easy scramble up one side tempted the rubbish climber inside me. The tip of this match-stick was the perfect spot for reflection, boots hanging over the edge, maybe 30 metres to the base and hundreds more to the tents. I looked up at the mountain with regret.

What on earth was I thinking?

I looked at the peak and instead of thinking how far I'd had left to go, I thought about how high I had climbed. I had learnt my strengths and weaknesses, that altitude was not my strong point, and I felt confident I had done the best I could. Having the chance to experience a true summit bid removed any doubts or unfinished business to deliberate back home.

It reminded me of the message from my teammate, Ingo, months earlier when announcing the expedition, who had questioned whether mountaineering was really my thing. In a world of doubters and naysayers, I knew that this was something that I could only find out for myself.

*

The Yaks left Base Camp first. Rob flew past out of Base Camp to catch up with MK and Dan.

'You've become your own man now,' he said. By putting his belief in others, Rob helped them to believe in themselves. Sadly, that hadn't been enough this time. He was disappointed too, having strongly believed that I was going to get to the summit.

Arthur had plodded his way to victory without one throb of a headache. Charlene had made the top from zero to hero. Susanne had become the oldest German woman to reach the summit. A simple discussion began about training for Everest, bringing a direct dig from Kam: 'Unlike you, I haven't failed anything.' I smiled. Failure seemed like my superpower.

'Why don't you just get a proper job?' came as a blunt remark from Billi.

'Why would I want to do that?' I was disappointed to hear this mindset somewhere so far from normality. I started skipping meals to stay in my room so as not to spoil their party. Thankfully, Arthur had become a friend along our way together. I sensed that his perception of me had changed for the better during the trip. Back in Tingri, he courteously offered me the first use of the shower, which I graciously took.

*

A question remained on my mind: *What was next?*

I could try to summit again, but the point wasn't so clear anymore. I believed that even after reaching the summit, I would only have been in a similar position, looking for more.

I felt out of the zone. I realised that my goal had always been externally motivated. The reward itself had mattered more to me than the journey.

*

We were summoned for dinner and, outside our hotel, met the same view we had contemplated weeks earlier. Everest and Cho Oyu were glowing across the plateau at the golden hour. Only this time, I felt nothing towards them. No goosebumps ran up my arms. They had stopped calling to me.

My life could have purpose without mountains, and I was never going to find my new purpose by climbing the wrong one.

PART TWO

CHAPTER 1

MIND OVER MOUNTAINS

"Your body can stand almost anything. Convincing your mind is the hard part." – ANONYMOUS

It was funny to remember that I had never considered failure to be an option.

*

The ordeal was far from over for Mum. Now she had to worry about how I was going to cope without these big mountains in my life. Worrying was part-and-parcel of being a mother, but I'd wager mine had it worse when I took it to these extremes.

Base Camp back home was full of questions, but I remained stoical about not summiting. Everest 2017 was off, and I had found peace with that. I knew that it would take time to re-adjust and come up with a Plan B.

But I wasn't the only one with ideas. I could understand why depression was often called the "Black Dog". It struggled to see beyond its nose and didn't want to hear what it already knew. My Black Dog had one hell of a scrapbook. It would try to convince me that life was uncertain and meaningless so I should give up and play "fetch" instead.

I processed what I needed to, caught up on sleep, and was eager just to get home and crack on with it. Clean-shaven and back in the oxygen-rich comfort of Lhasa, we were led into a grand hotel and a huge dining room. A large Peking Duck, complete with both head and beak, was laid across the table.

I made my farewells and I was happy to find my own space in the world of free Wi-Fi, spending the days alone in the gardens of Kathmandu Guest House, scribbling in my diary, and eagerly researching ideas. I couldn't really suss anything out properly without my laptop or mentors to help me weigh up the whole picture. Over lunch of egg and chips at Base Camp three weeks earlier, I had told Charlene about a wild future idea to run and cycle around the UK. At the time I hadn't questioned why my head was already looking beyond the mountain, but now it made sense.

*

There was nothing quite like getting home after six weeks away and appreciating the home comforts so much more. Hector the dog dive-bombed me in the hallway. Mum was relieved to see me in good shape, physically and mentally. So much had been suppressed in the anticipation and pressure of what was to come. I was excited to put the new strategies from the binge eating self-help book *Brain Over Binge* into practice after a few days of home-cooked food, and whatever training I felt like doing. Typically, there wasn't much time to dwell on things when I was thrown straight back into speaking commitments, first at the Chester Literature Festival, and then as the keynote speaker at a conference to over 250 people for Rotary International, with new stories fresh from the Himalayas to share. Without these commitments I may well have curled up in a corner and waved a white flag, but surrendering wouldn't inspire anyone.

Life was positively busy again and afforded little time for the negative thoughts. I went back to working part-time, managing a social enterprise called the One Mile Project which created sports projects for schools in disadvantaged parts of Manchester. The director, Jim Clarke, was an inspirational leader and community entrepreneur who had first contacted me after hearing about the expedition. It was incredibly rewarding to use my experience to make a positive contribution to others, rather than lining shareholders' pockets.

In the process of shedding my expedition coat and re-inventing myself, I started to sell my expedition gear. It didn't just give me closure; I think it proved to myself that I was serious about abandoning the high-altitude ambitions. The mountain no longer defined me.

Christmas was approaching, and I was scared about falling into the same low trough of depression as Christmas the year earlier. The effects of Seasonal Affectivity Disorder, appropriately abbreviated "SAD" were well understood. My Black Dog liked to hibernate in the winter and tried to maul me into the pit with it once the leaves dropped and branches turned bare. It slipped away equally quietly once the red flags turned to green shoots of spring. So I kept toying with challenge ideas for the year ahead and fleshing out the UK mountains idea.

In this period of uncertainty, I didn't want to give my anxiety the upper hand, so all I could do was focus on the things that were certain, with faith, from experience, that everything would fall into place at the right time.

*

After Everest, there were so many adventurers, fundraisers, and speakers jostling for space that I felt nobody would care about what I had to say. I had little hope of spreading a message without knowing what the message was either. Simply "inspiring people" was a little too broad for my taste. My own life had changed too quickly to plan very far ahead. Over the years, I had barely given attention to the long-term picture, and instinctively ploughed on doing what felt right.

The biggest danger was confusing this contentment with happiness and going through life like another hamster on the wheel, running away from everything in this pursuit of more, but getting nowhere.

Another coach within my support circle, Brigadier John Thomson, got me thinking in the right way whenever I hit the "grey zone" like this and asked me the same question I had asked myself in the tent at Camp Two on Cho Oyu just weeks earlier: How would you like to be remembered at your funeral?

I still didn't quite know the answer.

But I was working on it.

I took huge inspiration from Elise Downing, an English runner and writer, who at 24 had ditched her graduate job in London and embarked on a 5,000-mile run around the UK coastline over the best part of a year. What inspired me most was the way she shared her daily journey with such honesty and enthusiasm in videos to camera that inspired members of the public to run with her in every corner of the country. It set the benchmark and got me thinking about doing something similar. There was only so much one person could do on a mountain halfway across the world – but Elise showed me that bringing people along for the ride could really make change happen.

I still worried that, without Everest, I would fail to inspire anyone to set their own goals, and I could already feel the self-imposed pressure growing. I knew I had to do something, not only for myself, but for the loyal friends who had supported me from the outset. I could hardly go to buy groceries without being asked what my next challenge was. I worried that without Everest I would have no use to anyone and the last thing I wanted was failure to deter them from setting massive goals.

I knew that I wanted to get people involved in what I did. Doing a UK-based challenge – getting to know its curves and corners – felt right. I knew I needed a USP – something to set me apart, and encourage more donations. And, most importantly, I knew that I wanted to raise money for mental health charities to help make support more readily available. I was one of the lucky ones: I had an outlet to focus on, and a support network. But even then, depression could still leave us horribly alone, feeling as if nobody could help. Too many people were taking their own lives as a permanent solution to a temporary problem. I wanted to share the message that there was always hope.

A target of £10,000 sounded pleasing and significant to begin with.

I wanted to be a role model for what could be achieved in the face of adversity, especially mental illness. I knew that I didn't have it as bad as others; I was comfortable, healthy, and safe. I felt nervous about putting myself on a pedestal or appearing to undermine others. But the bad days were sometimes bad enough they were hard to visualise afterwards. I also knew that I was doing this for the right reason, and that spurred me on.

I still had the idea of doing "all of" something, be it peaks, miles or places, in a set time, and I wanted to reach people with mental health challenges in every corner of the UK. The possibilities were overwhelming.

High-altitude mountains were out, but the size of the challenge needed to be just as big. While I was still working through all the possibilities, the news broke that Lakpa Thundu, our beloved climbing Sherpa from our Cho Oyu expedition, had been killed by rockfall on the mountain Ama Dablam, in Nepal. I was stunned. Thundu was invincible; this had to be a mistake. I wasn't easily affected by grief or loss, but it had been a while since I had shed tears like this.

I wasn't just sad for me. Thundu's sudden loss devastated so many people in the stiff-lipped mountaineering community across the world. I knew how proud and grateful the Sherpas were to do what they did. They accepted the risks of their trade without question. But that didn't lessen the tragedy one bit. I was grateful to have spent time with him, and to count him as a friend. I remembered how he told me his wife didn't want him to climb because of the dangers, and how Ama Dablam was his favourite mountain. His words came back to haunt me now.

It didn't seem fair. After surviving the earthquake with us in 2015, he had been taken by an aftershock 18 months later. We already knew how unforgiving the mountains could be: even the best weren't safe.

It reopened the meaning of life debate for me. It challenged the idea of taking risks when life was fragile enough. Having our ducks lined up so neatly seemed like a wasted exercise, when chance could take it all away in an instant. Should you play it safe by not playing at all? Or go all in on life and win big, in spite of the losses along the way? I thought of Thundu and his achievements in his 40 years. His choices had created a legacy that inspired others to be better people, and questioned whether success was about living long or about living well. We could try both, but we were all on the same one-way street: and the biggest risk to me was taking no risk at all.

That night, I was booked to speak for a networking club. With the same resilience that Sherpas personified, I knew life had to go on. I went off page and told them all about him. It made me glad to know that his inspiration had touched the hearts of people who had never even met him, enough to donate generously to support his wife and two young boys.

Now that I'd sold my expedition gear, and given up on the big mountain in my head, my heart was closed to the idea of it too. Letting go of the big mountain freed me up: I had nothing to prove to anyone. Our own interpretation of the mystery of happiness is just as good as anyone else's, and I felt, more clearly than ever before, that my happiness was a by-product of being authentically myself.

I agreed to a series of outdoor talks and a mountain film festival without hesitation, even going so far as to accept an invitation to present a travel awards event in London, something I hadn't done before. The danger of saying someone's name wrong with my stammer was too high, but I did it anyway, and relished the challenge. Only the year before, anxiety had me pulling out of speaking at the biggest outdoor show in the UK; not a decision I took lightly – but it was important to acknowledge that the world didn't shatter as a result.

*

Earlier in the year I had been on a stammering therapy course at the Starfish Project, in Sussex. The course had taught me an intercostal breathing technique and other strategies that helped me take much better control of my stammer, and it worked wonders for my confidence. It was also to thank for giving me new friends quite literally all over the world, all with something special in common. One friend, Mikaela, shared a love for running and the outdoors, and invited me to visit them in Cape Town, South Africa, for the closest thing to a proper holiday for as long as I could remember. A week in the African sun was the self-care I needed to stave off the post-expedition blues.

I'd spent the previous Christmas looking back, but now I was looking forwards. I tried to enjoy the break as much as I could, inhaling the cosy waft of turkey and stuffing sandwiches from the kitchen. Not throwing up on Christmas Day was definite progress on the year before. A running race in Chester on Boxing Day was a deliberate safety measure to run away from the familiar urges and temptation.

It was all going fine until I received a box of chocolates from a friend. We were supposed to indulge at Christmas. It was wrong to blame them if they didn't know, but it was irritating, nonetheless. The urges came so quickly. That night, I climbed out of the lounge window to throw up in the garden, so my family wouldn't hear. I had been in a much better place but knew from the *Brain Over Binge* book that emotions alone were not to blame. These were just an excuse that gave the bulimia power.

I was fed up with making excuses for its ugly work and just accepted that it was going to turn up like an estranged relative at the Christmas dinner table before sodding off in due course. Everyone was having a good time without it, and it still lingered for a cheap meal. I hadn't cracked how to stop the urges completely, but I'd been doing well; just a couple of blips was an achievement.

Missing out on the festive celebrations or turning down New Year's Eve parties was a small price to pay for keeping healthy. Spending New Year's Eve doing my tax return was a safer bet. I never celebrated the start of a new year much when every day counted as an opportunity to improve. But this time around I was at least starting with hope; the motivation was building. I just needed the right challenge to prove it.

CHAPTER 2

The idea had been forming for a while, and then, finally, it came to me fully formed: I was going to climb the highest point of each UK county.

There were gaps to fill, of course, but the challenge had arms and legs. I had shared the idea with Steve Fives during a mentoring session and he had smiled back in agreement. The company, The Westgrove Group, had employees spread nationwide and that already boded well for getting people involved. The variety of counties would appeal to all abilities to come and join in along the way, or as Steve put it: 'the young, the wise, and those that haven't yet tried'.

Taking the concept to others was a bit like *Dragons' Den*. I was delighted that people seemed to share my excitement. There were still doubts, but they only helped me to refine the idea. For example, I wasn't sure if it ticked one final box – the physical challenge. I didn't think the counties would be hard enough considering many of the tops weren't even mountains. I was torn between the drive to test my personal boundaries by going far and fast, and the importance of involving people whose "personal Everest" could be to go for a run without stopping. Combining both narratives was difficult. But I knew that it should be more about the people and the journey, and less about myself.

An Instagram follower messaged to say he was thinking of cycling John O'Groats to Land's End. Although I wouldn't be able to join his challenge, I was happy to challenge his anxieties. I told him, 'Don't think – do it!' Advice I knew I needed to heed myself.

I still needed a name for it though ...

I'd met Mike Henshall the year before when the high school where he worked had fundraised for the Nepal earthquake victims. It helped to create a link with someone local and there weren't many young people from Cheshire in the middle of it. Mike came to one of my public talks in the summer, then dragged his wife, Sonia, and son, Dan, to another. An outdoor skills instructor and former scout leader with a passion for mental wellbeing and mindfulness, he had checked in regularly, especially after the disappointment of the expedition, and I cycled the 60-mile loop to his home in Congleton regularly for cake and a chat.

"Climbing The UK" was the first thing we scribbled on a mind-map of possible names at his house one Sunday afternoon. It quickly morphed into "Climb The UK" and it stuck like love at first sight.

But there was still one big unanswered question ...

Over a cup of coffee, Mike looked at me and asked, 'What's your why?'

To answer him, I described the moment I had visualised at the finish. I had settled on Moel Famau in North Wales for the big finale. It was close to home, I had trained on it for Cho Oyu; and the distinct Jubilee Tower on top lent itself to a big, triumphant moment. And I could picture the moment so vividly: a crowd of supporters and people we'd inspired along the way, all of us taking those final, exhausted steps of shared accomplishment, then standing as one, as I thrust a Union Jack into the sky. A drone flying overhead to capture the photo would frame the golden shot perfectly. I paused; goosebumps prickled my arms, and a tickling giggle caught me by surprise. I smiled at Mike broadly as the scene came to life in my mind.

'There you go.' Mike smiled back. 'That's your why.'

The challenge was finally good to go.

*

Like many things, the hardest part was knowing where to start.

Time was already against me and the worry about wasting time with mistakes only ended up wasting more time. Perfectionism in action! I enjoyed organising things but had no experience of managing something like this, with logistics, fundraising, marketing, gear, and training to consider. I knew that certain parts had to come first, but everything seemed to be a priority. The accommodation couldn't be done without the route. Encouraging people to come along and arranging school visits along the way needed advance planning.

I announced the challenge in February, and was delighted – if slightly overwhelmed – at the amount of support pledged and offers of accommodation on the route. My confidence was so tied up in pleasing other people that I felt obliged to accept the help, even if it added extra miles and complications along my route. Generosity also held me accountable so there was no going back or letting people down. Many things were put in a holding pattern until the right time, though I wasn't entirely sure when that time might come.

The date was a good place to start. 6th May was a Saturday at the beginning of Mental Health Awareness week. Through calculations, I realised it would take me just about 72 days to finish the entire thing, hopefully ending on a Sunday in July on Moel Famau.

Defining a "county" was the biggest dilemma. England technically had historic, geographic, metropolitan, non-metropolitan and ceremonial counties. Scotland had 33 historic counties or shires but had done away with them for council areas in 1975. Northern Ireland abolished the six counties in 1972 for unitary authorities, and Wales was plain awkward. I eventually decided on the combination which rounded up nicely to 100 counties in total and made the best possible journey. After that, it was just a case of finding the highest points within the current boundaries which had changed many times over the years.

It seemed that "bagging" county tops was quite a trend, but I could only find one individual who had the same idea of a human-powered continuous push, a writer, teacher, and mountain runner called Jonny Muir, who had produced a book about his journey years earlier. Now there was room for a fresh attempt. Once I had the county tops dotted on the map, a big game of logical dot-to-dot began, and more research to find the best way up each one. Some were more straightforward than others. Every mile, on wheels and foot, was to be pre-planned in the Strava fitness app and the ViewRanger outdoor discovery app.

Accommodation would largely be provided by the YHA, the Scottish equivalent SYHA, and Hostelling Northern Ireland. Staying for free in return for promotion was going to massively reduce the costs for a self-funded challenge. After foolishly sketching a vague itinerary first, many were already fully booked, which sent me back to the drawing board, tearing my hair out again. Each day had a knock-on effect.

Trying to make the route work around friends and family, and offers of a free bed, wasn't always practical for the sake of saving a few quid, and meant booking hotels and campsites instead. Adding to this was the desire to visit interesting places and areas likely to create public interest. I really had no idea of how many people would be likely to join in when some of the county tops were duller than dishwater, but I had to keep possibilities open and plan the route regardless.

It was an exhausting process and I quickly realised why few other people had attempted a continuous round since Jonny Muir.

*

In the past, I had cluelessly written press releases myself but this time, getting proper media support was a must. So I went to meet Mick Ord, a former BBC journalist turned consultant with 30 years' experience, whom I'd met the year before. He had sadly lost his own brother, Chris, to suicide which encouraged him to help even more.

I instantly warmed to Mick and knew he would be the person to get the story out, especially with his experience in crisis communications. The PR manager at YHA England & Wales, Anna, and Oli Reed at ViewRanger, would cover the other bases so everything would optimistically work together. Most of the fundraising would kick off once the challenge itself got underway.

In the meantime, I had the usual work and speaking bookings. March and April were always my busiest. Sometimes, I'd have four talks in one week, hopping on trains and staying in hotels. I loved the buzz of it all, getting to tell the story in so many different places. But the lack of routine and the pressure of being self-employed was also tough work. Sometimes I felt like an impostor standing in front of managers in my business suit. After one event a manager told me, 'I thought you were there to fix the projector... then you just blew us away!' After talks, my brain was usually barely any good for anything until the next day, and it all stole time from planning the challenge.

As I struggled to cope with the stress, I spent nights pacing around the kitchen, trying to outlast my urges to binge. It was ironic that something I had conceived to help others with mental health issues was compromising mine. The challenge was becoming exhausting before I'd even begun. These were the signs of burnout. Like depression, it crept in like a slow leak, until I couldn't make decisions and felt constantly on the edge of tears.

Running most days of the week helped me let some of the stress out, and aiming for personal best times gave me some goals to strive for that were not connected to Climb The UK.

At first, being stressed out fuelled some strong performances in directing the angst onto the tarmac instead of into myself.

Friends tried to offer advice, but it never really worked. I was so stressed that I saw their advice as a threat, assuming that they misunderstood my capabilities. Not taking it pushed them away and losing friends over a challenge wasn't worth it. I considered postponing the challenge to the summer to buy more time and step off the gas.

But I felt like I had one shot to make the challenge count and make the biggest impact possible, and I didn't want to delay and risk people losing interest. Besides, "just going for it" was my usual style. The ViewRanger team had produced a live map of the entire route from the collection of route files and ultimately followers could see my location at any point. This would either reassure Mum or drive me round the bend.

Mick was officially hired to manage PR for Climb The UK and invited me for coffee one morning. He wanted a better grasp of the cause and my story; to find the hook. As a journalist, Mick could probably tell I hadn't told the full story. Depression alone wasn't so much the problem now. While that was easy enough to share with friends, I had been terrified of speaking about the bulimia to anyone, even Mum.

I was supposed to be an adventurer. But an eating disorder surely didn't belong on the adventurer's job description. I hated that I was still unable to beat bulimia by myself, though it was my family, friends and mentors who had helped me through everything else. There was no shame asking for help here too. I had to be open and honest; I had to talk about my eating disorder. I even called it by its name: bulimia. Mick was pleased with my openness. The next leap of faith was to extend the same honesty to the world.

The memory of breaking down with fear in front of my GP came flooding back.

I had been inspired by a sub-elite runner, Tom Fairbrother, who had written about his similar struggles in *The Guardian*.

It had helped me see I was not alone in the slightest. Eating disorders affected over 725,000 in the UK and had the highest mortality rate of any other mental illness. Hearing this from another athlete made more sense of my own situation.

I came across even more examples of personal stories that liberated and lifted others by providing the opportunity to share their own stories and find mutual understanding, shared advice, and hope. It was an eye-opening and encouraging experience that cast new light on the eating disorder as an opportunity to help others speak out in the way that Tom had inspired me. There was a ripple effect of openness from one story after another. Completing a challenge around the UK seemed a fine way to push the narrative further.

My regular followers and many close friends had no idea and they deserved to know. So I penned a blog that explained the bulimia and how it all started. Writing it felt dirty and hitting "publish" took a while.

Why am I telling them this? Are they going to think any less of me? Are they going to even care?

Brushing my anxiety aside, I told myself that there was nothing to lose. Anyone who took offence was not worth impressing.

The second the blog went out, those fears were put to bed. An outpouring of support came instead. To my surprise, friends began to put their hands up and commented underneath to publicly reveal their own eating disorders. They had just been waiting for a door to open. Completely unexpectedly, I felt so much better now that it was out there, and the distant threat of it being revealed without my consent was taken away.

*

My chosen steed for the mission was a steel-framed Genesis Tour de Fer touring bike. Steel frames were supposedly more comfortable over long distances, and this sleek beast was undoubtedly built to last.

When it came to maintenance, our neighbour, Rich, was the usual port of call. He was an avid cyclist, often found pottering around and fiddling with the bikes in his garage, exchanging a friendly "hello" as we passed. He was always happy to help me fix the bike, and gave spare parts without hesitation. He was a testament to everything good about the cycling community. Rich must have been anxious about me heading off on nearly 5,000 miles, considering I barely knew the difference between a bottom bracket and a bar-end!

Getting the balance right in training was important, as ever. Like an expedition, I knew I could build specific fitness and conditioning during the challenge itself. In the lead-up to the off, I bagged my first ever Parkrun win in Delamere Forest. It was a modest event, but I was still chuffed. Dad was there to see it too, and brought the new bike fresh from the warehouse.

On the final weekend before the big depart I won another Parkrun to finish my season in style and it was time to rest up. I might not have managed to tick off everything on my preparation list, but at least I had managed to avoid any major dramas.

There was one job left. Mum always said I left things to last minute, but something always had to come last. By my standards, it was a minor storm. I laid out my kit for the first time and had to whittle it down to the bare minimum before working out how it might fit into the two pannier bags strapped to the sides. It was still nearly 30 kilograms when loaded. I gulped.

The pre-expedition self-doubts never changed. In truth I would never feel truly ready; I just had to start and find the way. I was prepared for the worst, hoping for the best, and would carry on regardless.

CHAPTER 3

On Saturday 13th May, I woke with a familiar nausea; a burden that would not budge. This time I was not flying to the other side of the planet, or to the worlds' highest mountain range, yet it felt the same.

It was an appropriately modest send-off on a drizzly morning at Derbyshire Bridge car park. We were met by Mike, Sonia, and Dan and a mix of friendly faces; some I knew, some I didn't. I was delighted – being joined like this by the public on day one was exactly how I hoped the challenge would start.

The first objective would be on foot – Shining Tor, the highest point of Cheshire. An outdoor journalist, Dave, had arrived to snap the obligatory photos with my worried mum, and to capture a quote from the moment. Starting such a journey surely warranted a distinguished speech of sorts but nothing decent came. In truth, I was anxious to just get going.

The walk climbed through the peat moorland of Stake Clough towards the soft hump ahead, flushed with purple heather. I enjoyed the brisk walk with David, a friend I'd met at a speaking event, and Chris, a keen fell-runner.

A figure watched us approach – Mike waited at the stone wall which led to the summit. Flag stones took us through the gate to the first summit of the challenge, where the weathered white trig point was draped patriotically in bunting, flags, and balloons.

Mike and Sonya had made it extra special for the occasion and stirred up support from other walkers on their own Saturday outing. Mum stood with our dog, Hector, who had immersed himself in mud to celebrate. Mum filled my pockets with too much lunch. Mike shook my hand and smiled. 'There are more surprises to come.' From the days of conception to now, Mike looked proud as heck; tinged with worry; to see it happening for real. I just felt sick with fear.

They left us to it, and we continued down the roadside towards Cheeks Hill of Staffordshire. Conveniently, this was quite literally over the road, and we blasted up a track onto Axe Edge Moor and found the true county boundary by a sheep pen at the corner of a crumbling dry-stone wall.

My routes were planned with the intention of being interesting and worthwhile, to encourage people to take part, rather than the shortest or easiest option to get them ticked off the list. The drawbacks were quickly clear when we opted to turn back the same way, knowing that staying on schedule for day one was more important than being too particular.

Back at Derbyshire Bridge and left to my own devices, Mike had not been joking about the surprises. With a reassuring bleep, the Garmin Edge computer started up on the handlebars, and my face dropped: all the pre-planned routes for the next 72 days had gone. Somehow, they had been wiped the previous night. I couldn't believe what was happening.

Luckily, the routes for the first five days of the challenge were saved on my Casio smart watch. It was only 25 miles to Edale, although navigating now meant cycling one-handed and focusing hard on a golf-ball-sized screen on my wrist.

Burdened by the weight of the panniers, the bike flew on the downhills, sweeping through the cosy Peak District villages of Hope and Tideswell in a flash. I sensed this machine would serve me well, until gravity started to work against us, climbing through the dramatic limestone gorge of Winnats Pass, where losing momentum for a split second would have flopped us onto the tarmac. Luckily, I had noticed the loose front wheel before roaring down the other side into the picturesque Edale valley and the car park in Barber Booth. Chris had come along for the third peak of the day with his partner and fellow runner, Amy. We were also joined by Mike, an aspiring Everest climber, plus Elaine, who by her own admission, had not walked hills like these for 30+ years, but had taken the plunge and thrown herself in to the challenge. Brilliant blue skies met us on the staircase of Jacob's Ladder towards the welcoming grassy slopes of the Kinder plateau, with gritstone rocks scattering the top like pepper. Up top, were polished boulders and a dull desert of peat that felt like walking on a different planet. Finding the true summit of Kinder Scout and the highest point of Derbyshire was not as simple. Only a few miles away was a warm welcome at YHA Edale youth hostel, along with second helpings for dinner, but I was more interested in the office computer to get the route files back on the Garmin. Trying to cycle without a route on a screen in front of me broke me out of my comfort zone.

It didn't look promising when the computer repeatedly failed. Having all these hiccups by the end of day one felt like some sort of conspiracy plot: they wanted me to fail, whoever "they" were.

*

In a serene Sunday daze, I set off later than planned.

A refreshing chill clung to the shade of woodland, whizzing through the quiet lanes to Fairholmes until glimpses of the reservoir flashed through the trees. Behind the gothic-style dam wall, Derwent Reservoir was perfectly placid and a beautiful mirror as I hurried past. I already had text messages asking how I was feeling. I appreciated all the concern, but was working on a laid-back approach like we had used on Everest where no news meant no bad news. But perhaps it was complacent of me to think that the British summer could throw nothing worse than the Himalayas, and maybe it was bravado to assume that I could look after myself.

A track led through the woods with scattered bluebells, and opened to the foot of Howden Moor rising gently ahead. Eventually the grassy plateau eased and opened for miles more until stumbling across a shy pile of stones marking the summit of High Stones: the highest point of South Yorkshire. The chain of reservoirs and dams dazzled down below, with gentle drop-offs from Howden Edge. The morning had turned gloriously still; it felt like a beautiful time to be alive. Returning over Featherbed Moss was less inspiring; veering off the path into peat hags and streams until finding my way south; descending towards the suitably named Lost Lad and back to Fairholmes now teeming with Sunday walkers and barking dogs.

The ride skirted along the eastern edge of the Pennines into South Yorkshire. With half my family hailing from the other side of the Pennines in Sheffield, countless drives across their hostile expanse on the Woodhead Road had always captured my imagination as a child. Through the window I had looked with fascination and trepidation; wondering what it would be like to cross them alone.

At Dovestones Reservoir the road went further than expected, steep enough that it was probably quicker to walk anyway, up to Chew Reservoir where I went on foot into the wild grasp of Saddleworth Moor. It was lonely, and barren as expected in those childhood visions; eerily silent but for the occasional breeze rustling the cottongrass. This silence was beautiful itself. The summit was marked unceremoniously by a snapped wooden post and cairn of stones nearby. At 542 metres, I was standing on top of the county of Greater Manchester.

Getting back to the Pennine Way was easy enough and I continued down to Crowden Great Brook. The path upgraded to flagstones, escaping the peaty black bog that gave the hill its name, and I broke into a run. My legs were resistant to the effort and could manage only short bursts until a white trig point appeared at last. Black Hill was the highest point of West

Yorkshire, perched on the mound known as Soldiers' Lump. It was almost 9.30pm by the time I arrived at Grandma's house in a leafy corner of Oldham where a huge roast dinner was waiting, regardless. Her partner, Mike, faffed with pouring gravy to make it look pretty; when I was hungry enough to have eaten it off the floor. Serving almost an entire leg of lamb had apparently been a prank to see my reaction; I hadn't thought twice about wolfing the lot.

After a 14-hour day, I found myself knocking on a neighbour's door at 11.00pm to find a laptop to try and fix the Garmin. My heart sank when the forecast showed continuous heavy rain from start to finish on the following day. Lying in bed, well past midnight, I began to question everything else. Arriving late on day two had damaged my confidence, knowing that many other days of the itinerary would be unrealistic too. But then, this was all part of adapting the plan.

*

My grandparents' home was a treasure trove of happy childhood memories. Of hearty home cooking in harsh winters, chocolate biscuits, and hot cups of tea in front of the TV, reading my favourite magazines until the early hours, and the rebellion of chocolate for breakfast, they were all triggered by the familiar comforting scent that still came in the doorway.

It was the one place that I had permission to be a carefree kid for a while longer. The only thing missing was Grandad, who had passed away suddenly four years earlier. It was painful to think he never had the chance to see me do this.

But he had never seen the rest either: as the eating disorder had progressed, this childhood sanctuary became a very anxious place to be. It was also where my bulimia had first raised suspicions in the bathroom after two years of secrecy.

Eating disorders were an alien concept to their generation. 'You haven't got depression,' Grandma had told me on more than one occasion when it slipped into conversation. This always packed one hell of a sting. She just couldn't see what I had to feel depressed about. She never "liked" the idea of depression. Funnily enough, I wasn't too keen, either.

We could talk about anything else, and any other problems I was facing, with compassion and shared life wisdom. Mental illness affected the older generation equally, if not more, than mine. It just didn't seem to be labelled or understood in the same way. My grandparents belonged to the "Silent Generation", a title often given to those born between the late 1920s and mid-1940s, when children were seen and not heard. Many lived by the notion that people did not talk about their problems, and it was considered stoic or noble just to keep calm and carry on. Times had changed, and they had a lot of catching up to do.

Perhaps Grandma's own upbringing was to blame for her unconditional spoiling every time I visited, and she took great pleasure giving her grandchildren what she had not had herself. Hearty portions of dinner, desserts, and bottomless tins of chocolate biscuits before bed had been a highlight of my childhood. Once the bulimia began, it became the precedent for a bingeing field day, or a prolonged battle with the urges. Her set ways were difficult to challenge when it came to food; in her world you could eat whatever you wanted if you weren't fat. I had eventually given up trying to explain my relationship with food, or making excuses not to eat certain things. When things were really bad, I avoided visiting entirely to prevent the bulimia flaring up again. I hated it for controlling what mattered in life.

Avoiding my eating disorder only gave it power; buying short-term gain at the cost of long-term pain. The eating disorder itself was only another means of avoiding an emotional problem. Getting on the bike and travelling miles, day after day, probably looked more like an escape plot than confronting these demons.

I didn't see it like that. (It doesn't count as escaping if the problem comes along for the ride too.) So there I was, fighting back, and I knew Grandad would have been proud of me for that.

CHAPTER 4

Staying with Grandma pulled me like a fish out of water; I was enjoying all the home comforts, but half-heartedly, knowing I had to leave again in the morning.

The 6.00am alarm was as deflating as expected.

One hundred miles of cycling was nothing untoward or beyond my capability and would also be much flatter than the day before, but my mind was still looking at 160 miles plus 69 more days of it.

Grandma had succeeded in sending me off about six pounds heavier than on arrival, and I failed to leave on time. Using a watch to navigate through the pot-holed roads of Manchester at the mercy of Monday rush-hour traffic in the rain wasn't entirely ideal.

My mind switched to the checkpoints and milestones ahead of me. Breaking things down into stages was a strategy I knew well.

The first stage was visiting the head office of my sponsors, Westgrove Group, in Warrington. Now they had the opportunity to see the challenge in action, warts and all. Jen met me with a look of concern the second I walked in and threw my dripping jacket straight on the office radiator. The team filled the boardroom, Steve passing on their support and I gave an impromptu challenge update between mouthfuls of coffee and chocolate biscuits, hiding behind anxious laughter and jokes to hide how I really felt, trying to stay positive and portray the same sense of belief that everyone had in me.

Seeing friendly faces and colleagues was a huge boost for the next milestone. It was a mad rush to St Helens to give a talk at a high school, which had been arranged by a school governor and friend of Mick Ord.

Arranging spontaneous talks along the way had been part of the vision from the very start, to raise as much awareness about mental health as possible. Turning up mid-adventure seemed the perfect opportunity to inspire.

For five years, I had cycled 10 miles to high school each day and was habitually late. Today my lack of punctuality was not through lack of interest but a one-hundred-mile day and discovering a fully laden touring bike could not match the effort my mind anticipated. Right until the 11th minute, the assistant headteacher was waiting anxiously at the school driveway, and understandably didn't look best pleased. The bike was dumped in the first-aid room before I was frog-marched into a full sports hall, still in cycling shoes, leaving a trail of rainwater down the hallway. This was a textbook example of how not to prepare. The slides were still loading as the students waited. Public speaking with a stammer meant having a script for every talk that was rehearsed meticulously until memorised. This time I was winging it to a whole new level. It was a pleasing testament of how far my speaking ability had come. The room fell silent as the headteacher introduced me, and over 200 Year 8 students looked up. Whatever they had imagined a real-life adventurer to look like, I guessed it was probably not me.

Those next 25 minutes came from memory, experience and luck. It was authentic, if nothing else – and showing the ViewRanger live tracker directly above their school quite literally brought it home. All the time I was finding out what I could pull off; though I was careful not to make a habit of winging it too often. All things considered, it went well. Over 200 students were more aware of mental health now. If only one of them had paid true attention, that was good enough for me. On the way out, a teacher stopped in the hallway to say I was an amazing inspiration to young people, while social media messages from the young people direct about their own "Everest" suggested this visit had been worth every minute.

*

The suburban roads of Merseyside made for quick progress, with unexpected pockets of countryside shoved between the towns and villages and bullish white van drivers.

The highest point of Merseyside, Billinge Hill, stood in the nearby village of Billinge. To my surprise, Mum had come along to join me for this one. She had planned this all along, and it was appreciated more than ever. The summit of Billinge Hill was marked by a trig point at 179 metres, but mostly by the beacon tower. For such a diminutive hill, the views across to Greater Manchester were impressive. Mum had never shared my physical drive, and my Mr Motivator approach had not always been well received, but even she declared the walk was a doddle.

*

There were 62 miles left to cycle and my attention switched to counting down the distance, rather than time, and these fresh targets helped me to recover quickly from the resumed isolation. 50 miles was not far from 40, and soon became 30. Time was not proportionate to progress like mileage; miles brought the goal measurably closer and this internal countdown was encouraging.

Cycling the A6 through the heart of Lancashire, I was lashed with hailstones that sent me diving under bus shelters, and doused with road spray that went through to my underpants. It eventually fizzled out towards the open pasture of North Yorkshire and the Yorkshire Dales National Park. Uphill and down dale; the scenic uplands, ribs of dry-stone walls across rolling fields and dramatic limestone landscapes said "God's own county" like the revered Yorkshire Pudding or a proper cup of tea. One hundred miles hadn't turned out too bad in hindsight and 60 miles tomorrow now felt pleasantly insignificant by comparison.

As I rode, I reflected on the distinction between a challenge and an adventure. The idea of being on a bike, or out walking in the hills sounded like heaven on earth. But I was anticipating plenty of discomfort and uncertainty along the way. Those kinds of pressures were obviously not enjoyable – at least not until the satisfaction of overcoming them afterwards. But they were all necessary. And if there was ever a line to be drawn between adventure and a challenge, it was this. Human nature instinctively looked for the easy option and chose to do the things we loved. But setting out to avoid struggles was no way to fully experience life; shying away from the struggle only cheats ourselves of the opportunity to grow and prepare for the harder times.

CHAPTER 5

Day four would be the first "proper" day, from hostel to hostel.

It was another soggy start, and I hurried up a stone-walled lane with my hood perked up like a garden gnome; the map right beneath my eyes like a poorly sighted pensioner. Reaching the top of Whernside was a long slog up the tongue of Scales Moor and West Fell, gradual enough to run the flatter sections and occasionally misjudge puddles above the ankles. In these first days of finding routine, I soon realised running uphill would inflict too much stress on the body to maintain myself for the remainder of the challenge, so I used the time to catch up with emails, social media, and messages instead.

Fleeting breaks in the cloud offered false hopes of the summit ahead and obscured everything in the dale below, with the iconic Ribblehead Viaduct somewhere far on the right. The bevelled top of the ridge plunged into murky nothingness on both sides, with a sense that you could roll off the earth entirely and nobody would know a thing. There was an easy descent into Kingsdale before a sharp ascent up the other side. This became a lumpy, pathless trudge up Back Gill that was nothing like expected. I was at the mercy of a red arrow and a blue line on the screen, dragged like a dog on a lead; not knowing where I was going but knowing no better.

The ridge of Gragareth came as quickly as the wind, with the highest point a few metres off the path. Running down was more appealing, and the Inov-8 trainers gave the option of both, without twisting an ankle. From Gragareth, the descent was like running on sponge with a penetrating wind in my face until the ridge met a series of farm tracks and dropped to the knolls of North End Scar. I was happy to be changing into dry clothes at the hostel and a hearty lunch at the café in Ingleton would see me through the rest.

Eager not to finish another day late again, I was standing up in the saddle until a pain appeared in my left knee and forced me back. This didn't feel good. Something must have pulled during the last 30 miles of cycling. Suddenly, any force was uncomfortable, and every incline had me grimacing. I tried not to panic.

*

That night in Borrowdale, near Keswick, my sore knee set my anxiety off. *What am I going to do? Is it just a little sore? Will it be better tomorrow? Can I bear riding on it?* I knew there was no good in panicking about it, I had been here before: only last time was on the Cho Oyu expedition. The principle was the same: worrying about a possible negative experience was an even more negative experience in itself. Anxiety was all talk and no action. I told myself I was going to have to wait until the morning, then adapt and overcome as needed. An obvious step was to try and reduce weight on the bike.

I was too late for dinner at the hostel restaurant and improvised with a sachet of chocolate protein powder drink, a Snickers bar, and bag of peanuts. There was no solid meal plan to live by; I had to improvise, be efficient, save money. It was still early days, but the prospect was easy to manage when my mind was distracted by much bigger problems and the calorie burn was so high that physical challenges were usually a welcome respite from the bulimia. I could eat my perceived "bad" foods without worrying too much about excess. I sometimes questioned how much this liberty was motivation for doing the challenges to begin with.

A big buffet breakfast of porridge and cereal redeemed the night before. I had quickly mastered the art of eating with one hand and phone in the other.

Within a minute of getting on the bike, the knee had woken up with stabbing pain. Panic set in and sent anxiety running amok. Ignoring it was going to be the biggest challenge of day five – never mind climbing Scafell Pike, the highest point of Cumbria, and England too.

It was barely five minutes to the hamlet of Seathwaite, the wettest inhabited place in England, and a popular start point for the Corridor Route to Scafell Pike and the surrounding fells. Joined by friends, Steph, Fiona, and Mandy, we followed Grains Gill to the old packhorse bridge of Stockley Bridge and headed for the cold waters of Styhead Tarn, guarding the entrance to this rugged cirque of the highest terrain of the Lake District. From the pass, the route fringed below the imposing cliffs of Broad Crag and carefully negotiated the ravine of Piers Gill. The loose rock on this rugged hillside could not have come at a worse time as each jolt and twist sent a bracing pain through the knee and into my hips.

Two figures appeared, running effortlessly up the path between the boulders. It turned out to be Rupert Bonington and another local fell-runner, James. Rupert was the founder of sports nutrition company Mountain Fuel, and the son of mountaineering legend Sir Chris Bonington. I shared my concerns about my knee problem to Rupert as we marched up the path. By chance, he had a physio appointment booked for himself that afternoon and offered it to me without hesitation. To say that I was taken aback by the gesture would be an understatement. He knew the chances of getting to a physio at this short notice would have been unlikely, and although this meant somehow being back in Keswick for 2.30pm, I had a solution at least.

Going to the physiotherapist was like dragging a young child to the dentist, only without the screaming. Five years earlier, a running injury had taken my freedom to run away, and the bulimia had stepped into its place.

Now, a physiotherapist had the same power to deliver news that could throw the entire challenge into jeopardy. I wasn't panicking too much because my experience had given me the ability to adapt and overcome. So instead, I focused on getting up and down again safely, with one final scree slope onto the boulder field summit, until we were stood on the top of England.

*

In a small room of King Kong Climbing Centre, I met Jim, Rupert's physio. After various prods and pokes, he quickly diagnosed a medial quad muscle strain. Obviously, rest would be the best solution, but one he knew I couldn't take lightly. He taped and massaged the area and said the pain could become self-limiting: I just had to go out and try it. There were no guarantees, other than I wouldn't make the 70 miles to Dumfries that night.

I was relieved that it wasn't anything more serious.

*

Pushing on 40 miles to Carlisle seemed an achievable target, but far enough to keep options open and stay on target. To avoid procrastination, I had to act quickly, and booked a B&B in Carlisle on my phone.

Fiona and Mandy rushed me back to my bike in Seathwaite and I found that a large satsuma had been left on the seat. This had clearly not fallen out of the tree above; most hillwalkers were already enjoying post-hill refreshments in the nearest pub. Bemused, I packed it in the bag and headed out of the valley to re-enter the world of mobile phone signal to find several missed calls. YHA Borrowdale had called to check on my whereabouts. The walker I'd met at breakfast noticed the bike was still in Seathwaite on his return. Being this overdue had concerned him enough to check at the hostel. It was a credit to the hillwalking community in looking out for each other on the fells, and I wish

I could have thanked him. With the satsuma now accounted for, I hurried through Keswick and past Bassenthwaite. Covering the knee in blue physio tape somehow felt better, even if it was just a placebo. I knew I'd probably need something stronger for the next two months.

I took the flattest possible option on the A-road towards Bothel, and a road closure sent me on a wide detour. Belfast was still two days away. It would have been easy to focus on the negatives, and I knew that a negative outcome was certainly guaranteed without putting positive thoughts in to begin with. So I thought instead about my friends: Fiona and Mandy and their impromptu taxi service, Steph taking her day off work to join and support me, Rupert giving his physio appointment, Jim treating me free of charge, the concerned hostel staff – and the satsuma – were all things to be grateful for. Donations were coming in steadily to the JustGiving page. People in Scotland were even offering a bed and shower for the night. All these acts of kindness were a reason to continue. Just the fact I was cycling, moving slowly into a bright, chilly evening; was a blessing – and carrying on felt the best way to repay those who not only made it possible for me to be doing this; but for the benefit of others at the same time.

CHAPTER 6

6.30am. I woke up into another day in a new place, alone again. I was already accustomed to feeling alone from my prior expeditions. It would have been easy to reflect endlessly on the feeling of being alone, but the constant time pressure stopped me from ruminating too much. Even when my mood was low, I usually managed to find something to look forward to every morning. Sometimes, the temporary relief of reaching the end of the day was enough to motivate me outside.

I really needed to get going, but finding the momentum was difficult, no matter how quick and efficient I tried to be. There was no denying that the day was going to be a grind, with 40 miles to Dumfries to catch up before 50 miles on the original route, and two mountains to finish the day. Breakfast has always been my favourite meal and a huge carb-loaded feast left me sluggish, and keen to get moving and burn it off. One main anxiety with bulimia, and food in general, was the health risks of having high blood sugar. Exercise was the quickest remedy. And that's why the lack of exercise after my first injury had left me looking for alternative ways to manage it: purging.

The first couple of hours, my "power hours," were a good chance for progress, and I tried to make 30 miles before stopping. The villages of the Dumfries and Galloway region passed in a slow crawl down the B724 without much to see but occasional glimpses of the Solway Firth across fields and pockets of trees. I arrived in Dumfries for 11.00am and collected the supplies from the Best Western hotel where I should have stayed the previous night. (They had made a better job of arriving on time.)

Each stop was a race to do as much as possible in a designated time. Combining things to be more time-efficient, or "concurrent activity", was something that had been instilled by our Everest expedition leader, Tim. I was well practised at charging the phone, posting tweets and replying to messages with one hand, blindly guzzling a sandwich and downing coffee with the other. Although I could drink while cycling and stuff snacks in my jersey pockets, needing to check a tyre, take photos, or de-layer felt like itches and it was often easier to just stop and get them sorted.

High on Everest, the exhaustion of altitude and the cold made everything take much longer than at sea level. Stopping one minute to take your gloves off and have a drink, only to put your gloves back on, continuing a few hundred metres before stopping again to dig the sun cream out of your bag, soon added up the minutes. This was time exposed to danger and the debilitating effects of altitude. Here, the time saved meant less time cycling or walking in the dark later.

I decided to get past Dumfries before stopping for lunch at a tiny convenience store in the village of Crocketford. The ham and cheese sandwich had probably been there six months, only to be scoffed in 60 seconds outside, though I resolved to save the Cadburys' Creme Egg until reaching the halfway point; like coercing a child to eat their vegetables before dessert. The Queen's Way road climbed out of New Galloway in an unproductive slog. I gave in to the Creme Egg earlier than promised. Setting a new target of reaching the town of Newton Stewart would be more robust – it was somewhere I could get dinner, and the comfort of a proper dinner had the power to change a lot.

Seeing the town nearing helped me to appreciate the beauty of these unspoilt uplands in good time. The expanse of

87

Clatteringshaws Reservoir mirrored the Galloway Hills rising behind the water. Forest cascaded down majestic slopes and heather-clad hills on both sides as the road snaked through the Red Deer Range. I was so late arriving in Newton Stewart that another packaged sandwich for dinner would have to do – a couple of chocolate bars and some nuts for later. The incentive of a proper meal had fallen flat again. Far too often, when I was up against the clock, these pie-in-the-sky milestones only gave me false hopes.

The Glen Trool Campsite and Caravan Park was a pleasant place to spend my first night under canvas on the edge of the Galloway Forest Park. It would never have been practical for me to find a bed for each night, though staying in a tent was no bother considering the time I had spent on expeditions in the Himalayas.

The lady owners were charismatic and when they found out that my challenge was in aid of a charity, they scribbled a zero in the box of the registration card, kindly waiving the camping fee. They laughed, saying it saved time doing the accounts anyway. They looked concerned when I announced my plans to climb Merrick that night and threw a pack of oatcakes in for good measure. A similar debate roared in the commons of my mind: whether to have an easy day and do the hills early tomorrow or grab momentum while it lasted and get it done.

If I needed any extra encouragement to get going, I had one ... Midges. I clambered back in to the tent after popping off to the campsite toilets, and then fell straight back out again, as they launched their assault. The people in the neighbouring campervans had their Thursday night entertainment sorted as the swarm of little bleeders had covered everything inside and went for the kill, triggering my own rendition of the can-can while rummaging for the Smidge repellent spray. That did it. I was off!

It was four miles down the road to Loch Trool and the next two county tops, The Merrick and Kirriereoch Hill. With my head down, music helped to set the rhythm through the forest and helped me switch off from the fear of coming back through in the dark later when it was thick enough to muffle screams.

The canopy suddenly disappeared to open hills and a good track climbing a grassy flank towards the minor peak of Benyellary. We were just getting started: from the saddle of Nieve of the Spit, the magnificent mound of The Merrick was presiding higher still. Long-drawn shadows fell behind in the grass, and knobbly mounds of the surrounding uplands sat parallel in the distance. There was a long way to go, but each step was one closer to collapsing in the tent.

After 8.30pm a trig point and a ring of stone appeared at the summit of The Merrick. From the highest peak in the county of Ayrshire and southern Scotland, the kingdom of Galloway opened wide below like a scene from Middle Earth. Spotlights of orange filled the deep shadows in Bog of the Gairy, and burns of water trickled down like veins of fire from the brilliantly named Fang of the Merrick, guarding the head of the glen. Loch Enoch glistened in the falling shadows. A stumpy finger of the mountain dropped steeply to a ridge below. My hopes plummeted too, as I found no sign of the Little Spean ridge on the map. Turns out I was looking straight at it, and Kirriereoch Hill was still further behind. I had also noticed an entourage of threatening black clouds rolling in, thinking: *shit! What if that comes in?*

It had gone 9.00pm. Decisions were made on adrenaline; I couldn't turn back now. I just hoped to make it back in daylight, accepting it would be late regardless. Descending the rocky pasture sent me over on my ankle twice, and my knee didn't enjoy the experience either.

On the summit plateau of Kirriereoch Hill was the highest point of the county of Kirkcudbrightshire, a tiny cairn on a crumbling wall, sitting on the border with historic Ayrshire at 786 metres. Thankfully ViewRanger had marked the spot precisely in the purple fog and it was a case of walking straight to the spot, else I'd have fallen over it. Phone battery had gone down to the final percent so after the standard selfie on each summit, I hurried back to the col before swapping the phone – at least getting the right bearing off the hill first. I zipped every layer and pushed on, physically strong; grateful for the oatcakes in my bag, but there was no time for complacency. The summit was only halfway, especially when the route meant going back over The Merrick again. With long strides in the grooves and ruts of the slope, I pushed upwards, maybe beyond the mountain itself, as if to higher places. A bone-chilling wind whipped up against my back, breeze rattled the tufts of grass violently, followed by eerie stillness. Over my shoulder, the sky roared orange and the shadow of the peak fell twice the length behind; gripping to the slope but losing grip on reality; vulnerable yet truly alive. I felt fortunate to be experiencing such a thing.

Second time round, there was nothing left but a silhouette against pink bands and a purple haze, drawn across the sky like fireworks. I wondered if darkness would ever come; at this time of year it never seemed to fall entirely into night. Across the saddle, Benyellary looked so far away. This illusion of the hills always managed to fool us. The headtorch came on for the penultimate stage as the path disappeared into the dark plantation. I wasn't out of the woods just yet, but I felt unstoppable.

The final four and a half miles back to Glen Trool were a slow crawl. Progress didn't matter now. Clear skies froze the park and numbed my hands, clenched to the handlebars. Reaching the campsite was pure joy and I giggled with relief. Their campsite bothy had a kettle and a mug – the Swiss Army knife of adventure worldwide. The warming malt of the chocolate protein drink had never tasted so good. Ninety-five miles on the bike, 10 on foot, and 18 hours later, nothing was going to rush this quiet moment of reflection. There was nobody to celebrate it with, but I toasted the friends and former strangers in Cumbria who had helped make this possible.

It was 1.30am before I slithered into the sleeping bag. To think I had nearly left the ultra-light Marmot bag at home and roughed it for the cost of saving a few hundred grams sent an even deeper shiver through the arms. Every scenario I had feared was exactly that: a fear. Reality rarely produced anything as extreme as the unbounded imagination. Experiencing the avalanche on Everest a few years earlier was an exception to the rule, and it lifted these bounds entirely. What it had left was a willingness to discover what scenarios I might be able to handle: forever preparing for the worst, hoping for the best, and carrying on regardless.

CHAPTER 7

The light filled the tent four hours later. I stirred in the sleeping bag contemplating running to the wooden bothy for my breakfast before the midges got me for theirs.

After the saga of the previous night, I was looking forward to an easier day with just one smaller county top before the port of Cairnryan and the ferry to Northern Ireland for the next stage.

Each morning started with this judgement of easy or hard, though the definition was becoming unclear – each tough day built the foundation and raised the threshold so that each smaller day should have felt easier. The morning was beautifully bright and warm as I rode to Polbae through cleared plantation forest down tiny, rough asphalt lanes. The fatigue of a 12,000ft ascent grew, and the bumps felt like sandpaper rubbing on my saddle sore!

Over the last few days a sore spur had appeared in my right ankle to keep the knee company, with the grimacing pain that had blighted each day since the Lake District and forced me to pedal at a painfully slow rate of progress. It was annoying, but I knew that I would just adapt – as usual. I took a huge amount of satisfaction from overcoming adversity and digging deep, in an almost masochistic fashion. It was where I found my strength, and continually disproved the limitations imposed on me by my childhood. My past experiences raised a mirror of my capabilities, so that taking the easy option always felt like an excuse, while falling behind schedule was also much harder to tolerate than the short-term doggedness of pushing on.

With some faint 3G, I managed to change the ferry to a later crossing, which let me take more time with the knee. It was the right thing to do; but it felt like a weakness. My Sergeant Major was never far away and kept playing the old tapes of childhood bullying. These taunts had wired an unhelpful insistence on high standards within my mind which instantly turned the blame inwards whenever I failed to meet my targets, however big or small. It couldn't recognise achievements either, dwelling on the failures rather than the much greater number of successes.

Deep down, I knew that, just like the taunts of bullies, these events were often inconsequential in the grand scheme of things.

*

A boggy track led off on the Southern Upland way until a clearance reached the grassy summit of Craig Airie Fell – the county top of Wigtownshire. The trig point just crept over 1,000ft at 321 metres high, but the views were magnificent except for the windfarm scarring the untamed green below. The reverse route was the same; and only now, with the time pressure taken off, did I notice the wildlife, upland birds and the skirting board of bluebells besides the track.

The final stretch cut through a sea of matted moorland and deep pockets of forest, nothing but occasional isolated houses. A lady stood by the road outside at a campsite near Loch Heron and said 'hello' as I passed. Just to be acknowledged by another human was like being given a hundred quid and the beaming smile and cheerful 'Hello!' I shouted back would have given an entirely different impression of how I was actually feeling at the time. But deliberate positive actions were enough to distract my mind and restore the balance for a while.

The carpet of the moorland was outstretching and tranquil, too tranquil. I was looking for anything to make it more interesting

– checking the map or phoning home for encouragement. This lack of distraction turned my mind inwards, focusing on only the negative: the knee, the fatigue, the dehydration.

All morning I had started to lag and the combined sore backside, fatigue, and rhythmless roads tipped the mental balance the wrong way. There was plenty of time to catch the ferry, but now anxiety was telling me otherwise.

The next hope of facilities was the village of New Luce where the saga of poor planning continued as the village shop turned out to be closed too. At the slow intensity I could easily have pedalled on fat stores all day, but it felt like I had left everything on The Merrick the night before. My body knew what it needed and would throw a protest until it got it. Feeling in despair, I tore open a packet of Mountain Fuel carbohydrate drink and necked the dry powder with a minor fit of spluttering and coughing a cloud of pineapple dust, hoping some sugar would give a surge of life. The road flattened along the River Luce and the crest of the moor loomed far ahead as it wound around each corner, stretching patience thinner each time. At the top I knew the coast and the next stage would be in view, but it seemed never-ending. After turning a bend in the lane, the grass really was greener on the other side. The blue of Loch Ryan and faint outline of Stranraer came into view – as did the Stena Line ferry I had originally booked already cruising outside of the bay. The pain and fatigue were suddenly balanced. There was double redemption with a sweeping downhill ride all the way to the coastal road at Invermessan.

The ferry port staff at Cairnryan had probably never seen someone so happy to be there. One problem was solved with a decent feed on the ferry ride. Cravings called for something nutritious: a roast chicken leg dinner, minestrone soup, an apple and coffee. For the same reason, after expeditions in the Himalayas I always asked for grilled fish and fresh vegetables for the first meal at home following six weeks of fried food and biscuits. My usual home meals were nourishing and fulfilling. The problem was everything in between. When the body felt good, it was difficult for the mind not to follow, and I enjoyed the feeling of eating well. The body had a clever way of telling what it needed, even if mine often got confused with what it didn't. I was looking forward to my first ever visit to Northern Ireland, the new experiences, people and places.

The enormity of the challenge had started to dawn on me. There was a sense of dread about everything still to come, the uncertainty, and the ongoing discomfort of long hours in all weathers and unforeseen circumstances as I moved away from familiarity and further towards uncertainty. In good time, my friend, Chris Spray, sent a message of encouragement on Facebook and I jumped at the opportunity to vent these fears and anticipations. His sixth sense as an executive coach was probably why he messaged to begin with. In starting a conversation, the door was opened and free to become whatever it needed to be. Sharing those feelings was important as it took them out of my head and accepted them. Another resident from my village, Chris had a passion for helping people to excel, that had first connected with my Everest ambition years earlier, and naturally adopted the role of a mentor. Nowadays the dynamic had changed, Chris had got me to where I needed to be, but I still regularly called on his advice.

A bracing chill and briny smell rattled me awake as I stepped onto the mainland. The docks were deserted, the seagulls long gone. It was only five miles to the hostel through rough industrial estates and grimy streets as locals poured out of pubs onto the pavements, the holler of police cars not far away in the big city. The shadows of this cosmopolitan city were lit by sickly streetlights as I passed through half-asleep, cocooned in the hi-vis jacket. Ugly electric gates opened into the car park compound of Belfast Youth Hostel and I locked the bike inside.

Rowdy Friday racket from the neighbouring pub came through the tiny window of the shower. I stood in the cubicle for what must have been 30 minutes, pressing the button over and over, savouring the simple luxury of hot water. There was little reason to stop, besides the late night and an even earlier start, clutching every minute of sleep I could get.

CHAPTER 8

My first morning in Belfast was unceremoniously drizzly and soggy. If only compared to the other days so far, today would be a tough one with nearly 100 miles and two walks.

Having two friends joining my first of the county tops, Slieve Donard, was something to look forward to. Creating these little stages was enough to get to where I needed to be, before adding a bit more and a bit more, and getting to the end of the day.

I left at 6.30am and made fast progress on the flat A24 road towards a pleasant day ahead.

I was enjoying the new landscape of Northern Ireland heading south through villages, and soon after Seaforde, Slieve Donard and the dramatic humps of the Mourne Mountains appeared. I pushed against the clock; arriving on time was more important than the knee pain. David and Sonya flagged me down on the high street of Newcastle where, as the old song said, the Mourne Mountains swept down to the sea. For once, timing had worked out perfectly as they watched the tracker online and kindly arranged with the tourist centre to leave my bike there, dry and safe. Local walkers and keen cyclists themselves, David and Sonya Coulter had followed for a few years on social media. I was glad they could join me and climb their local peak. Their conversation filled me with energy as we chatted enthusiastically, walking up through the dense paths of Donard forest. Nepal was close to

Sonya's heart after trekking to Everest Base Camp herself, and they told me in person how they had prayed for all of us stuck up at Camp One on Everest in 2015 when news came through on David's phone of a massive earthquake in Nepal.

The path ventured through the woods and crossing streams before leaving into open country and following the Glen River towards a subtle mountain bowl flanked by these hill giants. The path wasted no time in gaining almost all 850 metres of height from sea level and pulled towards a saddle between Slieve Donard and Slieve Commedagh, where it met the famous Mourne Wall, a dry-stone wall which stretched 22 miles over 15 mountains, and took over 18 years to build. My eyes followed it into the distance, cutting ruthlessly across sharp valleys and mountains capped by granite tors, and I tried to get my head around why anyone would bother. The final pull followed the wall on a bare flank of the mountain and my legs felt they would give way. It was not a route for the faint-hearted but soon rewarded us with wide sweeping views across Dundrum Bay and the town below; the rich blue of the Irish Sea dampened to grey by a flat cap of dark cloud hanging close above. The highest point of County Down was the Bronze Age cairn of stones, though another trig point stood on top of a stone tower. For an extra summit bonus, Sonya pulled a pack of Custard Cream biscuits from the bag. I had joked at the start of the challenge with an open plea for Custard Creams. Sonya had absolutely nailed the memo. My first Irish mountain sent us off with a battering of hailstones as we hooded up and backtracked down the wall. We aimed to get down by 1.00pm, and they had offered to treat me with lunch too. I was quietly doing the maths and contemplating whether falling behind schedule was a good idea, while my phantom ankle spur flared up another level, slowing me down, almost to a limp. We were back in Newcastle faster than planned: 3 hours, 36 minutes. David and Sonya were chuffed to have a new personal best time. In a celebratory mood, with my body feeling depleted and with 60 miles to go, I was in no hurry to leave. Getting a big refuel would save time by way of strength later that day. Losing an hour would gain much more in good company, and a hearty bowl of Irish stew and soda bread hit the spot. I was sad to leave, and a week in, I was still learning to deal with the natural come down after the high of good company. The Mourne Mountains were soon shrouded in a grumpy darkness behind as I snaked around their rear end, heading towards the town of Newry.

My mind knew better than to dwell on emotions and quickly switched to the next milestone of Slieve Gullion.

The dark clouds caught up and hailstones lashed hard like pellets off my helmet. Sun cream washed into my eyes. Salt tasted in my mouth. The blue strands of physio tape peeled straight off the legs and now I had lost my racing stripes, to the amusement of every passing man and his dog. These dark clouds quickly caught up with my mind too. Eventually I dived for cover in a bus shelter and rang home. Mum told me, 'You know you can do this. You'll only feel worse if you don't.' She was right – as usual – and this was the trap: once committed you had no choice but to keep going until the task was complete. Having the choice usually made enduring outdoor challenges much easier than depression, but sometimes I still felt indifferent. Maybe being alone again had forced me to confront this reality, never mind the saddle sore that fiercely resented wet shorts. Sure enough, the vales of green on the Emerald Isle lit up again.

The rolling hills smiled back, life felt good. From flatter farmlands, the distinct Ring of Gullion formation rose out of the fields like a dome. Eventually I found the start of the scenic Forest Drive and a sharp road gave no choice but to stand up in the saddle again. At least it gave a head start on the walk, which took less than 20 minutes from a layby on a staircase path through the mountain heath. The top of County Armagh was marked by two stone trig points at 576 metres close by. One side of the mountain was having a tantrum, casting ominous darkness on the ground below; the other was lit in glorious sunshine and fluffy clouds, glowing green across the patchwork of fields. The wind made for a chilly ride and the hefty neon cycling jacket had not come off all day. This final 30 miles felt much better than 30 miles had felt the day before. I was fast learning that it was not so much the distance that mattered, but the mindset.

Even when I could get food at the end of each day, it was becoming lazy routine to pick up dinner en route to save time and money once I got to the hostel, too tired to go searching for something fulfilling. So, after stopping in the shady village of Newtownhamilton, it was now downhill almost all the way into Armagh in fading daylight, and I certainly wasn't going to stop then. The hostel was larger than expected and I was very happy to arrive. Unfortunately, the Custard Creams hadn't made it, but had served me well.

By day seven, the elation at the end of each day wasn't wearing off. Having a room to myself, complete with a bath tub, gave the chance to wash clothes and coerce the essence of 14 counties out of my Inov-8 trainers. A letter was also waiting in my room. Mike and his wife Sonia had sent a card with a chicken suit mural printed on the front, and the message: *Could be worse, you could be doing it in a chicken suit!* made me chuckle. The surprise had taken me back to where it had all started. From the conception to the real thing, they were still with me, and I suddenly felt less alone.

Mornings were always sluggish. I wondered if this morning lethargy was psychological. I knew that waking up with depression needed a different outlook if you expected anything better than the day before. The previous day was proof that I could do it again. Knowing we could manage something didn't necessarily make it less daunting, only more do-able; running a hundred marathons beforehand didn't stop the last mile of a race being painful; only less uncertain.

It only took one mini-success to register as an achievement in the brain, and get the ball rolling. Doing the most difficult and least favourite task first in the morning helped to create momentum. Obviously, cycling all day then climbing mountains was just that, but beforehand, there was getting started and going through a mental checklist. I tried to get the bags packed, the bottles filled, and the bike unlocked first so that there was only breakfast to savour and a rapid Wi-Fi session before getting on the move. Trying to motivate myself to run during my low points often meant sleeping in running gear to get up and out before breakfast; the longer I had to get out of the door, the greater the chances of finding an excuse. In the same way, having company created milestones, breaking the day up into fuel stops gave something to look forward to. On these quieter days with little else to focus on I became infatuated with food instead. Food could dominate my thoughts for the day so much that I almost forgot about the challenge. In truth, it was more of an obsession than a love for food; it was hard to love something that caused so much grief. But I fundamentally needed to survive, which trapped me in what felt more like an abusive relationship. Bulimia was a controlling partner that expected my challenge diet plan to be mapped out to military precision. But in reality, getting from A to B meant eating what I could when I could. Anything else was a bonus.

This was the spirit of adventure, after all. Ultimately what I found in these places was usually a matter of pot luck, and each morning, I started researching cafés, shops, and even petrol stations on Google Maps to make the best of the experience, aiming for bigger towns in the likelihood they would have more facilities. Typically, the next village would appear soon after I'd made my breakfast stop, teeming with even more shops and better prospects, and I would kick myself for this too. Or was that the bulimia trying to make its cravings seem more acceptable? It was all about control, after all.

*

Cracks and crags of rock guarded the flat summit plateau of Cuilcagh, and a wooden staircase climbed to the top, offering a dizzying look down across the carpet of bog I had just crossed on a boardwalk. The wind kicked up a notch and threw me all over the place. The top of County Fermanagh was marked by an old ancient cairn of rocks with a trig point on the top like the candle on a 666-metre cake. From the car park it was only 40 miles to the town of Omagh. The Bed and Breakfast owner encouraged me not to kill myself getting there. I went hell for leather regardless in those final hours. Forty miles was the same distance used in most training rides for Everest, so the number was easy to manage mentally. And the Garmin Edge device on the handlebar helped. It was more than just a navigation tool, it logged speed, distance, calories, ascent and heart rate. This lifeless screen became a companion of sorts. It never said much but the details it gave had the power to change a day entirely, to taunt or encourage in equal measure.

To my joy, I had discovered a setting which displayed the remaining distance for the planned route. Counting the miles travelled seemed more encouraging than the miles still to go – until I reached halfway and switched, when the remaining miles became the smaller number. Miles brought the goal measurably closer – even when the miles passed more slowly. Hitting the 20-mile mark always began an internal countdown where the end felt in sight, I was certain to make it. It would soon become part of the daily programme that I would hardly notice. With this certainty I was happy to step up the gear, spinning as fast as the knee would allow, weighing up whether arriving in good time to eat, sleep, and recover was almost as important as taking things slowly. After preserving myself in the mornings – either to ensure reaching the finish or for lack of motivation – the second wind always came, albeit usually in my face. This physical capability and reserve of energy could only mean that mindset was steering the engine, rather than the other way around, as the pace picked up out of nowhere on the quiet A32 road, making the pleasing discovery of basic geography that towns and cities were usually found at the bottom of a hill.

Getting to Omagh before dark took priority once again, and I made do with a petrol station sandwich, nuts and coffee for dinner in the town of Enniskillen. After 97 miles, getting to Omagh at bang on 9.30pm put the usual smile on my face.

Up the pebbled driveway, Mullaghmore House was a bizarre place. The listed Georgian house on the edge of the town was once home to the *Jurassic Park* actor Sam Neill, and it seemed to have been kept as a historic shrine. I waited for a while at the door, and was hardly surprised by the elderly, wiry-haired owner in a gown who answered. Paintings and sculptures lined dusty corridors and an over-sized chandelier hung on a creaky wooden staircase, with hard-wood panelled ceilings and stag horn mantelpieces. The wet-room was like a royal suite with another cohort of artefacts and mosaics. I only hoped the complimentary Bourbon biscuits weren't 80 years past their expiry date either; dunking them into the chocolate protein drink and crashing out.

CHAPTER 9

The importance of balancing easy and hard days was becoming quickly obvious; this pushing and pulling created the hope and can-do attitude to get me through. Today was only 66 miles and one shorter walk, so I started in an optimistic mindset.

Finding the route up Sawel Mountain was going to be more inconspicuous than the rest so far but I would deal with the uncertainty when I got there. A gentle valley rolled between the Sperrin Mountains along miles of criss-cross hedgerows and pasture, with abandoned farmhouses hidden in their shadows, lost like relics. It was cycling bliss, but I quickly got bored at the pace of things, endless miles of the same, hedge after hedge, field after field, but my temptation to speed up was quickly thwarted by the knee pain reminding me of its presence. Any hope of it fading away after brief respites was soon knocked back by another stab of fire shooting up through the limb. This emotional see-saw of uncertainty had taken motivation with it. It felt like something out of my control was threatening to put all my efforts to waste. I was just going to have to find new ways to keep myself occupied, or learn to enjoy the art of doing nothing. After losing count of sheep too quickly, I kept myself occupied with practising my best Irish accent aloud with each passing road sign. After three days of trying, this still sounded scouse.

The Sperrin Road climbed towards a vantage point spanning the unspoilt uplands. Across this wide grassy basin Sawel

Mountain was appealing in the distance with its bald, open slopes. The road flattened until a second cattle grid marked the spot, and I locked the bike to a sturdy fence. Apparently, the solid lock could resist an angle grinder, so the bike itself was less of a concern. Peace of mind usually meant decanting everything into the rucksack and hauling that up the hill too. Leaving gear behind was a case-by-case basis. Here, the closest sense of civilisation was a sheep pen. A local passed once in a pick-up truck and took a good stare. Before finishing tying up my shoes, he turned and passed again; not saying a word. I felt a bit uneasy and kept glancing back until the road fell out of view. A wire fence for a mile and a half led the way, negotiating the best line through tufty grass and squelchy bog in places. On the summit I had killed two birds with two feet, as the counties of Londonderry and Tyrone met in the same spot. It was the standard affair of a trig point and a few wired fences marking boundaries, the obligatory selfie, and following the route back. It was a relief to see the bike still there ready for the descent out of the Sperrins.

I took advantage of the shorter day and the opportunity for a "proper" sit-down meal; not knowing when I would get the next one, as the daily plan of having a hearty dinner, putting my feet up and enjoying the sights at the end of each day became less predictable. The village bistro in Dungiven was ideal to escape the rain for an hour or so.

The day had come together perfectly. Arriving earlier at 6.30pm made a pleasant change and I almost didn't know what to do with myself. It was a chance to catch up with the niggly tasks that had been popping to mind when on the saddle. Staying in hostels was such a convenience that I considered cancelling some of the planned camps further down the itinerary rather than making things harder than necessary. In a Skype call back home, Mum showed the phone screen to the dog. Hector looked confused as if seeing himself in the mirror for the first time. Looking ahead at the schedule of hilly days in Scotland for the next two weeks depended on whether the knee would hold up.

This push of responsibilities always drained the last bit of energy until I fell asleep on the sofa of the hostel lounge.

Another straightforward day of 76 miles didn't bother me, the bike was cleaned with some dishcloths from the supermarket, and my jersey was cleaned in the bathroom sink after smelling like cheese and onion crisps for the last few days.

*

Bushmills was only a couple of miles from Giants Causeway, the first UNESCO World Heritage site in Northern Ireland. I was always hesitant to stop in these morning power hours; though this was a worthy exception. Turning around the cliffs felt like stepping back into prehistoric times. The beach had been ripped up and replaced with bizarre hexagonal columns of rock jutting out of the ground; almost too uniform to be natural, perhaps the artwork of some higher force. Waves crashed hard as they protruded into the sea, and as far back as the cliffs that kept them a secret. After a photo I got back to the day plan. The coastal road was decorated with bluebells, flashes of yellow gorse and golden bays plunging below the cliffs at the edge of potato fields. The charming harbour village of Ballycastle was lined with sea-front cafés and a beach coffee hut as I flashed through and began the long gradual climb to Ballypatrick Forest. In beautiful blue skies the Irish Sea stretched wider behind me, reaching across to the Scottish coast.

I was flying and felt strong; aiming to get to Cushendall for lunch. For the first time, I was genuinely enjoying the simple motion of spinning on the bike, despite the occasional potholes sending fire through the lingering saddle sore. I had enjoyed the scenery so much that I had texted Dad who I thought would appreciate this, being a keen road cyclist himself. With living down south, Dad had not been involved in my challenges to the same extent as Mum, and perhaps because I felt less able to share the emotions when things went wrong. Maintaining contact with challenges was difficult, especially when racing the clock, and Dad was more than happy with the odd message to let him know I was safe. As a hopeless mechanic, I was grateful to regularly call on his cycling and mechanical expertise. But on a deeper level, my close-call on Everest had brought us closer rather than turned him away from my selfish pursuits. Maybe he wanted to be part of something that clearly meant so much to me.

The lush greens soon faded into murky moorland where the mound of my next county top, Trostan, was so subtle that I didn't know I had cycled straight past. The thick cloak of the Glenariff Forest rose up around the road, marking the entrance to Glenariff – "Queen of the Glens" – one of nine glens in Antrim. The steep forested hillside across the glen led the way to Trostan. Although I was annoyed with myself for eating a whole pack of potato bread, it probably explained the extra strength I had felt all day. The Moyle Way made a promising start across cleared plantation with wildflowers rising high above the skeletal stumps. The gravel track soon veered off into a thick forest that my dog would have got lost in, waymarked by yellow tape hanging from the trees. There was pure silence except for the shoe-cleaning trickle of enchanting streams with mossy trunks and tangled tree roots.

Reaching the trig point 550 metres up, on the bare moonscape summit – the highest point of County Antrim – hadn't taken much effort. But someone had clearly had a bad day in the office: an office chair was lying upside down next to the three cairns of rock nearby. I span around for a 360-degree panorama of views across to the Antrim coast and sweeping patches of forests in the glens below; it wasn't a bad spot to take a breather.

I had been getting cravings for everything – from Irish treacle bread, to Subway sandwiches, fish and chips, and the local ice cream that seemed to call out at me from every corner shop I passed. Bulimia could pester for days on end, and like a crying baby, it went quiet when it got what it wanted. Considering I had been fuelling up regularly to avoid genuine body cues, these intense urges for food could have been the bulimia at play, or the perfectionist desire to make the most of the experience that came with me whenever I travelled on expeditions. I would want to try everything on offer and overeat for the sake of ticking things off the list, rather than genuine want. My perfectionist drive and the eating disorder were partners in crime, but I couldn't tell which was to blame. Maybe it was both.

Sometimes, it was just easier to satisfy the urges, rather than leave them free to fester all day on the bike. And I felt a familiar pressure to make the most of every experience; absorbing different foods, places and cultures.

The burden of childhood regret still loomed large and fuelled the desire to experience everything; to achieve more. I had missed so many opportunities because of anxiety around my stammering and epilepsy as a child. There was no point wasting more time in regret, only in making the rest of life count. It had driven me on to do things to the best of my ability, and to make the most of every opportunity. The irony was this constant expectation only stole the joy from those moments. Bulimia was home to a high court of judges who would question everything I ate and ruled that the sugary treats I craved weren't needed. When I felt particularly, pathetically low, I felt as though I had only ever been cycling for the freedom to indulge in the first place; conveniently forgetting everything good I had experienced so far.

It was important to be kind to myself. But that didn't come easily.

If I used food to help me deal with challenges at home, then it was unrealistic to expect anything different under this level of strain. The familiar worry around weight gain wouldn't go away. My calorie burn reduced as my cycling intensity dropped because of the knee injury, and it meant I couldn't allow the usual guilt-free face-stuffing on big endurance days. The challenge was in restoring a natural balance with food, trying to regard it as necessary fuel for the body.

That day, my bulimia was making its demands known, and the remaining distance, progress, and perspective all came second to how it made me feel. Luckily, it was less than 40 miles back to Belfast. I had enough fuel and water to reach the finish, so I knew that, if I ignored the emotional cravings for a while longer, I would soon find peace. After reaching the end point of the day these thoughts fell into order under other priorities that couldn't be processed during long hours on the saddle.

*

Dark gloomy roads led back to Belfast Youth Hostel, ready to catch the ferry the next morning. The parcel that had arrived a few days earlier to top up supplies for the Ireland stage had unfortunately missed the shaving gel, and a simple shave cut my chin, bleeding like a stuck pig. I was walking around the hostel kitchen with a towel clutched to my face; the other hand trying to microwave a can of soup for dinner. A Japanese tourist walked into the dormitory to find his room-mate half-dressed with blood dripping over the floor. I resisted telling him that he was next; he looked worried enough already. Some "holiday" this was turning out to be.

CHAPTER 10

On the early ferry back to Cairnryan the sense of time had truly started to sink in, along with the pressure to make the most of the challenge, engaging as many people and raising as much money for Young Minds as possible. It felt like this depended on my updates, blogs, and initiative. There was so much to share, and so little time – barely enough time to complete the challenge itself – I had never anticipated there would be so little time to do this once the challenge started. My inner perfectionist still expected better. The perfectionist drive had been with me since childhood – a long-term squatter in my head I was trying to evict. It was another part of the program wired in by bullying that had me instinctively aiming for high standards, whether realistic or not, in order to feel good enough.

That tendency to all-or-nothing thinking didn't take circumstances into account when evaluating myself at the end of every day. This vice continually demanded more of me, but the harsh reality was that on too many days, I simply finished too late for a warm meal or a shower.

In the exhaustion of each evening it was important to start being in the moment: to capture the vivid feeling of fatigue for when the perfectionist demands piped up, so I could accept that whatever I was doing was already the best I could. The same applied to binge urges. Overcoming them was about learning to evaluate myself based on effort, which was controllable, rather than the outcome, which was dependent on other things.

There were other pressures too. Sponsors were rightfully asking me to promote and tag things already which was not unreasonable, but another "big ask" when co-ordinating from afar. Past challenges had taught me to be selective, but it was always stressful. For what felt like a one-man army, having PR support from Mick was invaluable with so much to do and so little time. One follower had even commented how impressed he was that I managed to post anything at all. When people took the time to support and encourage me unconditionally, then making the effort to acknowledge it was important, too.

*

For what Ayrshire lacked in dramatic scenery it made up for with subtle beauty. Riding a stunning open coastal road, parallel to the dark rocks of the shoreline and green spurs of hills on the other side, had me stripped down to a jersey again in the warm sea breeze. Across the Firth of Clyde was the unmistakeable granite island of Ailsa Craig that distracted eyes off the road. Girvan was the first target for power hour and the busy A77 had me there in no time. After grabbing coffee and a croissant I was already pushing on towards the town of Ayr, the second milestone of the day. The artificial greens of Turnberry and Donald Trump's Golf Resort interrupted the scenery with white-wash buildings, pristine borders and generally being as tacky and artificial as the man himself. Gentle rolling hills pulled away from the coast with little else to see but fields of sheep, though glimpses of the sea were never far below.

There were no county tops to walk today, but the knee pain had returned with a vengeance, and suddenly deteriorated for no obvious reason. The stabbing pain now came almost continually, regardless of speed and effort, with the time pressure of catching the ferry forcing me to pedal through it.

Brodick ferry terminal was the first step onto the fascinating island of Arran, that showcased nearly every landscape that Scotland had to offer in one place. The oceanic climate felt like the Mediterranean. Colourful rhododendron bushes lined the coastal road with stunning flowers and bird life. Crawling along slowly gave me the opportunity to admire the pretty coastal cottages and I quickly decided that I wanted to live there. Further north, the dramatic mountains of Arran rose in the centre as if a volcanic desert island, reminding me of the otherworldly Isle of Skye. The mountains also meant one thing. An abrupt 400 ft climb: Lochranza Youth Hostel was on the other side. Another feature of the Garmin was an elevation map. The screen was the most literal model of peaks and troughs. Acceptance was better than uncertainty. It gave me hills to anticipate and downhills to enjoy; today, the sharp line meant a steep climb. Combining this with the saddle sore and high cadence was like fire. My face creased up, crying out loud in pain. Cycling in paradise was not distracting enough.

In the Lochranza youth hostel kitchen, Pot Noodle and a Snickers bar didn't fill the gap for dinner, but I struggled to buy something substantial whenever I felt hopeless about my situation, even though I knew that was only ever a recipe for disaster. No amount of bread, jam, and rice from the "free food" shelf was going to solve the low ebb that had landed after a gruelling day with my knee, but eating several helpings was the only control I could find in the situation.

It was the closest thing I'd had to a binge in weeks. I felt like I was losing control again; being stubborn wouldn't cut it, and now taking a rest was looking inevitable. Almost a week had passed since vowing that if I could get through the next few days then I could get through anything, and the injury was a different animal now, the same bait wouldn't work forever, and it was pushing the pain threshold high enough that necking ibuprofen tablets like candy, as I had for the last week, would only help so much. The fear wasn't the thought of quitting, but being forced to quit by something beyond my control, and admitting defeat to adversity that pissed on my personal parade. Ditching the weight of the camping gear somewhere to reduce the weight and finding proper accommodation for the next planned camps, or posting the camping gear ahead, would cost more money. Anxiety said that if I spent more money than I was raising then I might as well just donate the money itself rather than spending the money just to carry on. The whole point seemed defeated.

Knowing I could go home at any point, gave me renewed faith in my own agency. It was my choice to carry on moving forwards. Whatever might have been going wrong in life, being active was a guaranteed way to keep moving forwards and get over the next mountain. There was only one way off the island after all. And however hard things might get, moving forwards always helped me get past it all.

It had always been the case that after each episode of binge eating, it had quickly faded into insignificance once the day started and things got moving without it. After binges, I would usually try and compensate by exercising without breakfast until I felt hungry, as a way of punishing myself for the lapse in control. It was porridge as usual, which was the first step of taking control, pressing the reset button and letting go of the day before, rather than setting off with the shoelaces of my mind tied together. After chatting to a couple of American hikers in the kitchen and telling them what I was doing, I couldn't really change my mind.

I noticed how my mood lifted after the first mile bleeped on the screen. It was energising. The sense of progress slowed quickly afterwards, but it kept going. Making progress on a goal created more positive emotions and satisfaction. And in turn these positive feelings created motivation and action, and momentum. Once we had momentum it was a win-win situation that kept generating more action towards the goal, like throwing more wood on the fire. It gave me an element of control back. I knew that mileage didn't matter without the right mindset, but only 44 miles of cycling was still an uplifting thought, and I felt like something was in my favour for once.

Straightaway, the knee had woken up on the wrong side of the bed again; otherwise it was a bright and promising start. Goatfell was the highest point of the historic county of Buteshire. Finding somewhere to lock the bike in the coastal village of Corrie wasn't much of a concern when there was only one way off the island. The track from the village followed a stream. I was moving fast, with the threat of missing the ferry back more painful than the stabs in my knee, and the mountain ahead was a majestic sentinel shouldered by ridges and peppered with grey rocks like snow. Boulder-hopping had me on the summit within 90 minutes, and the white trig point rose proudly from this granite castle. The viewpoint across the island and the sea was confined to an eerie blanket of fog that added to its magical aura. I had never known fog to be warm. With the salt air and sand between the granite boulders and alpine shrubs, it felt like climbing a mountain and going to the beach all at once.

*

If I was going to stay and recover anywhere, Arran would have been the place. However, Glasgow would give a good base, with more options and facilities. Mum said there was a surprise waiting at Glasgow and refused to say what – that was the point. The first hour was miserably slow through the Garnock valley. The town of Dalry was the first milestone. I was advised a knee support might help, but at a tiny pharmacy the compression sleeves were better suited for Grandma than an endurance athlete. They were better than nothing, and in theory, would prevent sudden movements and swelling at the joint.

Back on the bike the tight neoprene quickly began to rub the skin like a rash. Somehow the muscle pain seemed to become manageable if only because the pain had moved elsewhere.

Keeping below the pain threshold would mean cycling at a slower pace which made the distance feel much further. But it was progress for all I cared, and would just take more effort to hold it together mentally.

At the top of a long climb up the scenic Calder Glen Road would be a 12-kilometre walk and still the matter of getting to Glasgow. This time I had positive thoughts at the ready: I looked across to the beautiful mottled green slopes of Misty Law – the three-mile downhill on the way back, and the thought of getting to Glasgow at a reasonable hour, knowing the worst of the hills were now done. I locked the bike near the quiet Muirshiel Visitor Centre and got to business straightaway. A gravel track led towards the old Baryte mine which had closed 40 years earlier. From the old mine shafts and safety fences it became a frustrating traipse through a giant pathless bog and old shooting country. Pleasing views opened to the right towards the Clyde, far softer on the edges than Arran. Hill of Stake was an obvious target ahead. Getting across Queenside Muir without plunging into bog water was less straightforward. Springy heather and knee-high grass made hard work of it, and the faint tracks were barely distinct enough for a rabbit; a tree or two wouldn't have gone amiss. The county top of Renfrewshire was marked by a trig point which unsurprisingly I had to myself. Descending via Queenside Hill as planned would have saved a mile but retracing the original steps, not that they existed, seemed a safer bet to save time.

The routine 20-mile countdown to the finish took longer than usual. *You're going to make it!* I repeated in my head, over and over. Using positive language had a propelling effect. A scientist named John Eccles had won the Nobel Peace Prize for finding specific signal transmissions among neurons in the brain, noting how using positive language created a genuine physical response of strength and flicked the volition switch to action, while negative language drained energy, and flicked it off.

By 10.00pm I was at the grand Victorian exterior of SYHA Glasgow youth hostel against orange streetlights; everything felt okay again. As expected, there was a shoebox with another pair of running shoes to help the ankle. Christmas had come early with carrot cake, chocolate granola from my favourite café, and peanut butter sandwiches wrapped in foil. Mums did know best, even if I didn't like to admit it. A text message made my appreciation clear:

You absolute legend!!!

It was all scoffed before an urge could even register, without any guilt for calories either. Normally eating treats so late was characteristic of a binge at home. Usually treats were totally out of bounds. But I knew how much these urges to binge were so tied up in how I felt about myself at the time.

And how was I feeling that night? I was still promising myself that the end of the challenge was just around the corner. Enough was enough. Just thinking that was so comforting, and enough to keep me going, yet it was a cruel decoy. At the end of each day there was always a little something left in the bag: it felt possible again. Surely my mind was going to sniff a rat in these false promises. Making it this far had taken away another excuse not to carry on tomorrow, as had the donations on JustGiving. I had done enough of these things to know that decisions were always best made in the morning. Deciding to run another marathon didn't come in the moment of exhaustion at the finish line, and it wouldn't now, so I slept on it, and slept like a baby as well.

CHAPTER 11

Not having a solid target to wake up for was like starting a car without petrol. The morning routine ran like a default program regardless; loading the bags and creeping out of the dormitory.

Breakfast was spent weighing up the options on a fresh mindset: making decisions in the saddle among other physical and mental noise was difficult, just like making decisions when depressed and seeing only one colour in the palette. I was still uncertain whether to stay or go. Was it really *that* bad? Staying didn't mean stopping the challenge itself, but changing the plan to something I didn't want: to rest, to let the injury recover properly, and then putting the schedule together again. But stopping felt like quitting, and wasn't something I wanted to even consider. The fear of losing momentum was more rational. From experience, getting back on schedule and finding momentum again was much tougher than hanging on to it in the first place.

I was honest about my feelings with my supporters on Twitter and Facebook, and the response came back: to rest. I knew that choosing not to risk breaking myself was a positive example of self-care. But I also knew that any challenge in the public eye carried the possible burden of letting others down. Inspiring people was a good enough reason to keep going, and I had a responsibility to be a good example. Plenty of people suggested taking it easy, but they clearly hadn't seen what was coming next on the map ... the biggest mountains and most unforgiving cycling passes in the country.

I was just on a mission, and anything worth achieving was always going to defy common sense. My default response clicked back in: "adapt and overcome".

Without getting at least one county top done it would mean falling short of Glencoe the following day. Everything was dependent on the Glen Affric day with no other accommodation available. With little or basically no flexibility in the schedule, it seemed obvious that I would just have to get the Scotland stage done; the biggest, longest, and hardest stage. If my body could get through that, it would almost definitely make it through the rest.

This was bigger than anything I had done so far. But against the odds, repeating the same routine had got me this far, over 1,000 miles in.

Decision made: I boxed up my waterproof trousers, naïvely assuming the extra layer wouldn't be needed in the British summer. Calling Mum and telling her I was going for it just felt right. There was no better judge of a decision than saying it out loud and listening to how your gut reacted. Some underlying uncertainty would always remain, while a stronger will spoke much louder and sounded more trustworthy. I was scraping the barrel for any excuse I could find.

I couldn't allow my knee, of all things, to end my dream. After all, I had been to Everest twice. Once I had ruled that the injury didn't have to stop me carrying on, there was no good reason to give up. Fighting back always felt like the right thing to do, as much as setting outdoor challenges had always challenged depression with determination. The simple act of winning against adversity brought me alive more than anything. Put simply, it gave me control, and created a victory mindset. Feeling out of control created a victim mindset, and led to hopelessness. Nearing the end of week two, it was probably time to accept the pain was here for the ride and I would have to get used to it. A torn muscle was nothing more than a threat to achieving a goal.

Leaving late in the day never felt good, though escaping the rough roads of Glasgow and finding the scenery of the Kilpatrick Hills was a relief. The power hour target was the village of Drymen, short on the usual 30-mile target, but it was the last chance for a good lunch. The ride to Rowardennan was blessed with blue skies and baking sun. Cycling seemed the perfect speed to take it all in, the knobbly ridges of the Arrochar Alps mirrored high across Loch Lomond. Sweet-smelling flowers lined the shores and ancient trees offered crisp shade from the sun. Buzzards soared high and birds sang, and it was turning into a good day. Rowardennan visitor centre was a mecca for hillwalking pilgrims on a weekend. A stepped path began through woodland before the open hillside and the scale of Ben Lomond was clear to see, the first of the challenge. On the summit, looking out over Stirlingshire, wall-to-wall blue stretched far over Loch Lomond, spread-eagled in full glory beneath the Trossachs. Looking further across to the Pentlands, it was hard not to feel good. Descending Ptarmigan Ridge was even better, with the scenery slap bang in my face for the hour or so back to Rowardennan, faster than expected.

*

The route to Arrochar went the long way back around Loch Lomond. In the late Saturday afternoon playful families packed the pebbled beaches, dogs splashed in the water, and the warming smoke of barbecues wafted over from the campsites. The Lochside restaurants were bustling. There was a familiar tinge of sadness at what I was missing, badly wanting to be there, feeding myself properly and happily wasting time. 'This isn't a holiday,' barked Sergeant Major; 'You don't *need* those things.'

After Balloch, there wasn't much to see except for the odd village on A82, and any negative thoughts were dragged away by the trucks careering past at 60 miles an hour. I had been on the road for over two weeks and the feeling of vulnerability had eased now. There was always the knowledge that something could hit me at any point, and quicker than an avalanche. All I could do was make myself visible. Avoiding risk altogether carried the certain risk of missing out on achieving anything worthwhile.

At the head of Loch Long was the tiny village of Arrochar and the Glen Loin campsite. Something about being inside the tent was a relief, no matter how the day had turned out. Being here, and back on track, for the second time, was encouraging. A message from Rich to say a yellow weather warning for rain was on the way would usually have put a dampener on things, but feeling in control of everything else gave me the strength to brush it aside. That day my friend, Jeff Smith, had also summited Everest on his second attempt, after making his first in 2014, like myself. I was genuinely thrilled for him and everything he had been through to get there, especially the legacy he created. It was fortunate timing for the selfish reason that it spurred me on too. Our Everest had become different mountains and I damn well wasn't going to fail this one.

Getting to Glencoe was an encouraging prospect, if only for a shower, to stop me feeling like a giant sheet of fly paper. The yellow weather warning had me up early to make progress before the drenching came. I had a short cycle to Inveruglas, where the power station road was better than expected and led right to the start of the walk; saving miles on foot. It crept around the bulky backside of Ben Vorlich until the dam wall of Loch Sloy quietly dominated the valley at the head of the road.

Getting to the summit of Ben Vorlich, the most northerly of the Arrochar Alps group, was a sharp upwards slog. Music passed the time when there was little to see through the hazy skies. It might just have been another avoidance strategy but using music to temporarily calm the brain was fine. It was often the only way to truly zone out from the constant momentum of the challenge and take myself somewhere else.

The open hill path eventually eased into a rocky ridge where I could truly appreciate the scale of Ben Lomond; there were two possible highest points to mark the county of Dunbartonshire. Frankly I wasn't keen on coming back and bagged both in case, with one marked by a cairn and the other by a trig point. Now in the "proper" hills, the transition process from dead legs to spinning legs was taking longer. I would have made a rubbish triathlete, though I was getting quicker at packing my bag; challenging myself to get faster each time, with these micro challenges keeping the pace.

The roadside village of Tyndrum and the famous "Green Welly Stop" was a favourite lunch stop during the long drives to Scotland for Everest training. After popping ibuprofen tablets like mints for the last week I was glad to see some Scottish Tablet instead, a favourite cycling staple, a crumbly fudge-like bar that was cheap, and high in calories. Chunks would melt in the mouth like lozenges and made a good treat when hitting milestones. The downhill to Bridge of Orchy was exhilarating and followed by a punishing climb to the inhospitable expanse of Rannoch Moor.

Each big uphill climb was like a model of depression in miniature. Fearing the struggle, knowing it was coming, and not always being able to see the top as it closed the space in around our heads. The struggle focused inward to thoughts of whether the top would come or would be good enough. A disappointing summit was still the end of the uphill effort, and so there was always something to feel positive about. Going downhill usually carried the negative connotation.

Glencoe defied this rule.

Free-wheeling downhill for miles made it a joy to be alive. It was unquestionably one of the most breath-taking cycling routes in the country and stopping to take photos was almost mandatory in the shadows of volcanic peaks and crags frowning from high, threatening to swallow me whole. I raced past the car park and opted to check in to the Glencoe youth hostel first, to top up water, find plugs to charge gadgets and dump my camping gear in the drying room. Much like having a safe place to return to after a tough day at work, creating a base gave me something to look forward to and visualise. Comforted by the warmth of the lounge and happy walking parties enjoying dinner, getting out again took a big mental kick up the backside, cajoled by fear – each minute here was a minute of walking in darkness.

Cycling back up the road again with empty panniers and the light rucksack, it felt like I was flying up the Lakeland passes on a racing bike. The knee didn't drag at the heels either. It was clear that the weight of the bike had a lot to answer for. There was no chance of missing the unmistakeable mountain trio known as "The Three Sisters" – the north ridges of Bidean Nam Bian, which was really a mountain range of complex ridges, crags and summits rather than a lone peak. Looking up at the rugged castles of rock was terrifying; considering it had just gone 7.00pm and I was headed straight into these turbulent skies. I always noticed the skies first; looking up, as if searching for a nod from higher places, or an "okay" for staying put.

From the car park, the path pulled straight up to Coire nan Lochain, or Corrie, a bowl-like valley with steep sides. In one hand, texts of encouragement pinged through from my cousin Sophie. The timing seemed perfectly coincidental. I really needed it. Breathing hard, I couldn't believe how high I had reached in a short time. Blades of peaks were tickled by a thick cloud inversion cutting us off from the glen, white sunset lighting it above, like being on top of the world. The ridge was a mess of greasy rock, damp hung in the air. Gaping gullies plunged off the sides with patches of snow a stark contrast to the greyness of the ridge, all choked in eerie silence.

The scrambly rocks made the remaining hundreds of metres to the summit slower than usual. For such an effort, Bidean Nam Bian, the top of Argyll, was an unworthy cairn of rocks. The summit selfie was like the blurred mess of a drunken night out:

I just wanted to get the hell out of there, with less than an hour of daylight remaining. Reversing the route was tempting, but for safety I stayed on the planned route. It wasn't the time for music either; only focus.

Looking down from Bealach Dearg was daunting as threatening clouds rolled in, keeping the Lost Valley a secret a little longer. Loose scree slopes gave way underfoot and sometimes a metre too far, falling on my backside and shouting more than once. I could only hope the paths would come before dark, figuring the Lost Valley got such a name for a good reason.

A clear path arrived by the burn, and I broke into a careful run. Out of the cloud the unsuspecting field of rock and grass was finally revealed between Beinn Fhada and Gearr Aonach, and strange acoustics from the closeness of the hills on both sides. There was just the wooded gorge left to get through. Getting lost was easy enough in daylight, let alone now. Mossy slabs of rock demanded care with a sobering plunge to the river below. Eventually, the road appeared. Now, I was laughing with relief. The feeling of overcoming and achieving was phenomenal; realising a moment that you never thought would happen at the start of the day was like nothing else. Soon I would be over the worst and with days like this in the scrapbook, I was going to be ready for them.

Just before I made it back to the hostel, the bike chain fell off. The hostel warden was shutting up shop for the evening at 11.00pm, when I burst through the door in a daze, bike oil smeared on hands and face, midges splattered on naked arms and bloodied knees like fly paper. As if playing up to the movie stereotype, he took one look, and nervously dropped his eyes back to counting change.

CHAPTER 12

Day 16 started on the sleepy roads along Loch Leven through Ballachulish, then Onich on the banks of Loch Linnhe. With no coffee in the hostel to satisfy my morning ritual, Fort William was the first milestone, albeit less than 20 miles away, and a quick stop at McDonalds got things back in order. Glen Nevis youth hostel kindly agreed to store the bike inside and saved the need for carrying extra valuables up the hill.

The stop-start motion of trying to sneak through the motorway of traffic on the main Ben Nevis "Mountain Track" slowed things down.

Across the Red Burn, the familiar zig-zags began snaking the wide flank of the mountain, the clammy heat of broken clouds starting to ease, with constant stunning views across the Mamores behind. A helicopter hovered unusually close above until a medic was winched down, which explained the hold-up on the path. A Mountain Leader ordered us to stay well back, and I knew from Everest how easily the downdraft could throw rocks and debris around like a leaf blower. Like the rest, I moved to the side and took the opportunity to layer up and drink. One of the ladies passed back word that a walker had suffered a heart attack. Soon after, a handful of men passed on their way back down, some broken to tears, others visibly in shock. Now I could only assume the worst. The entire mood of the mountain had turned upside down. It left a sombre mood. This could have happened to anyone, enjoying their day on the hills.

Suddenly I didn't want to run anymore. My ego had been squashed to a stark reminder of mortality that I knew already from Everest but had never expected to feel on a mountain close to home.

It was important to think rationally rather than emotionally. Thinking of the worst possible outcome in every scenario would stop us from doing anything fulfilling, and without doing things that made us alive we carried an even bigger risk, of living life, half-asleep. Everest had only given me a bigger appreciation of this. It didn't make us fearless. I had always been anxious about the health risks of endurance exercise and years of less-intentional self-harming with bulimia hadn't helped. All I could do was follow the usual procedure: slow down and put some music on, escaping into the lyrics of favourite music to take the mind elsewhere.

*

The observatory ruins and memorial appeared first; like a museum to the iconic mountain, the highest peak in the British Isles and Inverness-shire at 1,344 metres high. All of it appeared without much celebration, considering the possible outcomes for the walker down below, and the other translation of Nevis – malicious – felt more appropriate. I quietly retraced the steps, skirting around the plunging depths of the northern gullies and hurried down the same path.

Over a fortnight in, I was still underestimating fuel intake and got back to Glen Nevis completely drained. Climbing high out of town from Banavie gave Ben Nevis an even more grotesque appearance from the north, and I was glad to have the biggest challenge ticked off the list, still feeling every step lingering in my legs. The stunning Great Glen brought its own unique scenery as it stretched over 100 kilometres towards Inverness.

Back in Gairlochy, the swing bridge across the canal was now blocked by crossing boats. Another cyclist pulled up alongside, checked his watch impatiently, and suggested crossing further down. Going the long way around on the A82 passed the Commando Memorial and the next village of Spean Bridge was only a small detour off route. Little did I know this detour would prove a double blessing, since the only shop for miles in Invergarry turned out to be closed – being dehydrated and low on blood sugar was never a pretty combination somewhere so remote. I was glad for the supplies to get through. Without realising I was completing my very own gratitude check; thinking of something to be grateful for and to look forward to. Maybe feeling good was a reminder of things to be grateful for. Even when feeling bad, gratitude could be created by positive thoughts instead and tip the balance of any situation back in our favour.

Everything was back in order and chunks of chocolate were stuffed into the jersey pockets, allocated into milestones with the final half saved until Invergarry, which marked the magic 25-mile countdown on the map. Cycling through the magnificent rift of the Great Glen along the fjord-like Loch Lochy and Loch Oich was beautifully serene. Families enjoyed waterside picnics as I passed at the daydream pace of a Sunday afternoon. It was a steady climb out of Invergarry through ancient Caledonian pine forests; higher and higher above Glen Garry. This lonely road looked on the gleaming white of Loch Loyne far below. High peaks interrupted the skyline once more and inspired a game of "I spy with my little eye" knowing one of them must be Carn Eighe; trying to replace the depleted feeling with more positive replacement thoughts.

Today, I was spinning at full effort, not to burn calories and allow peace from the bulimia, but to arrive sooner, anxious of another late finish and the prospect of walking up the glen in the dark. This effort didn't pay back, and I stopped countless times, convinced of a flat tyre or catching brake pad. It was not the bike, but a reluctant engine. The final five miles took longer than ever before; lack of sleep had started to catch up.

Soon after the Garmin beeped to say we were there – there was still no sign of the Cluanie Inn. Panic set in, but after checking the map for another fluff-up, I found that I had only fallen half a mile short. As arranged, I stowed the bike at the inn, while I spent the night in Glen Affric – that was going to be interesting, considering the effort involved walking in a straight line, against the wind.

Glen Affric, or Allbeithe, was often referred to as the most beautiful in Scotland with its perfectly placed lochs and mountain scenery, but it was so off-the-beaten-path that there was barely a path. I had kept my head down, pushing as fast as I could manage up a good track into An Caorann Mor. The evening skies lost their warmth, the mottled green slopes turned to grey and came down to a gentle bowl where bogs started squelching underfoot.

I decided to walk until 10.00pm, then got the tent up in some form of daylight. In my exhaustion, I could have slept into the next week and quickly settled for a half-dry patch of grass behind a sheepfold. Another promise of an earlier finish had fallen as flat as my sleeping bag in the spongy grass. These promises were only a motivator though; without hoping for something positive we would only go out looking for the worst. Discipline took over, forcing some water and fuel down first – swilling a protein shake around the sachet and scooping it out with a toothbrush.

Sleeping in thick grass turned into one of the comfiest nights so far. Outside it was dry though the greens of the glen looked no less dull in daylight. The first target for power hour was to reach the hostel and get some breakfast. I wasn't sure what the reception would be, or if anyone would be there at all.

Despite starting off behind schedule I tried not to worry too much about timings – the whole challenge so far hadn't exactly operated like clockwork. Once moving, I felt upbeat from the simple fact of getting started. The quirky green walls and orange roof of the hostel finally came into view, swallowed by the vastness of the glen. After three miles of plodding through sodden moorland like a flooded football field, I even congratulated myself for making the right decision the night before. A small footbridge crossed the river and a Schnauzer sat outside, barking relentlessly while a few figures watched me approach. The hostel warden was a traditional lady who made me more than welcome. The communal kitchen was busy with English families preparing breakfast as I came in, and I was sad to have missed it the night before. The group of walkers were inquisitive about the scraggy fellow invading their cosy haven, stirring up porridge on the hob, but soon made me feel at home.

Another guest was about to throw away a spare pan of herby couscous. *No chance*, I thought, taking up his offer and loading three bowls full. It was positive bingeing that would set me up for the day; better too prepared than underprepared. After Himalayan expeditions I could stomach anything no matter the time of day. A chap called Adrian introduced himself and we shared hillwalking stories until he had to shoot off and catch his friends who had already left. It was soon time to follow them into the hills myself.

A steep path behind the hostel followed a babbling stream through purple heather towards the first peak. Soon after I noticed a few figures in the distance, presumably stopping for a breather. They were still there five minutes later, looking down, until I recognised Adrian. His walking group had waited back to give me some company. This gesture meant so much. We walked together for 20 minutes in what felt like a hillwalking speed-dating session, trying to chat with as many of the group as I could. They were from Burnley in Lancashire, and I couldn't believe the irony of hearing this familiar accent in one of the remotest parts of the entire country. As usual, the solitude had me excitedly talking away at 100 miles-an-hour to let everything out of my head. Their route headed left – and sadly meant leaving them once again. Before shaking hands, Adrian had said how the body was a finely tuned engine. 'It will do whatever the mind wants.'

Psychologically, returning to my lone devices always brought a mood drop by forcing me to refocus on the long day ahead and the exhaustion that didn't seem to get much easier. The encouragement to continue had to come from myself. The mental come down was still worth the boost of great company, and I found my own rhythm again.

From the summit of Stob Coire na Croiche, I was expecting a glimpse across to the target. But there was nothing. I was confused. Its sister peak, Mam Sodhail, looked close on the map and should have been in view by now. The wispy cloud hung below as if I could just leap off the hill and walk across. Suddenly, it split into two ribbons, and the black lump peered through the gaps. This behemoth of a mountain looked miles away and the top itself was buried further in cloud. My heart sank like the col below. Going so far down and back up felt like climbing the mountain twice. Hopefully it was a trick of the eye; all I could do was accept this frustration and keep moving; leaving it behind like a forgotten binge episode. I grabbed the camera to capture the emotions fresh in the moment, remembering advice from an old expedition teammate who said that when you least felt like recording yourself was the perfect time to do it.

'Ignore the watch,' I snapped, continuing up Mam Sodhail on an unrelenting grassy ridge, feeling depleted and strangely giddy. I had somehow managed to veer off the path onto loose ground, stumbling over mossy rocks and scree to get back on track. This brought another judgement call: whether to retrace, or carry on a little further in the hope of something better – another metaphor for the highs and lows.

With progress already delayed and patience tested, I stumbled again, cutting a knee. The frustrations piled on top of one another, the knee pain returned to say hello, and my body was depleted. This was day 17. There were still over 50 more days to think about. I knew better than to worry ahead but today, it wouldn't budge. Whatever uphill effort I had was lost as steps continually gave way and I slid down the rocks. Someone had shot the wild goose. And I lost it. Sobbing, like a baby. Sitting by a rock with my head in hands; everything came out.

The madness eased in less than a minute, and there was silence. Nothing but harsh whistles of wind and rain tapping on my hood. Then it dawned: I was utterly alone. Nobody was going to come and pick me up. Curling up and lying there wasn't going to get me down the mountain. 'The body will do whatever the mind wants' came back to mind. What did the mind want? Contemplating 50 days was obviously going to feel unbearable. Thinking about how I'd cycle 80 miles to Gairloch Sands later that day was too much to process. I wouldn't take the easy option, but I didn't have to think about the hard option either. Looking at the map for a glimmer of hope, Mam Sodhail was now less than a kilometre away. Once there it would be a similar distance again to the summit of Carn Eighe. This breakdown had forced me to break down the challenge into smaller milestones. Short-sightedness was the new strategy. Instead of Gairloch Sands, my new goal for the day was getting back to the Cluanie Inn, promising myself the long-awaited rest day. Getting to the pub was a certainty, I wasn't going to get far without picking the bike up, after all. Anything beyond that had no permission to bother me now.

Soon after, the path appeared. Life was good again. Little had changed, only now the steps were moving in the right direction.

Along the ridge from Mam Sodhail stood a summit shelter that offered no protection to anything but the mountain itself, and the trig point of Carn Eighe, I had never been so happy to reach the top of a hill before this. The county of Ross and Cromarty certainly took no prisoners. Descending Coire Ghaidheil was more straightforward. Once the cloud cleared and safety of the glen appeared below, I felt like a free man; no longer captive on the hill. I was able to spare some phone battery and play music for the first time all day. Biffy Clyro was first up. And I began to sing at the top of my voice. If only the singing had sounded as good as it felt to release the tension!

I called back at the youth hostel to dry out for 10 minutes. The warden stuck the kettle on as I recalled the day. Living out here intrigued me, and she explained how she spent her free time reading and embroidering, perhaps a wee walk in the hills when she could. It was another vote in favour of simplicity that shunned the complicated misery of our modern lives.

Adrian was already back from his walk and shook my hand as I rushed off again with a stash of cereal bars, promising to return here one day. It took two and a half hours to get out of the glen and back to the road. The night before I had clearly been so preoccupied in failing to notice the puddles so deep that they were full of tadpoles, and the wreckage of a Vickers Wellington bomber that had crashed here in 1942, now scattered like litter in the grass. The puddles helped to clean the bloodied knees and I arrived at the pub in a presentable state. At the gate a scraggy guy with the characteristic beard of a long-distance rambler asked where I had walked from. I wasn't in the mood.

Over a plate of fish and chips I found one final bed available in Kintail only 13 miles away and the only option within reach. Pushing to Ullapool tomorrow would keep things on track.

The road tumbled and fell through the spectacular pass of Glen Shiel in a fitting end to the day, along foaming rivers in high spate, thick pine woods and crumbling ruins. There was unease in the atmosphere, thick mist and lashing rain forming a moody ceiling over the narrow glen. Dad had taken the worry baton in watching the tracker moving late into the night and texted me to stay safe. I had no choice. There was so much left to do on the mental to-do list when I got there, but not all those things were essential, and I forced them to the back of my mind. Get there, get fed, and get to bed was the unofficial mantra.

The glen ended at Loch Duich with rusty boats bobbing off the shore. Evening darkness merged the green of the water into the vast forests on the far banks. Staggering into the hotel bar in a daze; barely able to speak, the barman probably assumed I'd had one too many. The lodge was decked by a green builders' carpet from the seventies and a musty smell of mouldy cheddar matured in wet socks that knocked me sick. The room was even worse, sharing with an old-school hiker from the US on the bottom bunk who snored like a foghorn. The passing thought of staying here had knocked the temptation of a rest day firmly on the head.

CHAPTER 13

Relentless forward motion. Repeat that dude, my friend Richard Whitehouse texted me. I had messaged him saying, *The long days are killing me – but I can do this*, in what sounded like confidence, and felt like it too. The drizzle was due to pass, there were no county tops to climb, and only 90 miles to cycle to Ullapool. It was the first morning without a twinge in the knee; things boded well.

For the first time I topped up the bike tyres and was naïvely impressed at how the bike felt entirely reborn. Cruising along Loch Duich felt effortless. I had been in the same routine for so long that I quickly noticed the slightest shift in mindset, and naturally began looking for an explanation. I felt dissociated, on some sort of natural high. Maybe the feeling of speed in my legs was simply unusual, though it was difficult not to feel spaced out somewhere like this, largely uninhabited, with silent lochs shouldered by forested peaks.

Kintail was a cliché of Highland scenery with the archetypal composition: sea; castle; forest; mountain. Eilean Donan Castle was a 13th-century icon that I recognised from a photo on Grandma's wall.

Like the previous Glen Affric day, having so few opportunities to stop gave me little to aim for. The next planned stop at the hamlet of Strathcarron had little to offer, and a hot chocolate did little to warm things up.

Otherwise, the scenic area of Wester Ross was everything a touring cyclist could ask for, a synonym for wild and lonely. Distinct mountain summits sat behind ancient forests, rhododendrons in bloom lined the roadside and becks tumbled down. A few surviving pines stood like hairs on a brush from cleared plantations. It was stunning, without a doubt. Deeper into the Highlands, life got increasingly secluded. Signs warned of children on the road and made me chuckle as I envisioned the local children appearing over the hills hiking for two hours to get to school each day; I had seen more civilisation in the high mountains of the Himalayas than here.

It was silent, though there was rarely peace. My mind was struggling to adapt to this silence, and instinctively tried to fill it with anything. The intolerance of silence seemed like a symptom of our 24-hour availability on social media. And the solution seemed to be learning to empty it, or at least fill it with something more positive. I needed to look outwards and appreciate the surroundings. But however hard I tried, the liberty of nature and counting lochs was quickly becoming monotonous. I needed a stimulus or something to break the journey down before it turned my attention inwards.

After Loch Dughaill the thick forests of Glen Carron thinned and the village of Achnasheen appeared. The promised café had been abandoned years ago. There was nothing on the map between here and the 46-miles to Ullapool. I was weak, dehydrated, and couldn't run off sugar all day. The only option was a grand Victorian shooting lodge, the Ledgowan Lodge hotel. Inside was as quaint as expected, decked with ornate chairs and mirrors, lined by tacky floral carpets, and trophy stag horns protruding from the wall. In the restaurant a couple of French cyclists sat finishing plates of pasta and chips. I grinned, subtly plugged the phone into a wall socket and hung the wet jacket on a radiator. Things looked promising. The smart bespectacled French waiter matched the situation perfectly:

'Sorry sir, the kitchen closed at two-thirty,' he squeaked.

I glanced at the dusty old clock above the fireplace. Five minutes after 2.30pm. I was never the sort to argue over something so seemingly insignificant, but hunger compelled me, and I pleaded, struggling to appear threatening in dripping wet neon Lycra and a boyish quiff of helmet hair. He scuttled off nervously to the kitchen.

'Soup is possible, soup is possible sir,' he explained.

The bowl of Leek and Potato was better than nothing.

The next stage started strong and the glen stretched wider to far-flung views of the Fannichs mountains and followed the river bed for miles. Things took a turn northwest and then a turn for the worst: directly into the wind. Momentum was stolen in a flash. No matter the effort, average speed barely got above about eight miles an hour on the flat; let alone uphill. It was like cycling backwards. My mind was constantly calculating and working out timings to feel a sense of progress and the wind had stretched the 30 miles much further.

Yesterday it had been the scale of the challenge that had tipped the balance, and I had learnt to cope with that. This time it was mostly the soul-sapping theft of effort that had turned my focus inwards. Despite the extra practice, finding replacement thoughts was a struggle, and I was in no mood for singing. Today was even more challenging and so it would take a bigger kick to distract myself than usual. *Relentless forwards motion* came back to mind – but that only focused on the problem.

From bleak to bleaker, it got wilder still on the slothful climb towards a dam wall and the grey shine of Loch Glascarnoch. Crosswinds tossed me side to side; trucks thundered past and barely acknowledged this flea in their midst. Everything seemed to be conspiring against me – the "victim" mindset. Frustration built up like steam, until I couldn't take any more – everything boiled over into an almighty wail. I sobbed and shouted, like on

Mam Sodhail the day before. Then it stopped. I looked around awkwardly; hoping nobody heard. I hadn't passed another human for nearly two hours. I ducked behind a power station hut to escape the wind for a moment and compose myself. It felt like the Black Dog had made an unexpected appearance; splattering clean carpets with muddy paws.

It will get better, I promised. *It can't be like this for 20 miles*.

It was, almost. There wasn't even the usual time pressure – I knew I would arrive in good time – Ullapool just felt so far away. I assumed that at the top of the road there would be a big downhill and everything would feel better. Infuriatingly, the wind turned out to be stronger than gravity and it took hard pedalling just to stop slowing down. My head swilled with over-blown conflicts and negative thoughts. Frustration naturally released adrenaline and other chemicals which carried the risk of acting impulsively and I snapped.

'Surely there must be a petrol station?' Mum asked over the phone.

I shouted back over the wind; 'Of course there should be, but there bloody well isn't!'

It helped to vent. The final hours passed much quicker until the river widened and became Loch Broom. Wind and rain stopped, the sun returned. I had not been in the mood for singing all day, but with the end in sight, I burst into The Proclaimers' 'I'm Gonna Be 500 Miles' through the giddiness of relief. I could hear the cackling seagulls at the finish line; the lovely fishing town of Ullapool sat on the shores of Loch Broom, with bobbing boats and ferries moored in the harbour. Despite its size, it was the largest settlement for miles.

For once I had arrived at a sociable hour, falling over my own feet and shivering from the fierce coastal winds. Debbie gave a warm welcome back at the hostel and was glad to have me staying. I was mostly glad for my first shower in days.

Day by day, strategies were coming together with and without realising. Breaking down mentally and piecing the mind back together again was revealing lots about how it responded in different scenarios. One thing I had learnt for sure was to never assume anything. The only truth was that relentless forwards motion would always get you to the finish eventually. Whether I believed it or not, I was saying that by overcoming so much in getting back on schedule; anything else could be overcome. The challenge felt possible for the first time. My mindset had shifted from wondering if I would make it to knowing I could, especially with good company; it was just about being able to hang in there.

CHAPTER 14

Scotland was truly battering the wee English kid. My research showed that the next stage on the west coast was going to be equally lonesome. Knowing that didn't help get me going, but being prepared logistically wasn't a bad thing and gave an opportunity to learn and adapt.

At Tesco, I was loading up on food to set me up for the day with a pack of giant cookies, chocolate, Scotch eggs, and bananas, plus extra water. I wanted to be prepared regardless of facilities on the route. With the mileage still to come that day, I would need the comfort of sugary treats as much as I needed calories. Bulimia's rules were corrupt, and seemed to change on a daily basis.

In the depths of my despair on Carn Eighe, I had posted a video, that had worried a few of my supporters on social media. They had noticed the visible weight loss in my face, and knowing I had an eating disorder, were probably concerned that I wasn't looking after myself. Mum had obviously been one of the first to notice. Two years later, I could vividly remember the moment she sat down on my bed one Sunday evening and softly asked whether I was bulimic. As I recorded, the tears blurred the vision of my laptop screen, but I knew a plan couldn't work unless others were in on it.

I didn't have time to worry too much about it now, and secretly loved getting recognition for losing weight, despite eating what felt like an excess of bad foods. At the same time, while my more rational voice knew I couldn't get away with junk food and sports drinks for 70 days, it had started to accept the most important thing was doing whatever I needed to make the finish, even if it meant eating the "bad" foods that put me at risk of bingeing and purging.

*

It was sometimes difficult to describe the places and my experiences in my own words. But as Ernest Hemingway once said, "It is by riding a bicycle that you learn the contours of a country best, since you have to sweat up the hills and coast down them."

I agreed. I was doubly rewarded with blissful cycling conditions, devoid of wind, and headed straight into an endless kingdom of triangular peaks that could appear impassable; bringing surprises at each corner. Being bored today seemed unlikely. We could ride to think, or to forget. Cycling and its fleeting distractions rarely gave the opportunity to think about things like walking did, but I preferred the routine and rhythm, while walking was a start-stop process that took longer to settle in to.

Like a roving geology exhibit, Assynt had it all. The area was regarded for its dramatic and distinct mountains, their sheer sides making them appear bigger, scattered like Lego on a lunar landscape. The peak of Canisp rose behind the township cottages of Elphin. I was puzzled by a sign advertising a local craft market when there were probably more people in the church graveyard than alive in the community itself. Living here seemed a mystery far from the comfortable countryside of Cheshire and the lonely cottages made me curious about how people lived here; what they did; how they made money.

From the hamlet of Inchnadamph, I locked up near the hotel and followed the river into the glen at a brisk pace through the pretty bell-heather of Inchnadamph Forest where cuckoos and songbirds flitted between the young trees. The silvery mound of

Conival peeped around the corner ahead, like Ben More Assynt, one of only two Munros in the region. Such a beautiful array stole attention from the watch, the map, and the numbers. Progress was slowed in toiling with scree and hopping grey boulders that occasionally gave way to a heavy clunk. The summit was topped by a miniscule cairn. From there the magnitude of Sutherland county and its desolate wilderness was unmistakeable. The impressive bulbous cliffs of Na Tuadhan below caught my eye among the circus of quartzite buttresses. Shimmering lochans dotted around like rain droplets. These mountains claimed their own shade of grey, never mind fifty. I had seen nothing like it before; another moment of appreciation for how lucky I was to be here. It didn't take long to look at the watch again. From the summit everything switched to "beast mode"; running down, focusing hard to spare an ankle or worse; scuttling over the boulders as the hillwalkers shook their heads disapprovingly. It was 5.00pm when I returned to the bike in Inchnadamph, thirsty, hungry, and weak. Leaving a banana and water in the panniers had been a good incentive. Rationing food was a fine balance to avoid running out of gas on the hill, and ensure there was enough for the next part of the journey too, especially considering the abrupt climb towards Unapool and the comatose legs that took a while to grasp the idea of pedalling again. Anyone would expect to feel proportionally tired at the end of the day. An extra reserve of energy was left untapped until the flush of relief came instead.

There was little more than an upmarket hotel in the hamlet of Kylesku and a friendly Australian barman asked where I was headed.

'Tonight? Ambition!' he cheered.

I overheard him explaining to an English barmaid colleague who asked where Durness was.

'It's 45 minutes even in the car,' he muttered sceptically.

*

I raced into the evening light. Sutherland only brought more surprises; a maze of turquoise freshwater lochans hidden in russet heathland. Coastal inlets brought the waft of salty shores. A huge polecat bolted across the road into the trees. The continuous rise and fall of the road made it difficult to hold rhythm, but I pushed hard, focused intently on cadence as the legs came around to the idea of effort again. Whizzing at 30 miles-an-hour on the final downhill ended the day perfectly; long shadows stretched behind, and the sunset caught the low tide of the Kyle of Durness like a golden scar. A short-tempered driver launched a tirade of swearing out of the window as he tried to pass, but speed like this was hard to come by, and to hell with stopping. Little things like this could linger on the mind all day and flip the mood, but smiling and waving took away their power.

Being bullied at school had had a similar effect. I was so used to being singled out that I instinctively learnt to blame myself for other people's disapproval, and the stammer felt like something else that worked against me. With time I was able to view their opinions as a reflection of their own insecurities and unhappiness, rather than my own failings, which took away their power to hurt me. It had taken practice but when I recognised myself worrying about other people's perceptions, I brought the focus back to myself and laughed at these meaningless insults before releasing them and moving on. There was still some work to do in finding my own approval.

Another rendition of The Proclaimers followed. The legs had delivered: we had made it. Suddenly there was nothing north but the sea, lapping gently onto the creamy white sands of Sango Bay. Grassy dunes were stained sunset pink. Rusty wire fences rattled violently in the breeze. Looking at the live tracker on top of the UK was satisfying to say the least. It seemed the best days followed the worst. Managing this rollercoaster of highs and lows was as tiring as the highs and lows of the coastal roads. I wondered whether the middle ground would come at all.

It was the contrast between these peaks and troughs that kept life interesting. Being in a dip brought the guarantee that another peak would follow – this peak and trough model became an instruction manual for life.

Close to Cape Wrath, the most north-westerly tip of the UK, Durness was a tiny coastal village with a quirky youth hostel – a duo of wooden shacks tucked back from the cliffs. I had arrived at 9.45pm, exhausted and buzzing in equal measure. Evenings should have been relaxing, but I merely switched from cycling mode to admin mode. Friends and strangers alike were messaging for meeting details, I couldn't be annoyed because it was all part of the vision. I just felt the angst of being unable to do more to help when they were taking the initiative. I was grateful all the same and excited at the growing interest.

As with any challenge, sharing my stories was important. Not telling them was a waste. Adventure stories ignited feelings and emotions, and that was where inspiration often started. Being close to home was even better because the possibility of going somewhere and doing something was much easier and less of a dreamy, distant goal than the Himalayas would be for many people.

Six hours of sleep was becoming the norm. Feeling tired in the mornings got me down because I knew that my energy for the day was already short-changed. I was frustrated at being deprived of this basic comfort before learning to accept it, and I was surprised at how well my body would adapt to perform regardless. In what looked like some new-found discipline, I was up and organised faster than usual. In the dining room, I kept my head so far down it was almost in the bowl of Alpen. Until I overheard someone talking about a young lad who was cycling to the highest point of all the counties. My head popped up like a meerkat. Had somebody else pinched the same idea? Looking over I saw Richard, from the Ullapool hostel two days earlier and I stayed quietly humble as he explained what I was doing. 'And there's the guy himself!' – Richard said, noticing me, and I joined them.

It all added to the sense of support building, with people online calling me "an inspiration". I pedalled on, asking: what inspired them? Refusing to give up?

Inspiring people was the closest proof of achieving my purpose in life, and it was an immediate answer to every doubt about why I was here.

After a brief hiatus, the knee pain had reappeared suddenly. Pushing hard the day before had been a test – and it had failed. I worried how it would cope for the rest of the day in the middle of nowhere and considered turning back for Durness. But I quickly noticed what my mind was up to. It wasn't a case of wanting to give up – I had started to enjoy the journey and believe in my ability to see it through – it was being able to continue through the pain. By slowing the pace and lowering the resistance, the pain subsided enough to manage. One voice said my stubbornness was stupid. The other said: 'follow me'. It was better to get there with a bad knee than not at all. The ferry at Scrabster would leave regardless, but I had already calculated that making it was possible, even at snail's pace.

Heading for the Orkney Isles was exciting. The ferry would arrive first in Stromness in Orkney when I would cycle to Kirkwall before taking a rest day on Shetland.

It was 9.45pm before I left into a drizzly unsettled night. Orkney was a mysterious place, with tiny settlements and a trove of Neolithic monuments scattered across perfectly curved hills, their cartoonish green still vibrant through the broody evening light. It hardly got truly dark this far north. Grazing cattle and the roadside villages of Stenness and Finstown observed this eerie silence. Thank God, the island seemed mostly flat until the Old Finstown Road. Sleepy lights of the capital town, Kirkwall, filled the basin below; lines of orange shimmered against black as a ferry left the harbour.

Kirkwall youth hostel was a former World War II military base, and still looked the part. Grant made me welcome, in spite of my unplanned and late arrival. He warned me about an aggressive seabird called a Bonxie that was known to attack people on Ward Hill, the highest point of Orkney. I had been so far attacked by weather, delays, low self-esteem, a sprained muscle, saddle sore, midges, and self-perpetuated tantrums; this bird was seriously going to have to up the ante.

CHAPTER 15

After visiting the grandeur of the Himalayas, it took a lot to feel excited about exploring new places, so feeling this excitement in my home country was a pleasant surprise.

Getting around the Orkney Isles involved a precise series of ferries and timetables which didn't bode well for someone as punctual as a broken bus. There had been nobody around so early to get the bike out of the hostel shed and leaving late required a hasty ride against the wind to Houton for a short ferry hop to the Isle of Hoy.

The combination of sleep deprivation and constant time pressure left me irritable and defensive. It was easier to be reactive to things that didn't matter, rather than processing them rationally. Letting this frustration out was still better than allowing it to fester within.

In Lyness, I dived into the Scapa Flow Visitor Centre to warm up with coffee. Cycling the east edge of Hoy was beautifully simple: ocean, road, and green. Odd houses, an ice cream parlour, and a building was painted in psychedelic colours so eccentric they fitted in perfectly. In the north were mushroom-top hills, easier on the eye than their Highland counterparts; perfect curves mysteriously seductive to any pair of walking boots.

Bashing through twiggy ankle-high heather and no recognisable path left imagination free to assume you were the first to come this way. The landscape made it difficult to contest, the incline eased onto the first summit of Haist, looking down at the turquoise coast like tropical beaches and emerald greens of the fields. The neighbouring island of Graemsay looked close enough to jump – it felt like the adventure was truly getting started. I was grateful for the challenge leading to such an experience and for a moment almost forgot about my punishing timetable altogether. Sandy, spongy ground underfoot was like walking on the beach itself. From the summit of Haist, a ridge led to the whaleback top of Ward Hill ahead. There was nobody there but a group of mountain hares bigger than my dog watching my arrival on their hind legs. On the plateau, it all felt stuck in time, as if the Neolithic folk had dumped their sandwiches at the cairn and legged it down.

Descending into the crater below was equally satisfying, hopping like a frolicking lamb without snagging a foot in the heather, or being finished off by the Bonxie. Ward Hill had jumped to the top of my favourites so far. Looking back at these mesmerising cloud formations and purple beacons brought a feeling of gratitude – a gentle lesson in what to do when I next told myself that I couldn't be bothered. It was only 30 minutes back to Stromness from Moaness on the tiny passenger ferry that took the local children to school each day, connecting this extraordinary place to something more like reality. A couple of locals sat opposite glued to mobile phones and muttering between themselves.

'How many peaks have you got left?' they called across. I was confused. They had been reading an article about the challenge on the website of *The Orcadian*, the local newspaper. I had emailed a photo to Mick at the foot of Ward Hill only a couple of hours earlier while simultaneously bashing through heather. One of the Glen Affric walking party had donated to the JustGiving page and it really felt like the journey was starting to touch people in the way intended; taking mental health awareness quite literally to the tip of the UK.

I made use of the hostel facilities in Kirkwall again before the late-night ferry to Shetland and went hunting on the characteristic cobbles of Stromness for the famous bakery; bulimia didn't like to miss out. Every day I was seeing new things in the shops and developing new cravings. I kept giving in to them, and like a childhood phase they went away for a while, but they always drew me back for more, hoping for something better. It was embarrassing how preoccupied I was by food. Even when I was taking on such a massive challenge, I was seemingly unable to manage a fundamental part of human nature, and this failure seemed to tarnish my other achievements.

Trying to plan these treats so rigidly gave little wiggle room for everyday surprises. Mum had sent another parcel of supplies with a surprise of Cadbury Creme Eggs. It wasn't long until I had eaten the entire bag. I panicked. Unlike Glasgow when the snack parcel came like an early Christmas, I had barely cycled further than a training ride back home. I hadn't realised that exercise was just a different means of purging calories – albeit, on the surface, a more positive one – escaping any blame under the guise of being supposedly healthy. Not for the first time, I wondered how much of my motivation came from this alone, rather than a genuine joy for doing the activity, considering how much I enjoyed a sugary treat after long training sessions back home. The challenge had given me a rare holiday from the disorder, with the daily mileage torching enough calories to allow relative freedom from the anxieties of eating the bad foods, or whatever I wanted.

Or so I thought.

Easier days upset the proportional equation of calories in, versus calories out. Sometimes, these surprise bonus treats were just badly timed and too problematic; I asked Mum not to send any more. It would take Mum a long time to understand how my mind worked around food as she met the multiple faces of my disorder, who said one thing, and then something entirely different. No wonder Mum couldn't tell which one to believe.

Other people clearly saw a different picture to my own warped self-image. A French lady had roasted a whole chicken that turned out too big and offered me the rest. A retired English couple had a leftover bowl of vegetables and offered me that, too. Next to my own massive plate of smoked mackerel, microwave potatoes and vegetables was a spread of plates and the wake of a human dustbin. I enjoyed the dinner. It was strange how my bulimia didn't care too much about tipping the balance with healthy calories, because they were a genuine need. Junk food was labelled more as a failure of my own resolve and discipline. Eating healthily was not another punishment enforced by my inner critic, or Sergeant Major, to compensate for the junk. Calories alone were not the culprit, they were just a number. My mind used them as bargaining chips while my body quietly tried to get what it needed, and I felt powerless but to sit and listen to their bickering.

*

Out of a curtain of bright mist, the Shetland Isles appeared the following morning and the chill of Lerwick harbour woke me straight up from four hours' sleep. The hills were less inviting than Orkney with deserted grassy fields, and sparse settlements of Nordic-style red houses so that a longboat on the beaches would not have looked misplaced.

You were never far from the black rocks defending the island from crashing waves, though the beaches were calm today. It was a lovely ride; soul-lifting, mostly flat, uncontaminated blue skies mirrored in roadside lochs.

As predictably as heavy legs on the bike straight after big walks, there was always a slump in mood and energy when the next hill came into view, as if the body knew and was preparing itself for fight; flight was no option. Four miles away from Collafirth there was still no sign of Ronas Hill besides a dark rise ahead, and the fog hung so low that it looked like snow. An unexpected tarmac road led all the way to the radio transmitters and saved some time on foot until it got so steep that pushing was quicker. A strange buzzing sound appeared, before lyrics. Word by word they became clearer. Hang on, was this Cher? Or Celine Dion? Now the soupy clag was playing tricks on me – two glowing lights. Headlights. I bolted to the side as a van came hurtling down. A group of radio technicians were working on the transmitters, and I wasn't as delirious as I first thought.

It was less than four kilometres to reach the top, across the bare plateaus of Roga Field and Mid Field, and an easier walk was appreciated considering everything the Scottish Highlands still had in store. Being the highest point of Shetland meant little to the acclaim of the most northerly point of the entire country, having to pinch myself to think how far I had come – and why. The true summit of Ronas Hill was supposedly marked by a large granite slab about 20 metres west of the trig point, so I visited both.

The roads of Shetland were slick but few and far between, so it made sense to go back the same way. As the adage of four seasons in two hours suggested, a sub-arctic breeze made it a challenge to grip the handlebars with numb fingers and I quickly understood what the volunteers meant about the Shetland winds going the opposite direction to where you want to go. The skies turned murky grey and the wind kicked up until I was hardly moving anywhere; an unavailing process. Reverse direction brought the reverse psychology, and negative thoughts crept in – I quickly replaced them with thoughts of the creature comforts awaiting that evening.

Calling in at the most northerly fish and chip shop in the UK in the village of Brae was basically an obligation and helped break up the three-hour slog. I was eager to try the local fish, but after booking the hotel later, refused to spend any more money on myself. Battered fish was hardly worth crying over.

On every expedition or challenge, the stress about spending reared its head at some point. Even when paying for it from my own pocket, it didn't feel like the right thing to do when raising money for a charity challenge. But that only brought additional pressures: refusing to spend money on myself created the mindset that I wasn't worthy or didn't deserve it.

The next day, in Lerwick, began with panic when I saw it was 9.00am and I hadn't budged. Then I remembered it was a rest day, and I flopped happily into the simplest luxury of the warm duvet and the extra pleasure of dry clothes on the radiator. The only alarm was to make sure I didn't oversleep the breakfast buffet. Breaking the rule of relentless forwards motion felt strange and some resistance was hardly surprising. My mind didn't know how to stop or switch off from the daily routine of the challenge. It needed some way of staying occupied. The ants-in-the-pants were almost as bad as the occasional sharp spots of saddle sore that sent me flying like a pin jabbed in the backside.

Walking in loops around the town sort of defeated the object. I couldn't stay still. After staying ahead of it for the last three weeks, stopping allowed the fatigue to catch up properly. Today was a good chance to catch up with the admin that had been creeping up, spontaneously doing things before I forgot. Paradoxically, now that I had stopped, finding the energy and motivation was difficult. This was fine too, and even browsing aimlessly was important to allow some mental space before switching back into work mode.

Taking days off wreaked even more havoc with food, since I wasn't burning calories as usual, and felt guilty for indulging. After weeks of pushing and pushing, my body needed a reward, before it started to rebel. Food was an obvious choice. Going to an Indian restaurant for an all-you-can-eat buffet seemed a dangerous concept with an eating disorder, but it was a cost-effective way to get a good meal. It wasn't something I'd do at home. But then I wasn't at home. And I wasn't doing normal things ...

It was an amazing feast, and I told myself that I deserved the three plates for everything I had been through so far. But it didn't take long for bulimia to put an end to the enjoyment and scald me with guilt. Rewarding myself didn't come easily when I always expected better. I started looking for the cause: I was feeling upbeat, I'd had a day off, and things were going well. There was no extra stress beyond that, only the lack of activity to compensate for the calories. Fatigue was no excuse either. In other words, it wasn't my emotions at play, it was my urge to binge. I still needed to find better ways of rewarding myself.

On the walk back, I bought a bag of cookies, and didn't stop at one ...

I felt like I had abused the privilege, but avoiding rest days to stop it happening again was no solution, it was only punishing myself. My new mantra of *relentless forwards motion* had a flaw: we had to learn to stop sometimes. Being in challenge mode – constantly on the go – had kept me focused on moving from A to B. Rest days allowed me to confront things. In theory, that could have been a positive thing, but the everyday thoughts had just managed to sneak in again. Confronting these feelings was the only way to learn from them and show proper self-care.

The islands were almost done and what an amazing adventure they had been; coming back to England was going to be an anti-climax. Literally speaking, it was all downhill from that point on. Or so I thought. I couldn't have been further from the truth.

CHAPTER 16

Being an opportunist had some perks. After catching another late ferry back to Kirkwall that night and arriving back at the youth hostel for midnight, I dragged myself up early and set off for Stromness with a large detour north. The opportunity to visit the settlement of Twatt was simply too funny to pass up.

After a quick stop for a coffee with Ian in Castlehill, where I was supposed to have stayed the night before, I carried on along the eastern edge of the North Coast 500. John O'Groats, the most northerly village in the UK, was slightly off my route, but too close to ignore. I did the usual tourist duties with a photo by the iconic sign before carrying on south along the A99, further into the mottled colours of "flow country" - the largest blanket bog in Europe.

After stopping halfway in the town of Wick for fish and chips, the isolated village of Dunbeath came quickly. Up on the hillside, Inver Caravan Park looked over Dunbeath Bay and the coastal winds kept the midges away. The tent only took minutes to pitch before I adopted the utility room as Base Camp to hibernate for a few hours. The tap got hot enough to have a lukewarm leftover sachet of Cuppa Soup and regular blasts of dunking my head beneath the automatic hand drier was another creature comfort. Eventually it was time to make a move for bed. Getting into the tent and sleeping bag was about as good it got after 84 miles, but the next day's forecast was a slap in the face, and my mood plummeted.

The concept of "wake up and hope for more" felt all too familiar – waking up in a sense of dread, like those hopeless days in the dark fog of depression, when black and white merged into one grey zone. Today I knew what was coming: repulsive winds and hammering rain. What choice did I have? One thing I couldn't avoid was the weather, I could only change my thoughts towards it and learn from the experience – I'd done it before.

My mobile phone hadn't charged overnight. The battery had gone entirely flat. The phone was my sidekick – it had the route, a means of emergency contact, and a camera for proof of reaching each summit. The spare would do well to last the day, so this was more than a minor inconvenience. The campsite owner, Rhona, took pity on my plans to climb Morven that morning – most of her guests usually made a satisfying day of it – never mind cycling another 80-miles to Inverness afterwards. So she plied me with coffee and fresh buttery toast before leaving.

Her generosity warmed me up on every level and the first few miles on the bike didn't feel so bad. Rhona spoke about a good café in Berriedale and that became the second milestone. Inverness was forgotten about for now. A single-track road led into the hamlet of Braemore. There was nothing but an old shooting lodge, a tiny car park and the homely red of a telephone box.

Morven was a proper peak, rising distinctly like an ice cream cone, on the photos at least. Today it was short-changed by a blinding ceiling of cloud that wouldn't budge. Huge red deer stags stood boldly ahead before the herd regrouped and scarpered across the moorland into the mist. The gravel soon disappeared into a boggy mess along the river, until the foot of Morven itself became a maddening trample, clutching for heather and bilberry bushes; slipping on wet rock and practising my unique party trick of falling uphill. The route had clearly gone astray.

The rain didn't let up and the wind exercised all five senses. I was freezing but judged that I could make it down in time before becoming a liability. Vulnerability focused onto footsteps, transferring anxiety into powering my legs forwards, bit by bit. Setting visual milestones was difficult when unable to see more than a few metres ahead. Fighting this fog was no less than fighting the treacle of depression, thinking you were about to reach the peak, and being cheated. The final 500 metres took forever, until the tip of this giant Mr Whippy got no higher and brought me to a lonely flat plateau and the summit of Caithness, serenaded by an underwhelming cairn of stones. There was a deceiving, fleeting moment of calm, before the wind screamed again and called time – this hill wanted me off. I gladly shared the same sentiment and hurried down to the main track before the phone battery died and cut contact altogether. Suddenly, the track appeared that I should have taken. My teeth chattered into a laugh; this was just another metaphor for the very nature of life. Often, when our vision was clouded and uncertain, it wasn't until the very top of the peak that we found clarity, and then the way down looked deceivingly easier than the way we had taken. When we couldn't see, we just seemed to exist and head blindly into the unknown, doing what we knew and trusted. Regardless, both paths led to the same place and then our route didn't matter too much.

Back in Braemore the phone box made a useful shelter to change into the spare waterproof jacket. Even this was damp to touch and with everything soaked underneath it was almost pointless. Stepping outside again, the illusion of Superman quickly washed off in the rain, and this drowned rat wouldn't fool anyone.

The cycle track on the A9 was narrow in places, only inches either side of loose gravel and traffic hurtling past, with occasional hollers of car horns. There was no time to think about negative thoughts, sing, look inwards, or outwards; I just had to focus on the road, weaving around cats eyes and keeping the wheels straight like a trapeze act. This accidental mindfulness was useful to keep things moving forwards when it was the last thing my mind wanted to do. It was interesting to see how my mind switched off any unnecessary thing when focused on staying safe, or when my body needed to perform at peak performance. It helped explain why I rarely binged in those moments at home. Life couldn't run at that pace forever. Getting through the lowest and most exhausting days of depression was about focusing on the fundamentals of survival – as simple as eating, drinking, resting, and sleeping – when energy was in short supply to do much else.

The only way to stay warm was to pedal harder and faster, and inevitably flare up the knee again. Timber lorries passing on my side of the road gave a secondary blast of heat and a warming waft of freshly cut pine; oncoming lorries on the other side sent showers of freezing road water towards me and there was nothing I could do but close my eyes and brace for the impact as it penetrated every layer. It did a good job of keeping the bike clean though. A scalding-hot pasty courtesy of the village shop in Golspie helped for a bit longer, but the wet layers soon stripped the heat away. Today's rendition of The Proclaimers sounded more like three cats dragged up the motorway. All that shivering and blurry eyesight were one thing, but when I failed the singing test, I knew enough was enough. For the first time, the weather had become less of an inconvenience, and a genuine risk – hypothermia was very real. Scared and vulnerable again, I booked a new hotel in the village of Fearn 26 miles away. The mostly flat roads would bode well, but getting there was still far from comfortable.

Winds roared above the Dornoch Firth bridge loudly enough to trick me into looking for a jet plane overhead as the waters thrashed below. I was barely able to speak my name to the landlord at the Fearn Hotel, a modest pub with rooms in a quiet village. The bike deserved better than being dumped in a shed dripping wet, but I had to get inside. Even taking a shower required some care to restore body temperature gradually, considering my legs were now a shade of purple and I sat with a towel wrapped like an old lady's bonnet, clutching a mug of tea.

The landlord was a friendly and upfront chap who called me "son" and wasn't taken with the idea of putting central heating on in June. I adopted a corner of the bar nearest the heater and spread clothes out to dry; marking territory like a dog cocking his leg. Business was quickly resumed with updates and plans for some followers to join me at the weekend. Expecting some company was a comforting thought. Despite falling short of Inverness, the relief was much stronger. Getting this far was an achievement and kept the door open for catching up with the itinerary – I was just happy to be there.

*

I was quickly running out of ways to describe the worst moment of my life. Every other day seemed to bring another one to the table.

The mental pain I was inflicting on myself in the process of fundraising for mental illness seemed self-defeating, though reading through the daily comments I was getting assured me that none of it was in vain. I had struggled, at first, to understand how it was inspiring people. But it was quickly becoming clear. One message told how Climb The UK had inspired him to plan a long-distance walk of his own. Others had been positively shamed into pushing harder in the gym, and planning their own long-distance walks, and another friend said their lack of motivation to cycle an hour to work some days was becoming harder to excuse.

Friends said I was made of tough stuff, yet holding it together mentally wasn't really a choice, if only for the sake of my own safety. Admittedly, I was even surprising myself at what I was learning to cope with. The challenge was sending out exactly the right message: that we could endure much more than we believed, and even falling short brought us closer to the better days ahead. The peak and trough model promised that something better would follow if we could hold out a day, and tomorrow was never far away.

CHAPTER 17

The weather forecast looked a far cry better than the day before. There wasn't a huge amount to see or do; Easter Ross was much busier, but riding the flat busy A9 road was still preferable to a cross-country hilly road when trying to make up for lost mileage with 75 miles until Aviemore. Barring the sawdust from passing timber lorries, it was a joyful morning to ride beside the narrow Cromarty Firth and across to the Black Isle.

The Cairngorms National Park was home to four of the five highest mountains in the UK. Falling short of Inverness meant the original plan to climb the second highest, Ben Macdui, that night was pushed to the following morning. Tonight, I could relax with a gentler introduction on Carn Glas-choire. I powered up a gravel track, almost all the way to the summit from the estate at Auchterteang, stepping over shotgun cartridges and crossing streams with grouse running around the heather. Everything was wonderfully simple for once and just what I needed. The highest point of Nairnshire was a mossy half-mile detour to reach a lonely summit cairn. For what it lacked in character, Carn Glas-choire was a fine viewpoint across the Cairngorms with their lofty domed summits, some still holding snow in their veins, dominating the skyline. As placid as they looked in golden evening light, these majestic mountains had a reputation of throwing their toys out the pram, and thinking I'd dealt with the worst of the weather already was royally tempting fate.

Walking the county tops was often the least enjoyable part, for the time pressure and the heavy legs from cycling, but today had been more forgiving, and I had already calculated that I would be in Aviemore at a reasonable time. Any bitterness towards Scotland from the day earlier had swung around into appreciation, and a strange urgency to make the most of this wilderness before looping the loop back to the less vertically challenged counties of England and Wales.

Reaching the end of each day was a pleasant thought, but when things were more relaxed, stress and anxiety often found a way in. I would busy my mind making plans for arrival; deciding what I'd do first, and doing things as efficiently as possible, and in the best order, to save time. Sometimes there was so much to do and that started to stress me out instead, especially when perfectionism stuck a finger in. But the relief of finishing was all that really mattered, and if my planning routines were another distraction technique to keep positively busy, then that was perfectly fine.

It was a fine morning, riding into the Queen's Forest as red squirrels swung from the branches. The shade of the pine trees held a brisk stillness along the beaches of Loch Morlich with the big boys of the Cairngorms reflected behind. Cycling to the ski resort gave a head start on its slopes, rising high above the carpet of forest below on relentless winding roads. My stammer had been unusually agitated for a few days, and asking a ranger to leave my camping gear in the ski centre storeroom was a struggle. Losing the weight made for quick progress on well-trodden paths towards the ridge above Coire an Lochain. After the characteristic clouds moved aside to let me in, the remoteness of this foreboding place became apparent. Only patches of alpine vegetation could survive high on these bare arctic plateaus – the highest, snowiest and coldest in the country – the scene of many tragedies and disregard for the humans who ventured into them. Steadily colder with height, it turned out pleasantly easier than expected and the summit of Ben Macdui knocked two historic counties off at once with Banffshire and Aberdeenshire squabbling over this giant and eventually settling for halves.

Heading east through the villages of Nethy Bridge and Boat of Garten was much calmer and less inspiring – the approaching Cromdale Hills more modest than the now-distant Cairngorms. The mileage was unusually low, and when the wind and rain lashed down, the sudden downpour put me in a dark place. Perhaps it threatened staying warm and brought the hassle of getting everything dry later. There was no denying that it spoilt the views and being cocooned in Gore-Tex like a neon alien was a rubbish deal compared to the rush of warm air across your arms, jersey unzipped, and the feel-good serotonin of sunlight.

Tomintoul was the highest village in the Scottish Highlands, where I found the Smugglers Hostel off the main road. I even had to knock on an old wooden door to be allowed in. I tried to look impressed while standing outside, drenched. I quickly threw everything on the radiators and set up Base Camp. Losing the physical weight of the rucksack was a relief, but the mental weight wouldn't budge. There was one county top to go and that meant getting Carn a'ghille-Chearr done that night. It was tempting to take an easier day and catch up with an epic tomorrow when better conditions would allow. But the itinerary tomorrow was already hard enough, and taking easy days was always bittersweet – it only made the next day worse – and catching up with the schedule was a game mostly played out in my head.

Going back outside again felt insurmountable. Once I had taken control with hot soup and dry clothes there was no excuse, and nothing but discomfort or fear was left to deal with. At that point it wasn't about making decisions, but learning to face the fear of the right one. Even when we removed every obstacle, our minds still managed to talk us out of something we knew we could do. We had to tempt ourselves with something positive, and the comfort of getting back here was enough. Setting off created a victory mindset by taking the harder option. With each step I reminded myself how much better I would feel arriving back at the hostel; collapsing happily inside with warmth, food, the satisfaction of completing another stage and seeing friends the day after. Forwards thinking was not always a bad thing when it was focused on the good to come.

Glenlivet was only six miles away. The famous Glenlivet Distillery was almost opposite the car park at Mains of Inverourie with a line of dead rats strung up on the fence. A dram of Scotch would have been a fine way to warm up. I felt suddenly happier in starting, and remembering it was only three miles to the top. The usual adrenaline surge kicked in as wispy clouds stroked the muddy heather like cigarette smoke, with patches of bare hill, burnt like acid. On the ridge and the first summit of Carn Eachie things got quickly worse. Rain crept under the seams of my jacket; wind stole temperature from beneath. Getting this cold couldn't be doing my body much good. I was annoyed at myself for being under-equipped and compromising my safety when I should have known better. All I could do now was get on with it.

An email from my friend Hems arrived with wonderful ironic timing.

Are you somewhere warm and dry tonight? it had said, followed by a notice on the screen of my waterproof rugged phone warning that water had been detected in the speakers.

"Featureless" took on a new meaning as I wandered across this bleak disgusting bog, led astray by occasional faint tracks. Grouse leapt out of the grass, cackling loudly and scaring the shit out of me as isolation intensified the senses. The line on my map was my lifeline as the hill howled; visibility dropped to about five metres in the greyness and I felt vulnerable, making a judgement that it was safe enough to continue. My mind knew there would be nothing to look at, there was no hope; anyone could lose hope in such a place. The trick was to focus on the basics – keeping safe and getting down as fast as possible – there wasn't room for much negative thinking. Feeling vulnerable was not a bad thing when the risk was real and not just anxiety causing mischief – it was designed to keep us safe and the adrenaline surge kept me going at speed. I worried that my energy would run out at some point. I was just desperate to see the trig point to mark the top of Morayshire. The wind-speed topped out on a scale of one-to-Scottish, and I forced a short film on camera, yelling over the noise to show the supporters back home far better than words could – if this didn't encourage a few spare pennies then I'd clearly have to come up with something more ridiculous. Suddenly, the trig point of Carn a'ghille-Chearr appeared like a shadow in this sea of hellish grey, a few metres ahead. The selfie resembled another one of those blurred drunken selfies from a Friday night. I couldn't get off the hill fast enough. The impact of running helped to warm things up, but every time my legs gave way beneath me through cold; my heart jumped an extra step. In good time the hellish clouds abated and revealed the planned track I had clumsily missed on the way up.

In hindsight, it was this final stage of the day, as I was giddily singing out loud as I rode back to the hostel, that I was at my most vulnerable through complacency. Looking up into the repulsive gloom closing in up the hillside behind brought the question of where I was finding the strength from, and I wondered when luck might run out after taking so many chances – my borrowed luck was already in overdraft.

CHAPTER 18

My only perception of the challenge was my own, and I knew my self-narrative wasn't always the kindest. I'd had little opportunity to offload my feelings face-to-face. Social media and phone calls didn't offer the same sense of connection.

I'd always preferred being independent, but I'd never had to entertain myself for so long before. It was disappointing not to share the experience and struggles with others firsthand to get a second opinion, a benchmark of normality, and some fresh conversation to distract from the boredom of my own thoughts for a while. There was also something comforting about having someone there in case of the inevitable down days.

The effects of being alone weren't obvious until I had someone with me. And I was thrilled to have company after nearly three weeks of walking alone. My friend Louise was driving two hours to join me, and I gave myself a boldly optimistic time for the hard 50-mile push to meet her. I always preferred to give myself a kick up the backside, bust a gut and race the clock; partly that was a result of me wanting to cram as much as possible into every day. Sitting still felt uneasy, like time could be better used elsewhere. I had yet to realise that being stressed out wasn't the best use of time, either.

Prolonged climbs made the usual estimations difficult, and The Lecht, the second highest road in Scotland dragged on.

I detoured into Aboyne to get sandwiches for later. Not much seemed to happen in this village. The elderly shopkeeper of the village corner shop was shocked that I had come from Tomintoul and I nearly told her to sit down, this wasn't even halfway. Having a coffee gave time for a chat when an older gent came in for his newspaper, and she told him all about it. I was reloading my panniers outside when a young mum pushing a pram soon caught the word on the street. Before I knew, she reached instantly for her purse with a handful of coins for the JustGiving page. I thanked her, taken aback by the offer.

'What's your name?' she asked – 'Take your glasses off, so I know your face, then I can say I've met you when you're famous!'

The unexpected generosity of strangers for mental health issues, in the most unassuming of places was an amazing feeling. Unsurprisingly I set off to Ballater with an extra boost in mind and body. Louise was waiting in the car park at the Bridge of Dye with her energetic spaniel, Pollaidh, chomping at the bit. We made a quick start through the forest clearing towards the distinct granite tor of Clachnaben. Olive green slopes of heather climbed onto a long upswelling of rolling, peaty moorland, lavished by sun and heat. Mount Battock looked painfully distant. Chatting away continued to make time fly, while Pollaidh bolted through the undergrowth chasing grouse and hares with undying enthusiasm.

It was the first time we had met in person, but it felt like we had known each other for years after connecting on social media. We had a lot more in common than just a love of mountains. Our Sergeant Majors were closely related, and the outdoors was our weapon of choice in fighting a battle that manifested in similar ways. Her messages of support had given me hope of finding light at the end of the tunnel, and Louise was one of my biggest inspirations in speaking publicly about my eating disorder in the first place, with her own openness reassuring me that it was okay to talk, however uncomfortable it felt. It triggered the question of who I might help by being more open myself, and I had never been one for missing out. We didn't stop talking all day. I rarely had the chance to speak to someone who understood the irrationality and complexity of these internal wars and I wanted to make the most of it. *Wow,* I thought – *it's not just me.*

After feeling like a one-man army as far back as I could remember, it was uniting to open everything up without brushing over the uncomfortable bits like usual. Louise said how much my first book, *Icefall*, had helped her to realise that she didn't have to follow the conventional things in life – she could do what made her happy. I was always chuffed to bits to know that my writing could have such a positive impact on people; for them to become part of the journey for real was even more pertinent. Louise was another oatcake fan and Team Oatcake had soon conquered the historic county of Kincardineshire. The summit was just a simple trig point looking across to Glen Esk. Going back down the same way didn't matter with such good company to pass the time, before a hilly 40-mile ride to Braemar...

My friend Richard Ellis was driving up from work in Dundee, and taking the weekend to join me. Rich had followed my challenges avidly before and since Everest; one of the benefits of social media. We had met for the first time in Glencoe, to walk the Lost Valley, before Everest 2015, and this was our first adventure since. He had promised I was in for a treat riding through the pristine countryside of Royal Deeside and Balmoral Castle. He was right. On this gorgeous midsummer night, the forests held an enchanting chill and another slice of Scotland's soul.

After struggling to find me on the live tracker, Rich pulled in at the roadside;

'You look fucked!' he said. Funnily enough, I felt the same.

*

The next morning, we hit the Cairnwell Pass – the highest public road in the country, steep enough that buses once had to drop passengers off at the bottom to walk up, and the AA had maintained a well in the layby for overheating engines. Luckily, we had come from the other side, which still took over an hour as the wind pushed back like a bouncer, and horizontal rain turned the road into a stream. Momentarily, the clouds broke, and the vastness of the patterned brown hillsides were revealed below. Rich waited with coffee under the shelter of the ski centre – the biggest in Scotland – as I changed from wet cycling shoes into wet trainers. Being at 2,200ft altitude gave a head start on Glas Maol, the highest point of Angus and a bald domed hill that was hard to appreciate in a bowl of pea soup, following the ski tows to the first summit of Meall Odhar and then Glas Maol itself. Rarely were Munros this accessible, and it took no time to reach the summit plateau with a few hardy walkers ahead. Two ladies kindly took a photo of this drenched duo as we shook hands and celebrated our first summit together, and Rich told them all about the challenge, while I stood there quietly. Between howling fits of wind, we agreed to change the planned route and descend the same way, as a longer descent over Sron na Gaoithe only to come back up the A93 road in these conditions was pointless and achieved nothing. I resented taking shortcuts for the risk of falling under the advertised 5,000-mile target – the last thing I wanted was the challenge tainted by animosity from others, and especially not from myself. Truthfully, only Sergeant Major would either care or notice, and without changing the approach I had no chance of getting ahead.

At least gravity worked in our favour as we dropped like stones into the wide plains of Glen Shee. Rich had offered to take the weight off by decanting the panniers into his car, and it felt like a different bike. With a boot-full of food supplies and water Rich wanted to help in any way he could, and told me to take the comforts while I had them. I felt bad that he was doing all this for me but was too weak to refuse help on such a grim day. He pulled up in laybys ahead, taking photos of anything amusing, and had a school photographer's knack of making me smile, regardless of how I felt. His piss-taking about my newly sprouted beard was quite literally taken on the chin.

A steady soreness had lingered in the back of my throat all afternoon and I'd assumed it was dehydration, but the fish pie came with a sudden side order of a fuzzy head, and hefty aches crept in with dessert. Weeks of pushing had finally pushed back and whacked my immune system for good. It felt like I was coming down with something right before going up something: which happened to be one of the highest summits of the challenge, and the 10th highest Munro in Scotland.

CHAPTER 19

'Can I sleep in your car?' I croaked through a heavy chest.

Luckily Rich didn't object as I hoisted the sleeping bag around me, though it did little to ease the shivering and dull aches all over my body. At six-foot-four, I was hardly compact, but sleeping upright in the passenger seat was vastly more appealing than pitching the tent outside in the elements. Any bravado had blown out the window because if I wasn't careful the entire challenge would follow suit.

Under the dim dashboard light, we sat discussing plans for the morning. If not for someone to weigh up the options with, I could never have noticed how weak my reasoning had become, subconsciously engineering the conversation towards what I wanted to hear, instead of what I needed to hear. I was fishing for a reason to call it a day, hoping he would agree and add weight to the decision. He didn't let up. Only when I failed to respond did Rich notice I had slumped forwards, asleep, mid-conversation. It was exhaustion rather than an insult; either way it looked like we would have to make the call in the morning.

After a saga of tossing and turning, the alarm hit at 5.30am. Things had only become much worse. A splitting headache and lethargy had me wriggling like a parasite, one arm poking out of the sleeping bag to reach for a pack of painkillers. Thankfully Rich took pity and made a dash for the stove in the boot. A hot mug of porridge only scalded my raw throat further and turned my stomach, but it was forced down anyway. It wasn't often that I managed to reject food, as much as I dreamt of the ability. Feeling sick as a dog was even worse than binge eating – at least I had some control over that behaviour, even if I couldn't always find it. Right now, there was no choice but to suffer. This was the lowest point of the challenge, and I hadn't even hit Norfolk yet!

The forecast had deteriorated just as quickly, and left me quite literally under the weather. Sudden downpours lashed the windscreen and dampness clogged the air like the mucus in my chest. A threatening blanket of greyness made it hard to determine whether sunrise had broken or not. Going outside seemed incomprehensible. Could missing one top really hurt? Coming back the next day would throw me behind schedule further without Rich for support. Friends could always see further ahead than the next few hours.

'There's always a solution,' he assured, leaving me to ponder the decision in my fuzzy head.

If I pushed on, then feeling rough was inevitable, but at least I would go to bed with one less problem to deal with. This dilemma reminded me of the days back home when binge eating had been the only means of motivating myself to run for a couple of hours. Something far greater had kept me going for the last 30 days and over 2,000 miles already.

The solution was simple: to keep moving. Because at least that way we were making progress. We must have sat for 20 minutes while my mind swung heavy like a pendulum, building momentum, counting to 10. Then another 10. It was now or never. Eight, nine, ten. I grabbed the momentum with both hands:

'RIGHT! LET'S MOVE!' I grunted, reaching for the door handle with power. I had to move before second thoughts saw sense.

Rich smiled and quickly followed suit like a willing sidekick; probably glad to escape a car now festering with snot and pathogens. The door slammed in the wind and the cold instantly chilled my bones. But heck, I had conquered the first step, and the hardest part was done.

Climbing a simple Scottish Munro had become more dramatic than a soap opera. It was only 10 kilometres – I'd be done in a few hours – it was nothing new. But in this state of lethargy, every step summoned Himalayan effort. The best we could do was put one foot in front of another. This simple forwards motion took us further into fifty shades of Highland grey where the weather grew wilder and wetter. An overgrown track led through a nature trail and peat beds, with any glimpse of the sprawling mountains above cheated by a dense barrier of fog. Sending my waterproof trousers home to save weight because skin was "waterproof" seemed utterly stupid when borrowing some from Rich took the chill off pinprick hairs. The path climbed through ridged pastures towards a broad flank of the mountain, and straight into the mercy of the wind, where an unexpected gust nearly swept me sideways. An exposed line led to the underwhelming minor summit of Beinn Ghlas. Chatting soon turned to shouting over the groans of wind before giving up altogether, repeating 'Relentless forwards motion' under my breath. As my face grew colder and my lips too numb to speak, the mantra was confined to my silent thoughts. Through a pulsing headache I couldn't discern the tune ringing in my ears and put it down to delirium. Then, in a fleeting moment of calm I recognised them as the cheerful lyrics of 'Bring Me Sunshine' by Morecambe and Wise, blasting out from Rich's mobile phone.

Sure enough, forwards motion brought us to an unmistakeable stone pillar that marked the summit of Ben Lawers, and the highest point of Perthshire. A century earlier, a group of local men had built a cairn of rock to try and push the height of the peak above 4,000ft. We caught the moment of success in a short film, with the words coming in slurred confusion. Even with my head in the clouds, there was no doubt that I wanted to get down before I got cold again. An ongoing ankle problem meant Rich would be slower to descend, but he was more than capable of making his own way down safely, so I hurried off down the ridge to a col, where shallow-cut trails snaked around the bulk of the mountain and back towards the car park; providing my legs didn't give way first.

Back at the car park I discovered numb fingers were as much use as a chocolate teapot on combination locks. I prised the cursed thing open impatiently with my teeth and made a dash for it, with a downhill blast that froze my backside solid to the saddle. Either way, it was done. Before I could work out what on earth would happen now, I simply had to get warm, diving into the first coffee shop I could find and clinging to a dusty old radiator. As I began a plethora of mapping calculations to work out a Plan B, the hot chocolate and cake brought core temperature back to normal, and another slice of motivation came too. It was undoubtedly the day for comfort food. The gentle patter of rain through steamed windows looked somehow less insurmountable. In meeting these basic human needs, the situation didn't seem quite so terrible after all.

Rich arrived soon after. Before even tucking into the froth of his coffee the announcement came;

'I have to get to Stirling today.'

Otherwise, I would be too far north and without chance of catching up with my schedule. It wasn't just a case of planning each day, but the following days too, since diverting to Stirling would mean doing the next three county tops in reverse and bypassing Edinburgh entirely. Could I even manage another 45 miles of cycling in the rain? There wasn't much excuse considering what we had just climbed. My body cried out at the injustice of it; for the last few hours I had tried to kid myself into believing I was going no further than Killin. Of course, I knew that wouldn't be the case, and there was always something left to give. Endurance was a cruel game, like teasing a dog with a slab of meat. Sooner or later my mind would stop trusting itself and stage a protest. If not for tricking myself I would probably have failed to leave the car.

Time always passed quicker when moving. My head was set only on Stirling and trying to keep the bike steady through fits of violent sneezing. On a sleepy Sunday, the A84 traffic was thin but a car slowed to my side and I primed myself for another aggravated anti-cycling outburst. Instead, a familiar tune appeared from the open window, as I glanced across to see Rich belting out the chorus of '500 Miles' by The Proclaimers. Fortunately, his humour was better than his singing. Passing through Callander, I happily hollered the lyrics back at full whack, to the obvious bemusement of a young lad standing at the bus stop. With the impressive sight of Stirling Castle coming into view I had every reason to sing out loud without a care in the world.

There were surely better ways to sacrifice your Sunday afternoon than leapfrogging a stubborn cyclist. Rich reminded me that the record-breakers, and even my cycling hero, Mark Beaumont, who was due to cycle the world in less than 80 days, all had a support outfit. Many had the full shebang of physiotherapists, nutritionists, mechanics, and a communications team. Until today it had just been Alex and the bike on the frontline. I quite liked it that way but had to accept that taking support and calling reinforcements for a couple of days was a necessity to get the 72 days done at all. He waved me on outside the city before making the long drive home.

I pulled up at Stirling Youth Hostel around 5.00pm and wasted no time with the usual evening routine: I tucked myself away in a quiet corner of the dining room to think clearly in the hope nobody would ask where I'd cycled from. Predictably someone did. Checking the weather forecast through mouthfuls of dinner, I did my best to appear interested in his delight with the Scottish Rail network and his first-class ticket from Glasgow. Only when he described the fatigue after his sightseeing tour of Edinburgh did I lift my bloodshot eyes from the screen in a second glance. He wasn't pulling my leg.

'So, how was your day?' he asked.

'Well,' I yawned. 'I guess it could have been a whole lot worse.'

CHAPTER 20

Relentless forwards mucus was the mantra for the day. My heart strained, thumping hard; I could have been cycling under the bedsheets. Shivers tickled up my arms and my head pulsed before the alarm rang beneath my pillow. Without question, the first target today was finding a pharmacy in Stirling.

The verdict was the onset of a chest infection; carrying on would almost certainly seal the deal.

'This is your body saying it needs a break now,' she insisted, surprised it had even lasted this far.

My mind had other ideas, as I bought a box of painkillers and skulked off towards the rotisserie oven. The warm waft of chicken brought some relief to the constant shivering. The chest infection deteriorating into pneumonia was a more legitimate concern. I knew that if I could continue with painkillers, then I damn well would – cycling over a thousand miles on a torn muscle, being pulled by every push of the pedal and enduring the day on Ben Lawers had become an unhelpful testament to what I could tolerate. After that, my Sergeant Major had no intention of letting me settle for the easy option. And that unhelpful, barking, glutton for punishment was an even bigger headache.

My supporters were saying to rest: nobody would think badly of me. Mum agreed; though I could barely hear through the waterlogged speaker of the mobile phone. What would I advise a friend in my situation? Slapping them round the head came to mind. It was always friends who got me to the other side of depression, waving at me from where the grass seemed greener, when it tried to send us off alone into the garden like an old dog when its time had come. They only meant well, but they weren't on the bike, nor were they going to solve my logistics – we only take advice we want to hear, anyway.

With mind, body, and gut tied up in civil war, the only hope was to step outside of myself, to switch off from the mental noise and deal with the here and now. It was gone 10.30am and getting to Edinburgh was out of reach regardless. The weather was deteriorating. While an element of bravado was useful, there would be no heroism in spending a day or more in a hospital ward with pneumonia. Whereas taking a rest day in the hostel could nip this in the bud before it could bite me in the backside. Why was I worried about falling behind schedule? I'd catch up again – I had before. Making the call to take a rest day still did not come easily. Cycling back to the hostel through Stirling felt pitiable, like I expected better from myself.

Rest days were somewhat of a disappointment. They simply created time to catch up with admin and solve the mess I had got myself into. Rhythmic hours in the saddle were somehow far more relaxing than hurrying around Stirling city centre, picking up supplies, washing clothes and buying a birthday card for Dad. This exertion only defeated the object. The marketing manager at the youth hostel, Donna, had come specially to meet me for a coffee, which worked wonders in releasing some nervous energy. Stress always aggravated my stammer. Trying to negotiate an unused rag to clean my bike proved to be a slurred mess, and with my alternative hand gestures, the cleaning lady probably assumed I was asking her to clean it for me. I didn't bother asking for a cable tie to fix the split crotch of my trousers.

Hours passed glued to my mobile phone, sprawled across a bunkbed, spluttering mucus over the sheets, though it probably explained why the hostel had given me a room to myself. I was making calculations, eye-balling maps, and deliberating how I would get back on schedule. There were always options, of course. It made sense to bypass Edinburgh entirely and tick Clackmannanshire, Kinross-shire and Fife in one hit. Having a plan for the next two days was all I needed for now. But my biggest disappointment came from letting others down. Three people had planned to come along yesterday; had I stayed on schedule.

The intense focus that the cycling and walking required didn't just stop, it had to be transferred somewhere. So once my mind was set on something, that was that, and now the engine had stopped, there was an opportunity to challenge the huge physical deficit. Perhaps I hadn't learnt my lesson from before, but the all-you-can-eat Chinese buffet restaurant in Stirling promised a cheap way to get calories. I was determined not to lose control, but a few full plates later, I felt disgusting, gluttonous and intensely anxious.

Being ill and in a low ebb seemed a fair enough excuse. Back home, these episodes of binge eating would have resulted in fasting for days to compensate and unknowingly wiring myself further into this vicious cycle of unhappiness. But back home I didn't have to fuel myself for consecutive days on bike and foot. This was a different animal and conversely, any attempt to punish myself with binge eating was actually nourishing myself instead. For once, I could most definitely have my cake and eat the lot. The feast lulled me to a heavy sleep; my body had got what it wanted, and didn't care for what the bulimia thought.

It took further discipline not to compensate by starving myself after the "binge". Yesterday had to be dismissed, and now was not the time to deprive myself. Breakfast was a croissant, cheese, two bowls of muesli, milk and honey, topped with cold butter, for extra calories. I smiled, in control. The eating disorder wasn't going to get me from A to B, but eating would.

The burnt-orange mounds topped with heather, shot up for miles and gave a striking backdrop to the A91. The hill was guarded by a thick band of forest; a deep gorge, waterfall and disused quarry hidden within. From this scenic beginning began the pull onto grassy slopes, steep enough to be both exhilarating and an effective decongestant for my chest. My heart went like the clappers and my jacket hood wiped the streaming snot clear; Ben Cleuch was as steep as warned. Straight up, like a staircase, but short. Legs went to lead. After this chesty effort, it levelled to a boggy ridge and the summit of Ben Law.

The flush of morning appeared late, and the cloud lifted to cap the Forth Bridges. It was bizarre how mood could suddenly lift with it. Even the darkest and dullest days could flip to the brightest, once someone opened the curtains. Nature taught me to find the beauty in every day. Everything suddenly seemed that much more optimistic. Perhaps the clear view could clear the mind, allowing thoughts to drift free (in a blanket of cloud, these thoughts condensed in one place). This simple phenomenon of weather was strikingly parallel with the peaks and troughs of the mind – we couldn't control the clouds coming in, we just had to let them roll in and out again.

Unlocking the bike from the railings in the street, it was only 10 miles for number two and another blast on the A91. Approaching from the beautiful Glen Devon, the highest point of Kinross-shire was still too insignificant to recognise. From Littlerig car park, a gravel track began through a greying graveyard of tree stumps and branches, where felling had left the landscape ugly and decimated. At the marked spot there was no gap for anything larger than a rabbit.

Instead, I committed to the blue-lined direction on the map. Following the planned route embarked on a comedy show of clambering over crumbling walls and carcasses of fallen trees, crawling under exposed roots, snagging on twigs, and cutting myself on razor-edged bark. Rotting trunks croaked and threatened to fall in a moment as the squirrels took liberty. A machete would have been more use than the map.

Before agitation took over, I had no choice but to admit defeat, and retrace to the track; it led almost all the way to the summit – where the fir plantation thinned like a middle-aged head of hair to reveal the trig point grinning smugly at me. Why hadn't I chosen an easier life, like the train-spotter in the youth hostel? This observation made me laugh out loud, and a simple laugh was the medicine I needed.

With the sun blaring down, I grew weaker – each slight incline of the track countered momentum, until I could run only for a few metres at a time. Back at the bike, I barely had enough water for a cactus: opting to back-track a mile to Muckhart and a quaint café, before leaving again at 3.00pm with 60 miles still to go, and that never felt great at this time of day.

The Garmin had gone ghost, which led to the discovery of a cycle route through Wester Balgedie and spared the A91 running parallel, roaring with rush-hour traffic, The former county town of Kinross dropped further along the banks of Loch Leven, shimmering over my shoulder, while the Lomond Hills rose abruptly ahead.

As usual, I was flying into gear, hurrying off through a copse and onto a broad grassy track that shot straight for West Lomond – these volcanic remnants like a castle on the horizon.

Up close, this slope was unnatural, near-vertical, and took hands on knees to ascend. The highest point of Fife gave an impressive vantage point across to the Firth of Tay, and a sense of wilderness from the industrial mining scars of Fife below.

Back at the bike, checking my phone and scoffing whatever remained in the panniers, I noticed a £100 donation on the fundraising page and a message from a mutual friend who had been trying to hunt me down all morning – with flapjacks. Hannah had come to the hostel in Stirling, missing me by minutes; she'd even hit the road for Dunning in search of this elusive bloke on a bike. She had wanted to let me know that everyone was behind me. This staggering kindness was every reason to smile – I'd never had a flapjack stalker before. It was almost 11.00pm when I arrived in the cul-de-sac of Boghall, and my pal Fraser's house. A broad figure came to the door with a hearty smile. Fraser had waited up especially for me. I felt immensely grateful, standing red-eyed in his porch, removing the snot-covered gloves for a handshake and pat on the back. An accomplished mountaineer himself, he knew exactly what I needed, ushering me inside to a bucket-sized mug of sugary tea.

His family were fast asleep, and the house was silent except for the muffled sound of a TV in the next room. After a quick shower, a roast chicken dinner was waiting, steaming, on the kitchen table.

I wolfed it down at speed. Second helpings turned out to be a second complete plate, though that too was gone in a flash. Fraser chuckled that his huge Alsatian, Murphy, in the corner of the room weighed nearly as much as me.

'You couldn't have chosen worse weather than you've had these last two weeks,' he sighed. I grinned with relief – maybe the weather really had been bad, and I wasn't just a moaning Englishman after all.

We chatted for hours, though it was time to get my head down in the spare room of the attic. I turned the phone off, popped some ibuprofen and put another day to bed. Adapting and overcoming had paid off wonderfully – the county trio had worked; I was back on track with a fighting chance. Tomorrow would bring its own challenges, as each day did, and the ability to adapt would overcome those too. This ability was no superpower: it was a human instinct for survival.

CHAPTER 21

Cairnpapple Hill was close enough that my coffee would still have been warm when I got back to Fraser's house. The Bathgate Hills were less than three miles from the door and there was more ascent cycling to the car park than to reach the top of Cairnpapple Hill itself. Fraser sent me off with lashings of porridge. I was hardly fit to go, but I was going anyway.

Fraser had followed in the car with his dog, Murphy, and it took us less than two minutes to reach the summit of the historic county of West Lothian, or Linlithgowshire.

A message had arrived from a follower on Twitter who had been following me closely and noticed I was staying about two roads away. The "small world" saying was over-used, but today it was beautifully true. Regardless of time, I simply had to go and say hello. Rose was delighted and surprised to see me knocking at the door, inviting me inside for a coffee, as her little Beagle puppy jumped up excitedly.

Rose had cystic fibrosis and found her solace in road cycling. Her son suffered with mental ill health too, and she had lost her brother just weeks earlier to suicide. Mental illness couldn't get any closer to home. Emotionally, it hit hard. She just gave me a hug. We had never even met – and were now connected by this warming sense of hope from the dark places. Rose hurried to fetch some homemade caramel shortbread and a few mini cartons of milk for the panniers. As I headed south, it became clearer than ever why I was here in the first place.

I felt somewhat fraudulent calling myself a victim when I was functioning, out here, doing this. Everyone had something they were dealing with. Mental health was not a competition. Leaving the advocate roles exclusively to those in the darkest battles was a loss, because not everyone would feel the ability to stand up and speak out. That's why it was so important to speak up for those who hadn't yet found their way. This battle was about spreading the message with as many advocates as possible, rather than leaving the war to a handful. If my own journey could get more people talking about mental health, then it could unite the troops in every corner of the UK. People needed hope to keep the lights on a bit longer; I was determined to fight for those who had lost hope.

*

The open farm country of South Lanarkshire was a gentler introduction to the Southern Uplands. A friend, Robin, was due to meet me for the first walk, and I was pushing hard to meet him on time. Rush, rush, rush – it never stopped.

Rushing only ever left us avoiding confronting our feelings. But it worked too well. In the rush, we inevitably avoided the wonder and delights around us. We're never really in the moment when we're under pressure.

There was no time for anything other than a whistle-stop in the town of Biggar to get food for later, and lunch plans were thrown into the wind. My time calculations were either based on my racing bike, or just grossly over-ambitious; either way, they were not working.

I rushed into Glenkirk and met Robin in a fluster. He assured me not to apologise. After stressing out for hours about arriving on time, there was always a sudden relief when I saw the person waiting for me. Then, the pressure was off, and I could just enjoy the company. Robin had asked if he could bring anything. Cravings changed on a daily or even hourly basis and some days my stomach refused sugar altogether – but the sight of Hobnobs biscuits quite literally hit the spot.

Robin was a chef and a fit hillwalker who had followed my journey from the start and jumped at the chance to be part of it, another reason for creating Climb The UK. Mental health had caused its share of grief in his family too, and I was humbled by his story.

Culter Fell was dominant at the head of the road, and we thundered up the tussock slopes of Leishfoot Hill towards it, reaching an obvious trig point in less than an hour, for another vantage point across the wind turbines, before a photo and jogging back down to the glen like lambs.

On my own, there was nobody to empathise with, and I just had to get on with it. But with company, I rarely noticed the distance through talking continuously, and Robin's patience was a feat of endurance itself.

An otherwise peaceful summit, Broad Law was marked not only a trig point but an almost extra-terrestrial beacon, and the quiet countryside below was intruded on by windfarms like ants on all sides. The historic counties of Selkirkshire and Peeblesshire met at the top again. Reaching trig points had become an almost passionless process in ticking counties off a list. They were appreciated a whole lot more when sharing the achievement with someone else.

It was getting too late to climb White Coomb safely that evening, which continued the debate of how on earth I would ever catch up.

The Tibbie Shiels Inn had an envious setting: water, high hills, pine forests, and a caravan around the back for me, triggering happy childhood memories of weekends spent in our caravan in North Wales. But waking up to the sound of rain hammering on the caravan roof, and the sensation of wind rocking it from side to side was an instant mood killer. The "tin tent" was still a better deal than fabric, with a kettle and coffee in the cupboard. A sachet of Morning Fuel oat drink in a mug, with a bag of salted cashew nuts, was the next best thing to porridge and peanut butter.

Getting to Innerleithen for lunch was the motivation – the county top of Dumfriesshire, White Coomb, was simply a step to get there. The Grey Mare's Tail waterfall was the fifth highest in the UK and it felt like I had already stood underneath it by the time I got to the car park. A seemingly obvious path followed the burn into a dramatic V-shaped gorge with wetness hanging around its ankles. Something had clearly gone wrong when the path was closed abruptly by a danger sign warning of unstable ground and landslips. I didn't like the idea of finding another route and losing time when I was already up against the clock, and just assumed it was the usual health and safety red tape. I carried on. The path disappeared completely into hands-on scrambling, but nothing beyond my ability. As expected, the ground soon eased until I noticed the correct path – across on the other side of the gorge. It was true – rushing only made mistakes happen faster. I shrugged it off; the photos of the waterfall were worth the detour. Fortunately, the shin-high wall appeared as planned, leading across squelchy moorland to a knobbly rise ahead, and the sound of crashing water fell silent. The summit of White Coomb had magical solitude; defended by deep valleys and a hand of ridges, with Loch Skeen tucked peacefully below. Getting down was considerably easier than it had been going up. Eighty miles and two walks were quickly falling out of my reach though ...

Defiance was the theme for the day as I passed straight through the barrage of Road Closed signs, and the workers eating crisps in their van didn't bat an eyelid. A car came around the corner screeching the horn, and I braced myself for some abuse.

183

But the chap grinning through the window was my friend Richard Mostyn, who had made a big detour from working in Edinburgh to find me. We pulled over for a man hug moment. Having company always helped take us away from the problem for a while. It had done years earlier when we first met in Delamere Forest during my first bout of depression. I held a fond memory of walking together in the Glyderau of Snowdonia with two of his friends. That glorious winter day had dug me out of the pit, and the company had allowed me to forget everything that was going on, for a day at least.

Another good friend, Jenny, and her parents, Ron and Ros, had been eager to host from the start. Their home in Melrose was too far off my original route, but having fallen far behind, I fathomed an idea that was a bit drastic – and I was about to ask more of a favour than they probably expected. The tiny village of Fala on the route was out in the sticks, with no accommodation, and everything was too soaked to camp. It would add overall mileage, but if they could drive me back to Fala in the morning, it would give me a big head start to catch up and make the whole thing achievable.

I set off reinvigorated. There was no doubt that physical fatigue was often tied up in the burden of anxiety and removing the chains sped things right up. Blackhope Scar was only 10 miles away. If not for a signpost by the road at Windy Slack, it could never have existed. Before even getting my trainers on, a car pulled up decked in Climb The UK posters. If saving the day wasn't enough already, Jenny and Ros had driven out to give moral support and supplies.

Blackhope Scar was the highest of Midlothian and the featureless heather-clad mounds of the Moorfoot Hills. The farm track followed Blackhope Water, with rabbits jumping, and fish clear to see. For the first time in a frenetic few days I was listening to music again and allowing my mind to drift. A ridge followed a fence up to Adams Rig on notorious boggy ground which made dry feet a dreamy vision. Blackhope Scar was a typically uninspiring low-level summit. Its white trig point stood feeling sorry for itself in the corner of boundary fences with the murky skies and brown expanse below almost blending into one. Running down in leaping strides allowed me to escape the worst of the rain and I ducked into a farmer's tin shed to change layers. Only three days after leaving me in Stirling, Richard Ellis was waving from the roadside as I ran back to the bike, shaking his head in disbelief that I still had the energy. A flask of tea and sandwiches warmed the hands before Richard had to get back to work, and I had to prise the bike lock open. These hills were his local stomping ground and it was great to see him again.

From Fala, I turned off my tracker before anyone noticed I was diverting 24 miles the wrong way down the A68.

The impressive Leaderfoot viaduct stood proud in a sunset glow and the homely village of Melrose arrived like a big hug. In a quiet cul-de-sac, I noticed Climb The UK posters plastered over a lounge window. The Anderson family welcomed me inside their cosy home, with a feast of a dinner. After the last few days, I was too exhausted to listen to bulimia, and I enjoyed it. They couldn't do enough to help. I stayed up long after midnight, updating the live tracker map on my website.

Before bed, I noticed some scales in the bathroom, and curiously weighed myself for the first time since starting the challenge. It was a pleasant surprise to see I had dropped over five kilograms, which possibly explained the struggle to stay warm. Getting a good look in the mirror, it suddenly struck me, just how much weight I had lost. Veins bulged with washboard six-pack abs. Besides the unsightly tan lines, men would pay for abs this defined, without sit-ups or a gym ball, but they were only showing because my body fat had dropped so low.

According to the bathroom scales I was now classified as underweight. Due to their natural physical build and the typical lean frame that benefitted performance, many athletes would fall into this category while still being perfectly healthy. But I doubted whether this was healthy for me, and vowed to up my calorie intake. I couldn't avoid it though; I liked what I saw in the mirror.

The familiar voices bothered me. Each time I managed to listen to my body, bulimia was manipulative and persisted until it managed to deprive me when I needed to fuel up properly. Battling these calorie control anxieties began by drowning them in my orange juice and coffee the next morning; croissants and porridge helped me load up for a big day ahead. Ros worried she couldn't get the clothes clean – I laughed and assured her they were the cleanest they had been since day one. They sent me off with an array of Scottish sustenance and an early birthday card, too.

Crossing the border back into England in a few hours was the best milestone to get things going. The Anderson family took me back to the exact point in Fala where I'd left off. It was great to be back on the road and climbing into the rolling moorland of the Lammermuir Hills.

Besides the farmer at Faseny Cottage, I was alone again for the next summit. Meikle Says Law quickly turned out to be the usual affair of a gravel track and lonely moorland that made many of the Southern Upland summits hard to distinguish between, with spent gun pellets littering the ground. The neighbouring county of Berwickshire was clearly lacking ambition and its highest point sat 100 metres to the south across the border fence. I walked around in circles for a while to make sure I'd got it and went back the same way.

After lunch in the village of Coldstream, the English border sign was underwhelming for such a moment. Passing cars must have sighed at this silly tourist beaming for a selfie next to a landmark of their daily commute. This wasn't quite the halfway point, but it meant so much. Scotland had battered, broken, soaked, and scared me; but it had welcomed, awed, scorched, and inspired me in equal measure. There was nothing to be bitter about and only everything to be grateful for.

Getting this far was entirely down to the support and generosity of strangers and friends alike; old and new. People showing up to give me moral support was all I had hoped for; it was humbling how they had gone above and beyond. I still felt conflicted about taking support while trying to remain self-supported, but I knew that accepting help in our times of weakness was no shame. It was easier to be given a leg up than peeled off the floor. And it gave us the benefit of other people's experience when they had got out of the same trough. I liked how it empowered others too – the Anderson family had even gone to the trouble of knocking on neighbours' doors with tales of this passing traveller on a bike, raising an extra £137 for Young Minds.

Scotland had thickened the skin like a winter coat. It went without saying that grappling with the outdoor elements built our resilience, like poison in small doses developed our immunity. This was beautifully dangerous: because now I was excited to find just what I could overcome next. If I could keep believing in myself as much as others believed in me, then anything was possible.

CHAPTER 22

Being in England felt suddenly different, as everything could with a different outlook. Physically speaking, the body enjoyed the respite of being in the geographical troughs, while they lasted. I just hoped it would last to the weekend when I would finally get the chance to recover. The county of Northumberland was by no means an easy transition as the undulation of the roads stole momentum. It was up, or down, and nothing in between, some one-in-five gradients thrown in just for fun. My mind was already programmed to this routine, but my body was less robust. Lacking the leg power to maintain effort was especially noticeable under time pressure. Racing against the clock to reach Langleeford for my 6.00pm target wouldn't help shake off the remnants of an infection but getting away with something once was enough to chance my luck.

Time was often the root of my anxiety and stressful anticipation. I had already managed some of the mountainous county tops alone in the dark, but it was still intimidating. Being in the dark, alone, left me feeling vulnerable, and unlike other challenges where I could tolerate finishing in the early hours to get the job done, this challenge never gave me long enough to compose myself before having to get up the next morning and go again. That night I had booked Alnwick hostel at the last minute to get a big head start the following day, and the hostel owner was generously willing to hang around until 1.00am to let me in.

Volatile black clouds hung ahead like hoodlums outside the corner shop, and I knew I was about to be mugged. After 65 miles I was heading straight into the Harthope Valley and this microclimate of greyness. Sometimes the good thing about being so rushed was having little time to procrastinate; I left everything on the bike and locked it to a fence as fast as I could. Security was much less of a worry than the walk ahead.

For each kilometre, I had one chunk of the fudge the Anderson family had given me, letting it melt slowly, like a buttery lozenge. This simple reward system kept the forwards motion. Scald Hill was just one rise ahead and The Cheviot further still. Wind pushed me back as if warning me not to bother.

I sank into peat hags and mud for most of the first hour, before big paving slabs on the track let me run and jump with the freedom of a child. Finally, an eerie white structure broke the fog. This trig point was special enough to sit on its own mound, probably to stop it sinking into bogs like everything else. The grey mist was surprisingly dry, the wind subsided, and the mountain took on a friendlier persona.

Scotland called with one final errand. The highest point of Roxburghshire hid itself on Cairn Hill West Top, like an overgrown toenail of The Cheviot. It was a quick trot down the slabs to find it, with no more chunks of tablet until I had. The highest point was an unmarked lump at the precise height of 743 metres off the path and a photo of my trainers in the heather was the summit memento. When anxious for time it took discipline to make the effort to find the spot, rather than a blasé wave of "that'll do". Losing a few extra minutes to get the true summit was insignificant when travelling thousands of miles to get here. After checking my headtorch to discover the batteries dead, and the spares were the wrong size, there was even more urgency to get off the hill. Once more, a strength flushed through me. Water would lead back to the valley and running down this muddy path alongside Harthope Burn was bouncy bliss without the weight of the camping gear I could have run into forever. The milky blindness cleared into peachy evening skies as Langleeford made itself known again.

The day had turned out much better than I'd feared. It didn't matter how often anxiety played the cards of all my bad experiences to unsettle me; the visions were only ever negative in my perception. And if my perceptions could change so quickly then maybe the perceived problems never existed at all. Preparing for the worst but trying – or even just hoping for the best and carrying on regardless – gave us the best possible outcome.

A flash of white crossed the road, a Barn Owl flew ahead, almost brushing the leaves, not much faster than the bike span, too beautiful to be a coincidence. I could worry about tomorrow – tomorrow.

'Happy days,' I affirmed out loud. Everything was going to be okay.

*

Day 36 marked half of 72. Psychologically there was just something special about reaching the halfway point that brought a massive boost. Earlier in the pursuit I had to look backwards at what had been achieved. Towards the end, I could look ahead and see the number of days getting smaller, while the fundraising total kept getting bigger. Truthfully, I was already well past half, and the second chunk would surely be much less physically demanding with most of the really big mountains done. There was no time for complacency though; it was the most inconspicuous things that could trip us up, because we least expected them.

The next day, getting to Alston for another logistical obligation felt like a big ask. Well before the challenge I was committed to lead a Walk For Nepal event on Scafell Pike, organised by the charity PHASE Worldwide, who supported people in rural Nepal.

Once committed to something, going against my word was not something I could ever consider lightly. I wanted to ensure the event was a success and like usual, had found a solution. It just meant riding 92 miles in an impromptu heatwave, having bust a gut for the last two weeks to stay on schedule. And then there was the knee injury ... it reminded me of the running injury of 2012 that had first led to my eating disorder. Now, as then, my stubbornness to continue was possibly out of fear of losing control in the same way. Ultimately, the injury setback had changed the chain of events in my life – and led, inexorably to this point. I knew that after the initial pain and resentment, there was almost always a positive side to each of these events, even if it took years to materialise.

The chronic pain had persevered so long that in hindsight it was likely that it lived on in my head, where my conscious mind began to watch out for it. The drama of the last week had undoubtedly diverted attention from it, but these quieter days confirmed that the injury had somehow resolved itself through changing my cycling cadence, losing weight, or by inadvertently strengthening the injured muscle by cycling through it. Rupert Bonington had messaged to ask about it. He said I had done bloody well to keep going. Earning the support of such well-regarded people in the outdoor world was a compliment itself.

The morning got off to a good start, and the county top of Tyne and Wear was conveniently along the way. Currock Hill East Top was a hillock near the village of Chopwell and the bike had done most of the work already. A neglected bridleway left the road through a plantation past radio masts and climbed a gate into an open field full of cows, as I followed the map to the highest contour somewhere in the middle. People would do anything to raise money for charity nowadays; even taking a selfie in the middle of a field to determine which cow pat was higher than the rest. Bagging county tops was becoming more ridiculous as each day went on.

Eventually the moor was no more, and I shouted with relief, breezing the racehorse all the way into Alston, to meet Sarah, the charity director, as planned. I was late so often that I apologised by default, but it was more important to have arrived intact. Shocked at my weight loss, she thrust a packed sandwich at me and pleaded for me to eat it. Once in the Lake District it was a late-night meeting the walkers, and organising last-minute logistics with the PHASE team. That night I lay restless, rolling continuously to escape the thumping in my chest as my heart strained and body struggled to recover from the day.

June 18th was my 22nd birthday. Truthfully, I had always hated birthdays. They were just a reminder that I was running out of time to fulfil my purpose in life, and it seemed pointless to celebrate something that came by every year with no effort required. Each day was equal to me. Anyone unfortunate enough to ask when my birthday was usually got the reply 'Every year!' with a sarcastic smile.

This birthday was set to buck the trend, just how I liked it. Today I wasn't just responsible for myself, but 50 people, climbing the highest peak in England. The scorching weather had hung around and added extra considerations. An older chap quickly succumbed to the heat, and I volunteered to take him down. Selfishly, I was relieved – before we had even reached Rossett Ghyll my strength had all but gone and it would have been far from ideal if the walk leader himself became a statistic.

Confined to the finish point at a pub in Langdale, I spent the day monitoring the radios from afar; albeit feeling too junior to manage an expert team of qualified mountain leaders who knew what they were doing and would keep everyone safe. From the beginning, I had decided to complete Scafell Pike separately and earlier in the challenge, rather than during this event, so that the necessity to reach the summit as a county top would not compromise my responsibility at Walk For Nepal. This had proved to be a very good call, and gave me some ammunition for the next time my Sergeant Major decided to have a pop.

In the pub, I stumbled straight into Mum and my stepdad, Chris. I'd been expecting them, but they'd arrived earlier than expected. Mum gasped at my physical state (I was more worried about my apparent sun-bleached blonde hair) and she threw her arms around me. So much had changed over the last few weeks but my family were still the same. Hector the dog seemed pleased to see me too, although he did love everything on legs.

Mum tried to pull me away from the event for a special birthday dinner, but I had stressed my responsibilities and wasn't leaving until everyone had made it down safely. As much as I hated birthdays, I did want some family time while I could, and any excuse to rest. Eventually we drove off to Grasmere where they had booked a hotel to surprise me.

We left in a hurry. Mum was worried about being late. There was a lot of faffing around parking, then a real urgency to get us checked in before last orders. All these demands played out over and over in my mind until they became something else. Suddenly, everything boiled over, and I just snapped, tearfully. All I wanted was to stop for a moment – I didn't want the fuss, the luxuries, or even the birthday cake – I just wanted to stop.

Having dinner together felt strange, but it was still the closest thing I had felt to normality in weeks. Back home we rarely ate together. I tended to cook my own meals as it was easier to control the calories, and I didn't want to be judged on what I ate, which often involved odd combinations. Eating mindfully without the distraction of the TV also made meals more satisfying, while eating later helped me to prevent snacking in the evening. None of that applied here though; I was still in challenge mode. With nearly 40 days of stories and experiences from the road it felt like I should have been talking non-stop, and I couldn't stop worrying that all the things I'd forgotten to mention would flood back when I pedalled off alone again. But this wasn't like the Himalayas. We had been talking regularly, and it took away the desperate need to tell all.

My mind didn't know where to start, and nothing came. There was just something comforting about being with Mum, and being able to express myself however I needed to. All the home comforts had come at once. So I just tried to enjoy them while they lasted.

Before going off to bed, I hugged Mum and apologised for snapping when she had come all this way.

'I'm really worried now ... you look anorexic,' she said.

It only showed how our nearest and dearest were often the first to notice changes in our mental and physical health. I hadn't been trying to lose weight, it was just hard to avoid on a challenge of this scale. However much I rolled my eyes and assumed she was typically over-reacting, Mum did know best. I felt guilty and selfish for worrying her so much when she was too far away to intervene.

The non-stop nature of always pushing onwards made it consistently difficult to juggle the physical demands of the challenge with the eating disorder. Too often, the bulimia won its bid to deprive me, and stripped away muscle like paint, until my body began to chew itself for fuel. Even the youth hostel staff in Alston, who were well accustomed to weary touring cyclists, had passed comment on my weight. It was all a wake-up call to seriously take the fuelling efforts up a notch if I was to reach the finish intact. At home it was sometimes difficult to see the long-term consequences of an eating disorder as they just became part of daily life and there was less incentive to change. Now it was an immediate and pressing threat to the mission.

CHAPTER 23

Grasmere was wonderfully relaxed in the sun and I wanted to lie there all morning. Mum had arranged for Hector to stay in my hotel room and the white ball of fluff on the duvet was in no hurry to leave either. While a cold tent was ultimately much easier to part with, this was no different to the other days of the challenge, and on the drive back to my bike in Alston I braced myself as usual. I had been busy ringing the Ministry of Defence to get the live firing schedule for Warcop training zone, which changed daily. Logistically, it had left a big question mark in the itinerary; once I found that live firing was taking place until midnight, completing Mickle Fell that afternoon, as hoped, was no longer an option.

'See you at the finish,' I said, with a lump in the throat as it registered that it would be a month before seeing them again. It had taken long enough to settle into the loneliness of the challenge that it would have almost been easier not to have seen my family at all. It just meant that I had to re-adjust to being alone all over again. This sudden change in routine had shoved a stick right through my mental spokes, with the anticipation of setting off into more uncertainty and discomfort. I would be far from alone during the next month, but there was nothing quite like the company of family. And I knew I'd need to find something else to look forwards to.

It was a low ebb, but I knew the feelings were only transitory; relentless forwards motion helped them pass faster.

However quiet and faceless, rhythm was a human sidekick. After getting on the saddle, the rhythm quickly returned, and I felt back in the zone. The shortest ride yet of 20 miles allowed time to enjoy the classic stone-walled roads of Teesdale, beautifully unbroken against a darker moorland skyline. The back-up campsite in Middleton-in-Teesdale was an idyllic spot, shared only with the neighbouring livestock, a guy and his Labrador, and a friendly couple of fellow cyclists from Lancashire, who quickly pulled out a £10 note for the JustGiving page as their own daughter had recently suffered with serious mental health challenges.

Getting up at 3.30am, the midsummer skies were so luminous there was no need for a headtorch. In the campsite washing room I improvised a carton drink of iced coffee to mix the sachet of Morning Fuel and get my caffeine fix. For the first time in a few days, my body had had a chance to recover; my heart had calmed down, and my legs felt brand new on the steady climb past Selset Reservoir.

Ellis, a friend and teammate from both Everest expeditions, was driving over from Hartlepool to guide me up his own county top. I considered the irony of two blokes from the two consecutive worst disasters of Everest history going to climb a peak within a military firing range which technically required a permit from the MOD. It could only go well. I couldn't find any reason against climbing outside of live firing hours. Today it resumed at 8.30am and that gave a pretty good incentive to get down quickly. Warning signs and guideposts appeared at a layby with the County Durham sign. There was no sign of Ellis, and lack of phone signal left me unsure what to do. I waited and slowly began walking up the hillside as far as visibility would allow. With the thought of being shelled still looming, there was unfortunately no choice but to carry on alone.

Managing disappointment began with looking for the positives and knowing the disappointments would pass with continual steps. I took solace in my own company and in music.

Mickle Fell formerly the top of Yorkshire, now claimed by County Durham, was reached with a four-mile trudge through heather moorland along a boundary fence with targets on the other side. The curved ridge of the summit plateau came easier than expected while a persistent fog stole any hope of a visual keepsake, and the dampness rolled down my cheeks. A post stuck out of the summit cairn like shrapnel before turning and following the fence back down. I finally got signal and a defeated voicemail from Ellis explaining he had been unable to find me. The red flag had been raised by the time I got back to the bike, and I had just about got away with it. In true expedition style he had left an eclectic lunch box buffet of a pork pie, Turkish Delight, spicy chicken skewer, Penguin chocolate bar, and a packet of mints in my panniers. He waited regardless, and we carried on to a coffee shop in Brough. Ellis and I were part of an exclusive club; we had been through the same rare experience and it meant a lot to have his support as we continued to find new mountains in life.

*

In both good and bad times; I checked the fundraising total a few times each day and noticed a sudden boost of donations that afternoon. One donation email confirmed we had passed the £10,000 milestone for the first time. A grin beamed back at the screen. While it steadily crept up daily, it took a milestone like this for it to really sink in. There was something significant in the number; 10 pounds either way didn't quite have the same ring. Fundraising gave a warming glow like nothing else. My excitement in hitting the target inspired more confidence, and in my mind, I had already decided to double the fundraising target to £20,000, with less than half of the challenge remaining to pull it off.

As a bulimic, compulsive behaviour was something I knew well. The compulsion that led me to give in to urges and binge uncontrollably on foods that broke the rules of my eating regime was not exclusive to food; I was often impulsive in other areas of my life, where I acted quickly on temptations without thinking through the consequences properly. A recurring resolution each year was to be less impulsive and focus on doing things well, rather than spreading myself too thinly in lots of places. I quickly found this selective restraint didn't suit me. When carefully controlled, the compulsive behaviour made stuff happen before deeper thinking could get in the way.

But the difference was knowing how the consequences played out with food. Letting the fundraising total sit there would be too comfortable and scaring myself like this would maintain the pressure, and keep the money coming in. This felt more like instinct than impulse, and it had been the same force that had got me to Everest and other places before.

I didn't see another person for a couple of hours over Arkengarthdale, and only the resident sheep heckled me as I took the chance to film a video blog thanking everyone who had donated. However fast I cycled, the surroundings didn't seem to speed up, soothing the usual battle against the clock in favour of just taking everything in. The non-stop routine had not only worn out the rider but the bike brakes too, and the local bike shop in Reeth was a welcome find before I ended up leaving a conspicuous gap in the stone walls of snaking roads. There were so many gems to stop and explore. Realistically, the trip would need to run 10 times over to make a good mark on the ever-expanding list of places to visit again. This limitless wonder made adventure an intensely rewarding pursuit.

The hills faded gradually into flatter plains and the city of York appeared just short of the 90-mile mark. It was a big transition from the Wild, Wild, West of Scotland where the threat of being knocked off my bike by deer had been replaced with white vans.

York youth hostel was busy with school groups as I recovered for the night.

From York, I had my longest ride yet. The historic city walls and cathedrals were bustling as I sneaked through into the countryside and my first county of The East Riding of Yorkshire. The low-lying open country hills were known as the Yorkshire Wolds, and Garrowby Hill was the summit of Bishop Wilton Wold. Trucks hollered abuse as they struggled past on the road almost directly to the top at the grandiose height of 246 metres.

Bishop Wilton Wold was playing silly buggers, with a trig point locked up safely behind a Yorkshire Water fence like a decoy from the true high point: right in the middle of the adjacent field. I carefully followed tractor tracks to avoid damaging the crops and hoped the farmer didn't see the helmet bobbing above the maize. The summit was in the undergrowth and I wondered if these trees had been planted for it to hide in embarrassment.

·Falling behind with Mickle Fell and staying in Middleton-in-Teesdale meant cutting mileage somewhere and bypassing my planned accommodation at YHA Beverley Friary for York instead. At this point I learnt the pack of flapjack from Hannah that had evaded me in Stirling had been waiting patiently at Beverley Friary instead. Sometimes things changed faster than I had time to update them on the website, and my honorary flapjack stalker had watched helplessly as the tracker showed me veering totally south through Market Weighton and over the Humber Bridge, completely oblivious to the parcel of oat goodness left behind.

The Lincolnshire Wolds were equally calm and rural with rolling hills of yellow crop fields and hedgerows. Occasional road cyclists gave something fun to chase, and minor distractions to break up the time spent in the saddle. I also had an interview lined up with the local BBC radio station and as with most counties, the locals liked to warn me about the hills. Every county had a localised pride about their hills; a geographical badge of honour, perhaps because there wasn't much else to brag about. After what I had been through, I just nodded.

Normanby Le Wold Top had been christened after its home village. Getting to the top of Lincolnshire was a 10 minute walk along the edge of fields to a trig point half-buried in the surrounding hedge.

A sharp descent out of the Wolds bid farewell to anything resembling a hill for the next few days. There was little to strain my neck for, cruising through the square farm fields of Lincolnshire. Instead I had another distraction – that night, the chairman of PHASE Worldwide had offered to take me for dinner. Finishing late tonight was not an option. What could have become a negative source of stress turned into a micro-challenge instead, and my focus switched to making calculations again, after a few days enjoying the freedom of getting there when I got there. Luckily the flat ruler-edged roads supported this target and the afternoon passed through the squares of freshly ploughed fields. With concentration, I could just about hold the required pace, but my engine felt the strain of challenging the clock. It gave a target, but the anxiety of being late was mixed with concern at demanding too much from my increasingly fragile body. My head throbbed from dehydration despite at least six litres of water.

The landscape changed once more to the outskirts of the royal Sherwood Forest in golden evening light. Twelve hours after leaving, I pulled into the campsite near Edwinstowe. One hundred and twenty-three miles down, only 6,000ft of ascent, and 3,500 calories later, I had just about made it. It had been a day of time pressure.

Nick was waiting as I quickly checked in, dunked my head in a sink, then under a hand drier. We ordered dinner over the phone, just in time for last orders, then drove off to a nearby pub to meet his wife Marie, and their close friend Rosie Swale-Pope MBE, an international adventurer and fundraiser. Rosie was the only person in history to have taken on a solo, unsupported 20,000-mile run around the world. Over dinner, Rosie was teeming full of stories, including sailing solo across the Atlantic in a small cutter boat she had found in a Welsh cowshed, navigating by the stars using her Timex watch which put me and my Garmin dependence to shame. At 70 years of age, Rosie had recently returned from an epic run across America. Her modesty was humbling too, and she continually commended others, including me, refusing praise for her own efforts. She also refused the title of eccentric, despite sleeping wild in Epping Forest the previous night, and writing part of her next book on a napkin in the restaurant before we arrived. Rosie spoke even more enthusiastically and quickly than I did – being completely frazzled from the day, I was more than happy to sit and listen; wondering whether this might be a glimpse of my own retirement in years to come.

Nick brought me back properly refuelled and recharged. I was so grateful for his amazing gesture and the company. At the campsite, I had no foam mat for my tent, which was fine for wild camping, but didn't bode so well on hard campsite pitches. It was like sleeping on an ironing board albeit I was tired enough that I could have slept upside down. A message from one of the young people at a school I had spoken to wanted to let me know it had inspired him to take steps towards his goal – having just completed his furthest ever cycle of 43 miles. Despite Scotland being safely in the distance, my body was increasingly tired, and the days were still long. Undoubtedly, the message behind it all was as important as ever: this was my reason to spin.

CHAPTER 24

On Newtonwood Lane near the village of Tibshelf, a covered reservoir and mast stood behind a serrated metal fence, and the highest point was supposedly where the fence met the hedge. I was struggling to find a way through an overgrown bramble hedge that had swallowed the promised footpath. Bagging the highest point of Nottinghamshire was a matter of just walking along it. Doing the research beforehand and knowing what the top looked like had paid off. This research prompted memories and these places started to feel familiar. In some ways, the challenge now wasn't huge physical effort, but precision.

Then, on to Matlock, and the head office of YHA England and Wales, a charity that aimed to transform the lives of young people through travel and adventure. I had become an ambassador for the charity two years earlier, quite by chance, after a cheeky request for free accommodation during my Everest training. It had unfolded perfectly since they were reaching out to the people I wanted to inspire most: young people. They had ideal accommodation available on a large proportion of the challenge route. Taking a slight detour to call at head office was a good PR opportunity, and somewhere friendly to shelter from the rain with a brew. We got photos before they sent me on my way.

Matlock Bath was known as the "Switzerland of Derbyshire" with its scenic forested hillsides and I passed through, people-watching on wheels. In this ever-changing environment I was finding new distractions and noticed how after a while, the simplest things could seem so good. I looked in envy at the people sipping coffee in café windows, sitting on a bench in the street with the newspaper; even waiting for the bus and freely watching the world go by. It was hard to tell whether these cravings for comfort were genuine or simply mind games. Back home, life would take over and most of these things would lose their appeal. More emotive thoughts regularly came to mind as I began to ponder my life, my purpose, and my future. These thoughts worked since they weren't problem focused and took me out of the current moment. These long hours alone in the saddle allowed our thoughts to travel much further before being interrupted, so it was only apparent how our busy lives distracted us from being in the moment.

The next point of call was the old mining town of Coalville, where I was joined by Dr Ash Routen, an arctic adventurer and lecturer from Loughborough University nearby. Like everyone else, Ash had been completely flexible with my timings, though it never stopped me worrying. Ash probably wondered how on earth I'd got this far independently, considering I managed to take the wrong turn out of the car park and race one mile downhill in the wrong direction. When alone, I rarely made a wrong turn; with good conversation the most familiar of places could be missed.

The highest point of Leicestershire, Bardon Hill, wasn't going to offer enough time to chat. We began walking through parkland and into the welcome shade of woodland. Even with company, I tried to stick to my pre-planned routes regardless of whether a better route appeared in the various wooded trails. Bardon Hill was a former volcano and an obvious trig point appeared on a mound, with perimeter fences guarding a ginormous quarry down below and wide-reaching views across the county. The industrial mining remnants and the towns blended with countryside were safely in the distance below; up here the hill kept us safely away in a pocket of nature. We remarked how we were never far from a good view if we went looking for it.

Eighty-two miles and 5,000ft of climbing constituted an easier day now. The receptionist at the Travelodge on the outskirts of Leicester still had to help as I lacked the strength to haul the bike up the stairs. Lots had changed in 41 days, steadily building a foundation of strength that smoothed the gap between the peak and the trough. The challenge might have produced different demands, but my engine was not the same as it had been at the start, and that meant accepting more support to produce the same goods. The bike could join me in the room.

I looked in the mirror to see I had lost even more weight.

This obsession with low body fat had started along with the bulimia five years earlier. Being naturally tall and lean wasn't something I disliked about my body; it worked in my favour with running and endurance sports, and it wasn't something I could control anyway. I was often lulled into the common misconception: "You can eat whatever you want – you're skinny!" Looking younger than my peers didn't bother me either; I never wanted to fit in, for the fear of being ordinary.

Stereotypically, men were expected to pursue the muscular, broad physique. I knew that my ectomorph build would never lend itself to achieving this. While I had no interest in pumping weights to gain the much-desired "manly" bulk, my appearance still mattered to me; I just wanted the sharp-cheek and low body fat tone of a professional endurance athlete.

For what I lacked in physical strength, confidence, self-assuredness, and the perhaps intimidating character of the Alpha male, mental strength was something I valued far more, taking me much further in anything that mattered to my life purpose. It was hugely satisfying to outperform the gym goers in running races. Being the annoying lanky kid who ran past them up the mountains more than made up for my lack of Alpha male physique. I loved defying expectations. My strength came from my ability to endure in the outdoors. That was my arena. And this resilience made up for the perceived weakness of an eating disorder. The flipside of resilience was always expecting better of myself, to be able to overcome any problem. Gender had nothing to do with it. Stereotypically, men were seen to fulfil their carnivorous appetites by cutting steaks rather than calories, and were more likely to self-medicate with alcohol or other means, while food was seen as more of a ladies' thing. But as far as I could see, both were essentially the same thing expressed in different ways.

*

The rest day curse came again as the next day I had to travel from Leicester to speak at a conference for high school teachers and education leaders about mental wellbeing across my county. Considering the talk was focused on the thing that I was fundraising for, it was too worthwhile to cancel, and my constant refusal to let people down had been resolved with the *adapt or overcome* mindset as usual.

Trying to prepare and rehearse a talk via notes on my phone wasn't ideal. The conference was at a hotel in Cheshire and as planned, Mum had dropped off my suit earlier in the week. Nobody at the hotel could find the parcel and I started to come to terms with the idea of speaking to 200 people in my crotch-split walking trousers and the red walking top from the last month. Luckily they found it, and I emerged out of the toilet cubicle in a business suit like someone from *Stars in Their Eyes*, dusting the crumbs of cereal bars off the jacket. I was closer to home than I'd been in a long time, and it felt like I was returning to normal day-to-day work mode; it felt like a cruel dunk into the reality that was waiting at the finish.

All 45 minutes were largely improvised, yet it came together better than expected. Despite going without my normal preparation and routine, the usual tickle of anxiety that always came before speaking in public, especially in unfamiliar circumstances, seemed to have gone. I hoped that giving the talk mid-challenge would excuse any shortfalls. Mostly, I just accepted that all I could do was stand and deliver the best I could. At least the opening line was easy: 'You have no idea what I've been through to get here today!'

When talking about mental health, there was something that didn't sit quite right. Sometimes I felt like a fraud; preaching about overcoming challenges when I was still dealing with the mental health demons, winning and losing in equal measure. So promoting a lifestyle or mindset that had inadvertently started this battle felt innocently misleading. I was no expert on mental health. All I could do was be genuine and say what I felt – if nothing else, to promote the benefits of the outdoors for managing the problem, as had worked for me.

*

The next day, my first walk of the day was 36 miles away. Getting to the county top of Arbury Hill was a summery bridleway frolic through wildflower meadows, as butterflies flitted around, with the chug of a tractor nearby. There was nothing on the top but a herd of cows in the corner keeping me a safe distance away. Without a trig point to aim for, the point of the field marked on the map presented as high as any other and I wandered around the thistles until satisfied. Northamptonshire had a joint county top, Big Hill, of the same height. Arbury was the best known and widely claimed the title.

Having the jersey emblazoned with text about the challenge and the JustGiving link was a perfect placard that had been mostly hidden beneath double waterproof jackets for much of the first few weeks. Now it was revealed, another keen roadie struck up conversation as he passed on the outskirts of Daventry. Jonathan was a PE teacher at a local school and took the time to ride side-by-side for a few miles despite it clearly slowing him down. Like positive thoughts, people sometimes came out of nowhere, lifted me up, and then pedalled off into the distance. Later, he found my website and posted encouragement on his Twitter account too. A chance encounter had now potentially reached hundreds of people. One of my closest friends, Ste, would join me that afternoon. Having company meant there was rarely much need to take pit stops to break up the long days, though the temptation of trying the famous Melton Mowbray Pork Pie at a prize butcher's in Market Harborough was too much.

Ste was cycling out to meet me in Medbourne. He was an avid cyclist, and played tour guide for his home county of Rutland, the smallest county in England. Having company was not only a distraction from the fatigue and worries, but the navigation too. At least it wasn't just me who made wrong turns. Ste continually poked fun at the lack of hills on my training rides back home in Cheshire, and was disappointed to see me completely unflinching on the steep climbs; they were nothing compared to those I had seen so far. We flew like boy racers along undulating rural lanes and neat farmland. The county top of Cold Overton Park was modest, with a five-minute walk down a muddy bridleway and along a fence through the field to find a trig point, but nothing close to a slope. Ste and I were similar in many ways, both perfectionists by nature, which explained why we got on so well despite the age gap. He had been like an older brother and a more logical sounding board for my initial challenge ideas.

After pitching my tent at the campsite in Oakham, Ste's family had invited me for dinner that night in their local Italian restaurant. Despite our close friendship, Ste's family were yet to meet the slightly barmy mountain-climbing adventurer friend they had heard so much about. There was probably no more authentic way than now, in the thick of a challenge itself, still wearing my outdoor gear because I had nothing else. It was lovely to meet them at last. Ste's dad, Tim, was intent on refuelling me as best he could.

*

Oakham was a sleepy Sunday town that captured the charm of Rutland perfectly, and the views across Rutland Water made for a good start towards the east coast the next day. Cycling into Norfolk was a new experience altogether. Everything fell into sync; the sweet spot of resistance in the continuous pulling of pedals, and warm air tickling arms. The motion of spinning legs was quite hypnotising. With a westerly wind pressed gently against my back, momentum was a wonderful thing. These miles were like the minutes and hours of a "good" day at home that had to be appreciated while they lasted. Even the slightest turn against the wind brought a noticeable drop in speed. A chap on a flashy racing bike appeared to the side and the usual cycling conversation began. More cycling club members appeared until I was surrounded, like a peloton.

'How far are you going?' one lady asked. Another lady asked about the charity and said mental health was something that meant a lot to them in their club. I silently pushed hard to keep up, drafting behind the group. Time flew by until two of them were going to be late for their pub lunch and apologised, wishing their best as they picked up speed, and their thin tyres left me spinning. The chatting pulled me along, as good company always did, and 105 miles had lost a big chunk already.

Feeling fresh after cycling 100 miles with 25 kilograms in tow was almost disappointing. In a minor moment of losing the plot, I worried the challenge was becoming too easy and losing the sense of achievement too. The physical challenge was important to me. Taking one step at a time had conveniently meant I'd forgotten about the final battering to follow in Wales a few weeks later.

Thinking things were getting too easy almost invited a low ebb to descend on me. In the first few weeks, I had wished the whole thing to be over. As the days passed, the accumulation of ever more highlights helped me to appreciate the journey. But it wasn't until after the halfway point that I really started to absorb the experience. Now, suddenly, time seemed to be running out, and I didn't want it to end yet. I felt as if the challenge was dragging me along, not giving me the chance to enjoy the experience.

This paradox was a key frustration of feeling depressed. It stole the precious time of life to enjoy these opportunities, then left us rushing to make do with whatever good days we were lucky to get, and whatever energy remained. Perhaps that sense of being cheated could be a positive thing, it shaped our decisions to choose our next move more wisely, rather than grabbing anything on autopilot. My Everest ambition had only become a solid goal when coming up for air from the black cloud, and this had created the urgency to grab it hard enough. Choosing to venture into these high places was a reminder that I had some control over the difficulties in life and could appreciate the home comforts much more. Even here, there were plenty more good days to balance out the bad days.

My goal had been to get from A to B, but I didn't want to fall into the trap of travelling without stopping to admire the view. Our hectic modern lives sent us running around like busy idiots, meaninglessly, rarely being in the moment or having enough time to answer why.

That night at YHA Sheringham I talked to my friend, Mike, who reminded me it was never too late to start enjoying something. It wasn't so much about the physical hardship or surviving the elements, but telling the story while I could, and experiencing more of the places along the way. This was just a new phase in the journey. Having fun on a challenge didn't feel right. But Mike had a good point; followers wanted to see me enjoying the journey and be inspired to try the same thing themselves. They already knew what suffering looked like. They needed to know that there was some fun beyond the pain, and something worth pushing for.

'You're doing all the right things,' he said. 'This is yours now.'

The amount of time between now and the finish was going to pass regardless. All I could do was fill that time as positively as I possibly could.

CHAPTER 25

The next morning, 30 students were joining me from a local high school, Alderman Peel. I was not only responsible for myself but partially for them, too. Although a five-mile walk wouldn't take much effort, it wasn't the day to run out of fuel and live with the acclaim of being finished off by Norfolk, so I loaded up on the breakfast buffet. On a fine sunny morning, it was only a couple of miles to West Runton beach where Rob Mack was waiting. As a Young Minds trustee and a local mental health nurse, I was really pleased that he had taken the time to join us. A minibus full of boisterous year-seven students arrived soon afterwards. I gave a bit of a welcome talk before we strolled out of the village in a rabble. All of them had volunteered to take part and raise money for Young Minds too. They were asking questions as we walked up the road, about staying motivated; the challenge – and Everest, of course. They had been reading my book *Icefall* in school and seen videos in assemblies; hopefully the real-life adventurer didn't disappoint their expectations.

Keeping the group together was easy enough on lovely forest trails, and I handed my phone to one of the kids and let them take charge of navigation on ViewRanger, while I chatted to Rob, Kirsty – the assistant headteacher who had made it all happen – and the teaching assistants. Hearing about the work being done by Young Minds, and about some of the mental health challenges they dealt with in school, was both eye-opening and concerning.

At first glance, nobody could have known what challenges some of the 30 students happily walking around us could be facing. Mental ill health was invisible, and that was its secret weapon. It took me back to high school and how grateful I had been for drop-in sessions with the school nurse when I had been struggling with anxiety attacks.

The scale of the mental health crisis in young people felt very real, but Rob and I agreed there was lots of awareness, and more people were talking about it than ever. We never went far without hearing about mental illness – now the priority was doing something about it. I only hoped Climb The UK was making a difference and chipping away at the problem. Kirsty was one-in-a-million in the teaching world and I only wished other schools had someone so proactive in the wellbeing of students. She had annotated my book *Icefall* like a teacher would, highlighting her favourite quotes. The atmosphere was buzzing.

*

Norfolk had stuck up for itself against the regular jokes about being hopelessly flat. The county summit, Beacon Hill, was marked by a huge pole in a grassy meadow with a clearing in the trees revealing a deep curtain of blue. We got a big group photo and enjoyed lunch before strolling down bridleways and tracks.

We were soon back on the beach at West Runton, and the students sat on the sea walls with ice creams in the sunshine. I was beaming. Twenty of them hadn't walked Beacon Hill before. To them it might just have been a good excuse to escape the classroom for the day; to me it was a moment of realisation and accomplishment, to see them here achieving something because of Climb The UK. It was the best day of the challenge to date; the epitome of what Climb The UK was supposed to create. I had trusted that getting closer to home would gather momentum and support. New ground always felt uncertain. All I could do was believe in my vision and that it would happen – hope for the best, expect the worst. Now it was becoming real.

There were only 40 miles left, and I soon stopped at a popular café called Rocky Bottoms. Outside in the sun I tucked into a Weybourne crab sandwich for lunch, with the beach itself in sniffing distance; a proper taste of Norfolk. This was exactly what Mike had meant, and it felt great. I was staying outside Great Yarmouth in the village of Belton with close friends of my grandparents, David and Jane.

With a few miles to go, I was lagging, depleted of fuel, but I knew from experience what my body could do when the fuel light came on the dashboard. Working up an appetite for dinner in this way was a pretty normal behaviour. The empty weakness of low blood sugar eased the anxiety of having a large meal and excess calories on what was, after all, an easier day. I recognised a familiar problem wearing a disguise – exercise bulimia – and kept a close eye on it. My relationship with food needed to become properly interdependent, not a maths equation of calories versus exercise. I wasn't going to let it stop me enjoying dinner as it usually did on easier days. David and Jane were fantastic cooks and I knew my grandad would be delighted they had taken such good care of me. It was saddening that he had never had the chance to see this unfold. He would probably have followed me in his car with binoculars and a radio, like we had when we'd watched planes at Manchester Airport when I was a kid.

I felt rude hijacking the opportunity to borrow a laptop to catch up with logistics instead of chatting to the friends who had put me up so generously for the night. I was ruthless in my priorities and fortunately friends always understood ...

One hundred and eight miles took me around the Norfolk Broads past Caister Castle. The landscape was unthreatening but seductively undulating. Everything seemed much of the same – including the relentless rain. Even the slightest change in road surface vibrating through the handlebars was exciting and it seemed the challenge today would be managing boredom and resisting the sandwiches in my bag for at least an hour.

Suffolk was the most easterly county of the UK and the last place I had expected to be shivering and cold again, pedalling hard to create heat. The rain had been as relentless as Scotland. Spray from passing trucks and vans forced me into the flooded margins of busy A-roads and whatever lay beneath. The centre of Bury St Edmunds boasted romantic architecture like a BBC period drama where I found a quintessential café to warm up and watch rain pounding the crooked cobbles.

'Nice day for it mate!' laughed a young worker in overalls as I shivered at traffic lights.

'Only 40 miles left now, thankfully,' I replied.

'Bloody hell mate, at least you can have a rest day tomorrow then!' he shouted back over the sound of a hydraulic breaker.

'I wish – got another 27 days yet.'

Great Wood Hill of Suffolk was a new contender for the most uninspiring county top. The local farmer had destroyed the trig point years earlier, and there was no obvious high point besides a big radio tower. A grassy bridleway led to a service reservoir, fenced off in a concrete compound, surrounded by fly-tipped litter and spilt animal feed. The highest point was anyone's guess – my research said it was not on the marked spot height of 127 metres, but where the trig point had originally been, in a field by the lane just before the mast, where I stood and got some photos. I was speaking on the phone to BBC Radio Suffolk and trying to sound enthusiastic about the countryside as I walked back. My PR agent Mick had said the journalists were so short staffed in the summer that it had been a struggle to get any interest. This awareness was crucial for the challenge to reach its potential. Like the rest, time was ticking, but there was only so much that I could control.

It was a relief to find the YHA hostel in the outskirts of Cambridge.

'How was your day?' asked the manager at check-in.

'Wet.'

He handed me an unexpected parcel as I left a trail of water on the floor, tempted to shake like a scraggy sheepdog and regretting buying my usual pack of mackerel and vegetables for dinner while students tucked into pizza nearby.

Go Postie Go! This boy's on a mission so don't be slow! was scribbled on the back on the parcel. Inside was a slab of homemade flapjack that brought a huge smile to my face. It was the flapjack that had evaded me in Stirling about two weeks earlier. Hannah had persuaded the Beverley Friary youth hostel staff to post it onwards, along with a postcard and a £20 donation. It was an amazing gesture that had captured the British generosity in a single bite – or three. Unplanned treats were sometimes problematic and there was a stab of frustration at the lack of discipline in eating half of the pack, before being rational, reminding myself about the 100 miles of cycling that day, and seeing I was still very thin in the mirror once my cycling clothes were spread over every inch of radiator. I had to accept that putting the weight back on would mean losing the toned physique I had started to like and changing my eating disorder that clearly seemed to be giving the results I wanted. I couldn't have it both ways. The eating disorder was not a friend, and it wasn't going to help me finish the challenge. Unlike me, the flapjacks had got better with two weeks of travelling, and still tasted fantastic. As the journey progressed and the scenery from the saddle continued to change, it wasn't so much the places, but the people, that mattered.

Oli Reed was next to join me; he worked for ViewRanger, the navigation app that had got me this far. As a Yorkshireman now exiled in one of the flattest counties of the country, he was eager for any challenge he could find and cycled out for the day. It was another drizzly morning as we barged our way out of the city at rush hour, and it was great to hear about the challenge from the other side of the coin. Everyone felt it was going immensely well and seemed surprised to see me moving forwards almost by default. The first county top was Great Chishill of Cambridgeshire which involved the grand effort of cycling 200 feet along a dirt track which was adjacent to someone's back garden. Another county was so poorly endowed with elevated spots that the local utilities had to build a reservoir on the spot to make the most of any elevation. This reservoir was fenced off and walking around it had bagged the true county top. Great Chishill had kicked the can down the road to Essex.

A couple of miles down the road, and an accidental long way round, the hamlet of Langley was surrounded by fields of rapeseed and barley more golden than the county stereotype. On a Wednesday afternoon it was deadly silent as we pushed our bikes across the cricket pavilion and curtains twitched. On the hill-bagging website, Chrishall Common, the high point of Essex, was described as being 10 metres from the corner of a field where a path emerged from the woods, and much less obvious than the trig point nearby. It was even more laughable trying to find the highest point in the undergrowth of Roughway Wood. A much bigger challenge was had in finding a pub open for lunch when it seemed the villagers had battened up the hatches and scarpered. We were like excited kids to find somewhere with the fire roaring to dry out clothes. Oli headed off back home towards Cambridge and left me in good spirits. Later, Oli texted saying how knackered he was after 75 miles of cycling – his furthest ever ride – and further than I had clocked the same day. I was especially chuffed that he had now achieved something for himself and Climb The UK had catalysed something else positive. Hopefully the sense of achievement would eclipse his difficulty walking for the remainder of the day.

I wasn't far from Dad's house but getting there was far from straightforward. I took a wrong turn onto a dual carriageway and had to drag the bike down a bank of decaying McDonald's wrappers, then haul it over a wooden fence laced with barbed wire. When I got to his house, Dad was banished to his man-shed to service the bike – the chain was apparently about to fall to bits. My step-mum, Debbie, was another great cook. I had always enjoyed hearty dinners when visiting as a younger child, when I had eaten "normally". The oven was always on, and I would wolf down food as soon as it hit the table; always having second helpings for the simple enjoyment of it, rather than binge urges. Hospital visits as a child and consulting Doctor Google had left me more health conscious than most my age but I didn't even know what bulimia was back then.

I had still been anxious about eating out, after my epileptic seizures during fast food and restaurant meals, and the thought of going to a restaurant for dinner was enough to ruin my week. Treats were kept in the portions that they were intended to be. It was saddening to have lost this innocence around food, but I'd learnt to dismiss it like any other life milestone. After turning 16, my dad had moved down south and I had spent less time with them, just as my relationship with food turned sour.

I'd always just assumed that people were aware of my eating disorder, but I revealed the truth about my struggles with food before starting the challenge. Most people didn't mention it – perhaps because they were worried about making me uncomfortable – and they certainly wouldn't have guessed as I tucked in happily after another 100-mile day. This mismatch between my behaviour and people's common belief of what an eating disorder was only added to the confusion.

*

It was Dad who had inspired me to start running years earlier when my step-mum had put a bet that I couldn't run a couple of miles with him during a holiday to France. Wheezing and suffering, I had fulfilled the bet and proudly bought a pain au chocolat with my earnings; my first and probably last prize money as a runner. Now I had embraced the fitness drive. Dad's knees were less enamoured of running marathons now, and he had now made a slow return to cycling.

217

We set off together at 9.00am. Dad took his time, and we rode side-by-side, when traffic allowed. It was a great opportunity to hear things from the other side of the coin. Dad said he had enjoyed following my updates, and told me he hadn't wanted to play the worried parent when the tracker had gone down, or when I'd been pushing alone late into the night. He had never completely subscribed to Everest – and the risks it involved – and considering it had nearly killed me, I couldn't blame him. Fortunately, this near-death experience had also brought us closer. There was no doubt he was fully onboard now though, and it meant a lot that he had taken the day off work to be a part of it himself.

My friend Kim flagged us down in the village of Woburn as we headed south to London. Kim had been a London 2012 Olympic Torchbearer, too. Being chosen as one of the Olympic Torchbearers in Chester, in recognition of my charity fundraising, had given so many friends for life, and it meant a lot to still have their support, five years later. Bedfordshire was a hillier and less picturesque sibling of nearby Cambridgeshire, but the countryside of the Chiltern Hills was an uncrowded display of rolling green. Dad's chain came off with a clunk on the steep crawl up Bison Hill – luckily, he didn't fall off too. It was steep enough that we walked the final hundred metres to the car park. Dunstable Downs were the top of Bedfordshire, and the trig point was just metres from the road. If not for company, I could have ticked the top on two wheels instead. But I was happy for the opportunity to walk and talk instead. We were joined by Dan and Rachel Pidcock, friends of a friend, from nearby St Albans. The Chiltern Way took us through fields, birch woodland, and pretty meadows to the visitor centre at the top.

One thing Dad and I had never really spoken about was mental health. I knew he knew about my difficulties, from reading my blogs, but speaking to him about mental health just seemed too daunting. The earliest male influence in our lives was usually our dad, and that was true for me too. Most young boys naturally wanted to impress, and be like their dad, and I had wanted to do everything he did, from learning to play the guitar, to running marathons, and scuba diving. Being sensitive, I was always scared of being told off by him – and worked hard to get his praise. But aside from being a perfectionist like me, we were quite different.

Mum had let me get away with anything, and we had spent more time together, so we shared things more openly. When they had divorced, she had bust a gut doing three jobs to keep me in my childhood home and minimise the disruption. She always fought for what she believed in, so I had clearly got my fight from her. Dad was more easy-going and not the sort to trouble anyone with his own problems. This didn't discourage me in revealing mine, and I never felt the need to uphold any image other than my true self. Perhaps I feared he would be as disappointed as I was in myself. But deep down, I knew that was irrational; the eating disorder was not a choice, and it was no different to an everyday physical condition.

I wanted to confide in Dad. He had been so supportive through my childhood epilepsy and stammering, and had always said that we could talk about anything. I had never been afraid to ask for his advice on everything from navigating adult life to marathon training, but mental health was something I assumed he hadn't experienced before. And I was torn; it seemed pointless giving him a problem he couldn't fix, and I was scared of spoiling our relationship. Once somebody knew these things, they wouldn't be forgotten. I wanted to keep the happy memories of us fishing together when I was younger, or mountain biking around Delamere, and walking the dogs around the forest.

Although telling Mum had only turned out to be a positive thing, much of my family and many of my friends were a place of respite from the eating disorder, where life retained a sense of normality. And I wanted to protect that.

*

After the town of Tring was a steep climb to Haddington Hill, mostly covered by Wendover Woods. Somewhere near the Go Ape adventure centre and Forestry Commission car park was the highest point of Buckinghamshire, and the Chiltern Hills, hidden in the trees. Dad finished lunch at the café, as I walked off to find the treasure in the woods, like one of the excited school children. A large boulder with a plaque made it straightforward. I had checked my phone for the first time to see missed calls from Mick and Oli Reed from ViewRanger too. The BBC wanted me for an 8.00am interview in London two days later and there was mention of the *Chris Evans Radio Show* too. It was all happening fast. I made sense of various voicemail messages and lost patience with the internet signal as I tried to work out if this would be achievable on the way back from another talk in Snowdonia. Dad was totally chilled and keen not to get in my way, but I wasn't going to let this spoil our time together.

We pushed on to our third of the day. The county top of Hertfordshire was described as the "northeast shoulder of Pavis Wood" and I had little else to go on. Research said it was the layby by the road near the hamlet of Hastoe. The spot height in the adjacent Pavis Wood was possibly higher and I joined some dog walkers in the woods to cover both bases, working out logistics for the radio interview and texting Mick to confirm. It wasn't fair to pester Mick for media coverage then miss the opportunities when they came. With three ascents by father and son, it was time for Dad to head home, having already cycled further than he had done in months. Dad typically said little, just that he was proud of me, as he always did.

I wasn't looking forward to the chaos of London. There were 40 miles to go, made more miserable by being alone again. But I was soon forced to focus elsewhere when the leafy Chiltern Hills faded, crossing through Berkhamsted into the ugly suburban roads and constant traffic in Watford. I was quickly exiled from the wilderness into the big smoke. Cycling into London was an assault on the senses. It was a world apart from gazing into nothing and dreaming of what life in the countryside would be like. There were more people on Edgware Road than I had probably seen for the last 48 days combined. Here, the wide berth of the panniers on the bike offered as much swagger on the roads as a rabbit through Notting Hill, and I needed to concentrate. The stop-start motion of traffic lights was infuriating.

I had always enjoyed working and speaking in London; getting dragged along in a faster pace of life. A day in the big city was an ample dosage to give me a renewed appreciation for where I lived, and getting safely back home again always brought the gratitude that I had the choice of both worlds.

The contrast of peaks and troughs was much more interesting than being stuck on one level, literally and figuratively. It didn't take long for one place to affect mood, either, whether as a result of withdrawal from my usual countryside environment, or the pack mentality of city life.

This was the last place I would want to be when depressed. Everyone quietly carried on in their own world – but emotionless faces of the London Underground could convince you that nobody cared. I strongly feel that we are vulnerable to the energy around us – if we don't give off our own positive vibes, we can sink into our surroundings instead.

CHAPTER 26

For what it lacked in mountains, London wasn't short of people, friends and supporters. My friend Leah had dropped off two giant cupcakes from her favourite bakery at the St Pancras youth hostel for when I arrived. After a testing day, there were heaps of messages and people asking for timings to join in walks over the next few days – 'Leave the logistics to me,' I had to say, before my head exploded.

London was split into two ceremonial counties – Greater London and the City of London. Months earlier I had no way of knowing whether anyone would want to walk to the top of London with me, but figured that St Paul's Cathedral would be a more pleasant place to start than Euston Road at rush hour. The next morning Leah had arrived first, and another torchbearer friend, Holly, came with her boyfriend, Dan. Will, the fundraising manager from Young Minds, joined this bunch of intrepid mountaineers heading off from St Paul's Cathedral in search of the top of City of London: High Holborn, the lowest county top in the entire country. We joked at the slightest incline in the road as we chatted away. The junction of Chancery Lane on High Holborn road was supposedly the highest point at 22 metres above sea level. In my research, the hill-bagging website had described the top as "very flat". We asked a confused passing commuter to take our group photo. It was positively ridiculous. But without a doubt, everyone had now been a part of the journey; even if thousands of others bagged this county top on their way to and from work each morning.

I walked to the Young Minds offices with Will, for a photoshoot, and it was reassuring to hear from Will how the money was being spent. It was great to hear how much of a difference it could make.

For the rest of the day, I had another obstacle: getting to North Wales. Stu and Tracey Breese, who had also "sponsored" a county top in Wales, were organising a charity walking challenge called The Snowdonia Challenge. Months earlier, I had committed to be one of their evening speakers on the assumption the challenge would be finished by the end of June. I caught the train to Betws-y-Coed where my friend Jacha, who owned a pizzeria, gasped at the state of me, shoving pizza towards me and telling some of the diners to go along and hear the talk that evening. The unshaven and helmet-haired guy sitting in the corner, with his trousers held up by a drawstring and a cable tie in the crotch, probably didn't raise excitement. My appearance was low on my list of concerns considering my PowerPoint slideshow hadn't been received, and I had to borrow a laptop to throw some photos together from my website and online. There was no script, or anything rehearsed in the slightest. Winging it had jumped to another level again.

The talk was authentic, if nothing else. I had taken so many powerful messages and lessons from the journey already that would make inspirational content for future talks, once I had time to reflect and collate it together in a more polished format. Still, everyone seemed to enjoy it and lots of tweets afterwards said the same.

One chap in the audience was going to buy a copy of my book as a positive reference for his friend who had just hurt her leg, with the caption "Get the **** over it". I thought this was fantastic – hopefully she felt the same.

Kev, one of the walkers, and a regular follower, caught me outside before Jacha took me back to Llandudno train station.

Kev shook my hand. He wanted to know how many people I was inspiring – going out there, day after day, inspiring so many; inspiring him, too. He added that a lot of the girls from the Walk For Nepal event had been worried about my physical state and he wanted to make sure I was looking after myself too. His words stood out, particularly as he had gone out of his way to come and see me.

Interrupting the challenge for these errands was nothing like a rest day, but they were worth every throb of their logistical headaches. Sometimes stopping for a moment was the only opportunity to hear the feedback and truly feel it through the emotion of others. It was easy to get carried away in *doing*, and forgetting why.

*

There were no dramas getting back to Crewe in the early hours, where the receptionist at the Travelodge looked at me with pity, like a lost soul. My trainers were still damp from the Cambridge day, and the hairdryer in the hotel room soon blew up after another failed attempt at drying them out. The 5.00am alarm left me feeling more than just sluggish from anticipation of the day ahead; I felt physically sick from exhaustion, and only hoped my body would hold out a little longer.

My phone rang almost instantly as I stepped onto the platform at London Euston station at 7.30am for an interview with BBC Radio Sussex while still on the platform, as far from the Tannoy as possible. I was so tired, I ended up at the wrong Tube station – Victoria instead of Oxford Circus, and there was no way to call the BBC to tell them I was running late for my big interview on the BBC London's Breakfast Show. The phone buzzed angrily in my pocket as BBC Radio Kent tried to ring too. There was no time to stop as I ran frantically to Broadcasting House in Portland Square. This interview was mega, I couldn't afford to miss it. In the offices, flustered yet relieved, I had a moment to compose myself and was led in to the studio to meet the lovely radio presenter,

Joanne Good. Mick had struck gold in landing the big slot we wanted. It was a great discussion about mental health and unlike many producers, she let me go into enough depth to do it justice. As Mick suggested, I managed to sneak in the JustGiving link subtly before time ran out. Kent persevered, calling me about our interview and I did a pre-recorded interview in the archway of a closed shop. It all felt worthwhile, when a sudden boost of JustGiving donations came in. For strangers to donate over £250 could only mean something had touched their heart.

Now there was just the matter of cycling 85 miles to Brighton! My mentor and friend, Chris, had come to join the day and was waiting at YHA London St Pancras, along with my bike. The hostel manager, Fizz, was excited to see us off and take photos. She was another of those connected to the journey by what it stood for, drawn in by what mental health meant to her. For now, these everyday heroes were a quiet but powerful army, and with the growing openness of mental health there would never be a shortfall of cavalry. Months earlier I had been in the same regiment. Only now I had taken a step forwards, hoping to be an advocate for better mental health, and encouraging others to join the fight.

Chris had ambitions of cycling around the world and led the way over Blackfriars Bridge and out of the city. After Biggin Hill airfield we were coming up to the first substantial climb of any sort, and I realised that the county high point must be close and signs for Westerham appeared. The county top of Greater London wasn't worth touching with a barge pole. It was unmarked, on the left-hand verge of this busy A-road, and somewhere in the hedge. It was probably more dangerous than any of the other tops so far and a photo with the 60-mile-an-hour traffic was passed for one standing in the farm driveway opposite.

The highest point of Kent, Betsom's Hill, was supposedly just over the road on private land and down a gravel track to a few houses. A lady picking the weeds in her bungalow garden looked confused as we pushed our bikes up her driveway.

'Excuse me, this might sound a bit odd, but we're looking for the highest point of Kent, and ...'

'Are you the lad I heard on the radio?' she said. I was astonished.

Lynne was mellow and friendly. She knew we were coming, and I was just glad not to have said anything offensive on the interview.

'It's up here, I'll show you,' she said happily. The original high point was on her garden lawn. Lynne even offered us a cup of tea as she invited us inside to see the head of the original trig point; now engraved into her fireplace. Lynne was used to weird county-baggers visiting like us. A county top had yet to give a greeting like this one. We thanked her very much and left, feeling warmed by her hospitality before hurtling downhill to Westerham like boy racers for lunch. Having company helped keep me on track. When the quieter roads allowed, we chatted endlessly; the ideas flowed and Chris challenged some of the negative mindsets I had picked up on the challenge so far. Getting stung inside the lip while hurtling downhill, trying to stay calm as it swelled and throbbed for ages, was probably a sign to shut up talking for a while.

My mind was distracted; one of my speaking clients, Ruth, was meeting us at Leith Hill, which created an extra pressure to maintain my usual business etiquette and arrive on time. A route mishap took us down a one-in-six gradient that we now had to reverse, and Chris was probably bidding to throw me in the sea in Brighton. We were 90 minutes late reaching the Broadmoor car park. I was furious with myself. Time was, without doubt, the biggest stress of the challenge. Being disrespectful to others constantly goaded me and clashed with my values. Circumstances outside of our control were a fact of life, yet I had spent a lifetime apologising for my stammer in conversations when there was no need to apologise for being myself. The same applied to mental health. Apologising for something only suggested it was our fault. Preparing for the worst, hoping for the best and carrying on regardless was not going to change this habit of poor organisation. My mantra that life was too short to wait in queues had wiped a smug smile off my face enough times that Mum just shook her head – her punctual nature as a taxi driver had yet to rub off on me.

As usual, friends were more concerned about my physical condition than my punctuality. Ruth and her husband Roger were waiting with a smile, on their Surrey stomping ground, with their spaniel, Poppy. We chatted away happily, and it was the first time Ruth had seen me outside of the business suit, doing the thing that created the speaking stories in the first place. It took 15 minutes through an inviting rhododendron woodland and sandy trails. The county high point was technically a grassy mound topped by a bench, out-shadowed by Leith Hill Tower and its spiral staircase that was unexpectedly still open. From the top, the tower commanded extensive views towards the London skyline, with The Shard, Canary Wharf, and even planes lined up on the runway at London Heathrow. The shelter of majestic giant redwoods and Monkey Pine were still on the edge of our contemporary lives.

Ruth and her business partner, Jane, had generously sponsored the top of Surrey and we took photos together on the summit; Roger sponsored the summit with a round of carrot cake and coffee from the tower café, and we enjoyed the view together.

We had a joyous afternoon through immaculate Surrey countryside.

Apart from the dry heat and occasional stinging climbs that tried to shake us out of our rhythm, I was on autopilot. It was enough of a challenge to look after myself, and predict my own timings, that I wasn't so good at judging the physical cues of others. But I knew that physically breaking them, and putting them off getting outdoors would be a disaster. We stopped at another pub where peanuts, salty crisps and Diet Coke missed the nutrition memo, but did the job. The final assault was the climb over Saddlescombe, and the aloof mounds of the North Downs, where the skyline turned pink and the emptiness beyond could only be the coastline. The lights of Brighton twinkled beneath an early moon, and we flew four miles downhill towards it, before a pannier came loose on a pothole at over 30 miles an hour and bounced across the road, without taking Chris out in the process.

The seaside town was alive and vibrant by 9.00pm as we straggled through with the lights of Palace Pier rippling across the sea and music drowning out the waves. All day my mind had been set on something else – fish and chips. And after 85 miles, I wasn't going to forget about my reward too easily. Sadly, Chris had been unable to find a hotel room and caught a late train back to London, but he had got me from A to B in good spirits, and it meant a lot that he had been involved with my biggest challenge yet. Brighton High Street was a clash of bohemian flare and Saturday night rowdiness, as I sat with my fish and chips. Then I made a dash back to the hostel, too tired to care for a shower, and struggled to sleep with the sound of nightlife pulsing in my ears.

By the next morning, the vibe of the UK's hippest town had fallen to the arcadian quiet of a summer Sunday, and an unrelenting climb into the countryside for me. The South Downs were unpretentious and painted red by poppy fields, a perfect blend of dramatic white cliffs and chalky grasslands. We had been too late to tick Ditchling Beacon the previous night, which meant a paperboy errand in the same direction. It was just five minutes of walking to the summit from the crest of the hill, where cyclists recovered from the sheer technical ascent on the other side.

At the top of the steep northern slopes of crooked trees I was out onto the broad spine of the South Downs, with a startling 360-degree vantage point out to sea. The true top of Ditchling Beacon, East Sussex, was 40 metres off the path, and none of the passing walkers or wheels came close enough to take my summit photo.

At the foot of a driveway in Pycombe was a stall selling Emily's homemade chocolate brownies with an honesty box. I had Emily to thank for an especially fast push over the hump of the South Downs as paragliders soared overhead, then through the picturesque market towns of West Sussex. Another passing cyclist asked whether the JustGiving page on my jersey was still live and pledged to donate when he got home.

There was clapping and cheering as I pulled in to Haslemere Cricket Club; my friend Annick had gathered the troops – nine in total – from her family and running club. Annick was another of the torchbearer crowd who had followed and supported my fundraising wholeheartedly ever since. The torchbearer bunch were unsurprisingly the sort who got things done. Riding high in the competition of obscure places to lock my bike was a cricket cage.

Handshakes and hugs came all round as we made introductions and set off for Blackdown, the top of West Sussex, through sunny meadows and fields. I tried to move through the group and speak to everyone. Annick and her daughters, all keen runners, struggled to comprehend the daily grind of the challenge, and said that I was regularly talked about in their house. It was good to know that, however lonely we could feel at times, we were never too far from someone's thoughts.

The banter was rife, and like the Galloway cows traipsing around the heather, I lost sense of time in the surroundings, carried along by the company. Blackdown was an unusual sandy plateau of lush forest and sun-kissed heathland. The county top was hidden within the trees off the path. Maybe these relics were conspiring to try and wind me up now. Tom knew the spot, and I needed longer arms to fit the group into our celebratory summit selfie. For most, it was their first time on their own county top, which only added to the sense of achievement. Temple of the

Winds gave a panoramic viewpoint far across the green rug of countryside.

Everyone waited to see me off at the cricket club with the cheers buzzing in my ears for the final 17 miles of the day. Self-belief was essential for an adventurer to get moving, but the belief of other people took you much further, by giving that extra cheer when we stopped cheering for ourselves. We all needed cheerleaders sometimes.

*

I pulled up a gravel driveway to a lovely rustic house in the village of South Harting, where I met Rebecca Stephens and her husband, Jovan, a Yugoslavian artist, who had kindly offered to host me. A legend in the mountaineering world, she was the first British woman to climb Mount Everest in 1993. She was wonderfully modest and inspiring – someone who had made a huge success around sharing her adventures for the benefit of others. After climbing my own mountain of logistics and social media updates, we had dinner out in the porch, looking over the country gardens in the glow of a perfect midsummer evening, with as many fresh strawberries drowned in cream as I could manage without looking rude.

After dinner, I sat transfixed by her stories, as she showed me her photo collection from the Himalayas and Tibet; story time could have gone on forever. I had somehow gained membership of the Everest club without even climbing the thing.

CHAPTER 27

Getting an early start didn't look likely with pancakes and coffee arriving continuously at breakfast, with me nodding shyly and raising my plate like Oliver Twist. I was speaking at a primary school that morning and we chatted about the challenges faced by young people, and how, without a plan, young people were vulnerable to falling apart when they hit the storm.

My updated route wasn't on the Garmin, and I lost time poaching Wi-Fi outside Marks and Spencer in Petersfield but the children at Townhill Primary School had no idea as I pulled up to the school gates and they cheered excitedly. Hopefully they couldn't smell me coming. The PE teacher, Andy, introduced me to 90 students while I frantically tried to download my PowerPoint slideshow in the classroom. Beaten by technology again, I just loaded up the tracker, some YouTube videos, and let it come naturally. It worked. Some of the teachers were even welling up with the stories of how I'd turned my life around.

Most people assumed the best way to meet an adventurer was with a mountain of biscuits and sugary treats. It was difficult to explain the problems with food and sugary treats without offending people, and taking the family-sized sharing pack of millionaires shortbread, flapjacks, and biscuits would cause too much anxiety: stashes of food like this were usually reserved for bad episodes of bingeing and purging, and Mum would hide them away at my request. The challenge was like therapy in itself, giving me some more practice at dealing with these situations so they would become easier to deal with back home. They had kindly sorted out some lunch though, which was appreciated too. It was a long time since I'd had a school dinner – being crouched up on the tiny stool with my knees higher than the table attested to that. One young boy came over to say that now, he wanted lots of cycling stuff for his birthday.

It was nice not having to rush for the afternoon. Another friend, Simon, had kindly offered a bed for the night in Marchwood, west of Southampton, and treated us to an Indian takeaway too. Simon was a mountain leader and outdoor events organiser, so was entirely understanding that I had to shut myself away in his office for a few hours to catch up with everything, although I still felt awful about it. Socialising and challenges didn't work too well – sometimes I had to make do. He knew the Snowdonia mountains well and was the perfect person for second opinions as he supplied coffee on tap until the night turned late.

The following day, on the Isle of Wight, was to be one of the biggest logistical headaches yet. Being as human-powered as possible meant kayaking four kilometres to get there. It seemed a good idea at the time. Considering I had only kayaked about twice in my life – once on a school trip – getting a support team was a sensible idea. An adventure company on the Isle, Tackt-Isle Adventures, had been completely supportive of the idea and stepped in to help. So much could go wrong. The anxiety had hung over me for months. But the last few weeks had kept me too busy to grant it much attention. By the time the bridge had come to cross, I had become like a cycling monk in a meditative state, and everything sorted itself out by just letting things happen, one at a time.

*

The New Forest National Park was like nowhere else. This sparsely populated kingdom embodied the last wilderness of

England and had even escaped phone signal as BBC Radio Solent had tried repeatedly to call without luck. Two guys were waiting in a black RIB in the shallow waters close to the beach at Lepe Country Park. Ben waved, and I quickly locked the bike in the car park as the instructor, James, brought two single kayaks ashore. The kit from the panniers was sealed into a waterproof liner onboard the RIB. Fortune was on our side since the waters were perfectly calm. The Solent was busy, but the larger ships were safely far away as we bobbed in their wake, navigating between buoys, with the Isle deceptively close.

I quickly discovered that I was useless at paddling in a straight line, and felt seawater seeping through the bare patches in the waterproof jacket with each stroke. It hadn't quite sunk in that I was finally here and on the water; and I was happy to be there, chatting to James about life on the Isle, and enjoying the calm.

The trip took about 90 minutes. The ramp of Gurnard Sailing club and quirky green beach huts arrived sooner than expected and James dragged the kayak up onto the shingle of beach. It was like *Baywatch* – without the babe. He soon appeared with a mountain bike from a storage shed at the club, and then I realised that I had left my pump, toolkit, and puncture repair back on the mainland. They hadn't got one either.

'Ahh well. I've come nearly 4,000 miles without one flat. It's only 30 miles. What're the chances?'

James said we would need to start the crossing back no later than 4.00pm because of the tidal conditions. He and Ben would be chilling out in Cowes in the meantime.

The island felt instantly warming and far enough away to forget the gripes of the mainland for a while. At only 13 miles wide, it would be difficult to get dramatically lost. Before putting this theory to the test, I dropped straight in to Gurnard Primary School where a friend, Sophie, was a teacher and had jumped at the idea when the challenge was announced months earlier.

The children were so excited by the arrival of this unshaven adventurer.

Sophie appeared with a smile. 'Do you want to get changed first?'

'This is all I've got!' I laughed.

A hundred and twenty kids were crammed into the classroom as I dripped with saltwater, hoping they wouldn't notice the gaping hole in my shorts. The local newspaper photographer had snuck in for a photo without me even realising. Afterwards they lined up asking for autographs on scraps of paper until a teacher dragged me away to get on the bike. We got a photo outside, just like in my vision months earlier; truly getting people in every corner of the UK involved.

It was 16 miles to the south coast and St Boniface Down, the highest point of Isle of Wight, a ceremonial county, once voted by Lonely Planet as the best place to cycle in the world for its tranquillity and self-contained charm. The Sandown cycle path made brilliant use of an old railway track, since steam trains weren't too keen on hills either. It hadn't occurred to me that I had no mount for the Garmin, so for the first time in nearly two months there was no perception of speed. But by now I had a sixth sense of judging it by the surroundings and the force of the wind alone. With the extra time pressure, maybe this was an omen from above that stressing myself out with the clock was not the answer. Newport came with a sigh and a reminder of life back across the water, before another bridleway escaped off into roasting fields and the grounds of an impressive country house. The bold chalk escarpments of the Ventnor Downs loomed like sunflowers and blocked the ocean views. Dust powdered into the air on a downhill trail before a loud pop. This was one sound that registered from the days spent cycling to school at the mercy of Cheshire farmers. A whooshing sound. A flat tyre. Bugger.

I could only laugh. Of course, it could only happen here, the most southerly county of the challenge, without a pump, on a bike that wasn't even mine. There was another life lesson in the fact I had spent so much time worrying about the kayaking that I had completely overlooked the basics.

I had enough practise with counting blessings. The hill was only two miles to walk. Pushing the bike was much easier on the road. Best of all, there was a solution, too.

Ben laughed when I called him.

'The irony!' he chuckled. 'No worries, we'll sort it,' he said in typical outdoor fashion.

Ben called back within minutes and had a colleague driving out with a spare bike. There was no substitute for having a support team like these guys; the island was their playground.

The road from Lowtherville would have been too steep for a mountain bike, I told myself. Walking was the right speed to enjoy the view across my shoulder towards the English Channel, the deep blue expanse dotted with ferries. Finding the highest bit was less staggering. I knew already that the true high point was behind a high security fence of a radar station. Like a child at the zoo, the best we could do was look. Even with my new-found approach to finding solutions, scaling a barb-topped fence was probably a step too far. The ground on the verge of the bend in the access road was widely accepted as the high point, just half a metre lower. This would do just fine. St Boniface also had a lower trig point for those who wanted a finer souvenir than the perimeter fence.

Ollie arrived in a Land Rover with the replacement bike. He offered to take me back to Newport for a head start. There wasn't much time to debate options. I had been defiantly human-powered for so long that it seemed a waste to ruin it now. But I was already too far behind and missing the crossing back, just for my stubbornness, would have been nothing to celebrate. I had to stop the tracker and bite my lip – I could make up the lost mileage another time. Ollie dropped me and the bike in

Blackwater, which had shaved eight miles off the ride, and just enough to make it feasible. From there it was a frantic push down the cycleway; worried about pushing too hard, but more worried about missing the crossing altogether. I took a shortcut down Cowes high street and dodged idle shoppers like hairpin bends on a downhill red run before the final jump down to the sailing club. Surface currents had doubled in speed and the guys looked cautious.

'We're going to have to work really hard and make a big push now,' James warned. We had to paddle along the beach to allow the wind and tide to push us back in towards the mainland.

Rush hour on the Solent sent much bigger wave swell from passing traffic that made tough work of staying on the right side of the water. Ben shook his head when James asked anxiously if we were halfway. The profitless slog continued for a while longer, until he eventually nodded. We cheered; we were going to make it. I told James about the radio interview that morning. He shouted over to Ben who whacked the radio up to full. It wasn't delusions from sunstroke when a familiar soundtrack rang across the water: it was the soundtrack used in a documentary film about my Everest journey years earlier, followed by my voice. Here we were; two kilometres across the Solent; listening to my interview on BBC Solent from earlier that day. If I'd had the time, I would have pinched myself. 'Road to Nowhere' was the next song on the schedule. Ben stood up, lapping the sun, pumping his oars in the air in time to the tune. It was a brilliant moment. So many people had strongly doubted the kayak idea; getting the ferry would have been the sensible option. Bouncing in the waves and paddling as hard as I could was probably not sensible – but this was adventure. With the right support it had not only been possible; it had paid off beautifully.

Seventeen miles to my accommodation should have been like the paper round. Feeling so tired was no big deal now the timer was off, the pressure of the day uncoiled. I hadn't eaten for hours, and the emergency cereal bar in the panniers didn't go far through the taste of salt on my lips. But even my exhausted eyes could appreciate the enchanting New Forest. Wild horses and ponies grazed quietly by the road side, as common as squirrels. These natural caretakers barely flinched as I passed between idyllic open glades and deep swathes of native woodland, where it fell mysteriously dark and magical enough to believe the tales of pixies. From a rise above the moorland, the scene behind looked like an oil painting and prehistoric skies faded to a palette of orange. I was quickly running out of superlatives for this one road wonder.

Eventually my energy had completely dropped into dizziness, and confusion, with less momentum than a flat tyre. For once, there was no wind to blame and it was time to take control. Low blood sugar was much faster to reverse than the binge eating episodes. It only took a small hit of carbohydrate to resuscitate me from roadkill to Duracell bunny, after raiding the discount aisle at Tesco Express in Brockenhurst. YHA New Forest arrived soon after, with the waft of BBQs and happy families relaxing in the gardens. The wooden glamping pod was the shameless luxury I needed to get the Solent out of my clothes.

With only 64 miles of riding to Litton Cheney and no counties to climb, I was in no hurry. My friend Mike had suggested sampling the local area and posting photos showing me enjoying myself for a change. Burley was a timeless place of folklore, witchcraft, and quaint shops cashing in on the otherworldly hype. Wild horses wandered around like locals beneath the shade of gnarly trees. Cake, coffee, and cycling was a combination that needed no explanation – it just worked.

*

The days were merging into one. I had stopped counting the counties, and only started counting the days and the fundraising target which had crept up suddenly after donations from the recent radio interviews and strangers I had met. Hitting the ambitious new fundraising target looked increasingly likely.

Bournemouth was the epitome of a day at the seaside, with sandcastle beaches, a pier, and imitation palm trees. Luckily, there was a regular ferry making the four-minute crossing over the mouth of Poole Harbour to Studland on the "island" of Purbeck, for cheaper than a chocolate bar.

Technically Purbeck was not actually an island, although it was relaxed and wild enough to feel insular. Coastline occasionally appeared across the peninsula, as did a Chinook helicopter, and the white horse monument on Osmington Hill required a double take. I was now on the Jurassic Coast, 95 miles of coastline and England's first World Heritage site. From the outskirts of Weymouth came the chocolate-box village of Abbotsbury, overshadowed by the final crawl up Limekiln Hill lifting me higher, in both senses, until the crest of a hill. Few sights had the potential to elicit as loud a 'wow' as this. The Jurassic Coast stretched as far as my eyes could squint through glistening sun, an immortal blue haze and dizzying white cliffs.

Litton Cheney youth hostel was another countryside hideaway. Being truly switched off from the internet and not being able to look at a map and plan the day ahead was both frustrating and relaxing at the same time. It was a people-watching paradise in the local pub; and listening to the village gossip kept me occupied.

Getting away early the next morning was much easier with so little to do. Stoke Abbott stepped back a century or two, with its orchards and deep lanes, now decked in bunting for the village fete. A sign warned of *Hobbits and Hippies Crossing Ahead*; I had seen it all. The 12th-century church seemed a good place to lock the bike up. Crickets croaked in the tall grasses, and besides the birdlife, there wasn't much else. That was the beauty of it. Lewesdon Hill was covered in a National Trust woodland and the high point was unambitious, a mound in a grassy clearing of ferns, with gaps in the trees offering some views to the afternoon ahead.

Despite the unfettered calm, my lack of planning or milestones in the sleepy countryside, combined with the stuffy heat, left me frustrated for most of the day. Stopping impulsively and making do with sustenance in deserted village stores was annoying when the next towns emerged full of life. Not getting enough miles under the belt only caused more restlessness. It was hard to plan without knowing what might come – like filling our diaries with events and commitments without knowing what frame of mind we'd wake up in that day. Building success on how we felt was unwise. It was more about commitment, about doing what we had to, regardless of how we felt. Sometimes taking things as they came worked out for the best.

Negotiating the gridlock of Exeter at rush hour was far from ideal timing. It was a final sprint into Okehampton and along the Granite Way to reach a strange campsite situated idyllically next to a dual carriageway. I must have looked like a broken man, adopting a corner of the petrol station to charge up gadgets and get dinner, sitting awkwardly on a stool long enough to cut off blood supply to my leg so that I nearly fell in a heap, and then hobbled back to the campsite.

CHAPTER 28

Dartmoor National Park: this bleak expanse of granite tors was known for having four seasons in one day. The Royal Marines trained there for good reason. Early the next morning, the tussocky moorland was more placid and the skies a tad overcast. In a world first, I arrived on time at Meldon Reservoir to meet Oli Broadhead, albeit it was only two miles from the campsite. Oli was an adventurer, photographer, and scientist who had already travelled to places I'd never even heard of. We were the same age and similar in many ways, though he fitted the adventurer bill perfectly. He'd had a shit time at school and had worked in kitchens to pay for his adventures. Likewise, the outdoors had been an outlet for the frustration and challenges that school had perpetuated.

At the summit of High Willhays, dense cloud stole any view from the moonscape plateau of over-sized rocks and heightened the eerie silence. After a few handstand photos on the county high point, we bagged the nearby Yes Tor with the bog giving way beneath wet feet as we improvised our way down over Okehampton Common and back to the reservoir before twelve. Despite my incessant prattling, Oli was already making plans to come along to Cornwall at the weekend. Spinning behind the wind and ahead of progress for the first time in history, a massive downhill led into Tavistock and a rush for a taxi to Plymouth train station 20 minutes later.

My friend Richard, and his bride-to-be, Katharine, were just buzzing to see me at their pre-wedding dinner in Hereford that night. Richard was a close friend, who had even come all the way to meet me in the Scottish Borders weeks earlier, and I had promised to make it for their special day at whatever cost. They were possibly surprised that I had made it at all, considering the state Richard had seen me in in Scotland. Their family-run campsite in the countryside was holding the wedding reception the next day and Richard suggested I sleep in the wedding marquee. It turned out to be the comfiest sleep of the challenge so far. Sunlight through the marquee woke me just in time for an interview with BBC Devon, and I hurried off with my phone pointed in the air for signal, like a talisman.

With a few hours spare, there was nothing to do but stop. I enjoyed listening to music again for the first time in weeks and it was a relief to re-evaluate everything that had niggled away since the beginning and hatch a plan to maximise the final two weeks. Planning social media posts and being creative didn't come easily when exhausted. Although 57 days of experience told me that trying to create more energy or time to get different results wasn't going to happen easily. In the campsite toilets I got changed into the wedding suit and looked in the mirror. An overwhelmed and agitated person glanced back weakly. The weight on my shoulders was invisible, but clearly there. What more did I want from myself?

The wedding ceremony itself was heart-warming, though rising for each hymn in the church almost finished me off. I was even looking at ViewRanger routes in the pews, praying for some divine intervention as the challenge swung back to the heart of England with a list of people on standby for more plans and timings.

Friends and family had travelled far and wide to be at the special day. 'Someone has travelled over 4,000 miles to be here,' Richard said in his speech, thanking me, as I stood up red-faced.

He went on, telling all one-hundred guests about the challenge, and lifted a big jar with the Climb The UK logo on, asking for any charity donations and spare change. The last thing I wanted was to take anything away from their big day. Being there for a friend was the least I could do – returning with over £185 of donations for Young Minds from their family and friends was flattering. I felt guilty to have to leave early, but I left with a tray full of the first and only part of the hog roast that was cooked. Only God knows which part! Salty, protein-rich meat was my latest craving. There was no doubt that these bodily cues were legit.

On the station platform, a man asked how the challenge was going; Chris worked at Cardiff youth hostel and had recognised me in spite of the suit disguise. We grabbed a selfie before his train disappeared. The biggest wonder of the challenge was having absolutely no idea just how many people it could be reaching, inspiring, and helping.

The next morning took me back to Plymouth as if nothing had happened. Paul Arnold was waiting with the kettle on in Moorshop. Paul was a great friend and one of my main confidants. He had known about the eating disorder before we had even met in person and it was so helpful having him involved during the bid to fight back. Sadly, there was little time to chat, with six more people waiting in Cornwall. We pushed the bike up his steep dirt track driveway to the main road.

'You're doing amazingly well. Even if you packed up now and went home then I'd still be bloody impressed,' he beamed, proudly.

The county of Cornwall was in the way of going home. There were 32 miles to reach the start of the walk, and Tavistock was the quickest bet to fuel up for the forecast heat.

The grass was quite literally greener in the Tamar valley and into Cornwall, where abrupt climbs followed the untamed spread of land and made catching up with the late departure unlikely, and I swore at each incline. Everything flew by in a blur.

The amusing place names were always a delight. From Crapstone, the pendulum of roads flattened like a table across the edge of Bodmin Moor. Whether unfortunate or simply ridiculous, the county top of Cornwall was a hill on Bodmin Moor called Brown Willy.

The pine trees looked misplaced within the bleakness, clutching onto a sense of wilderness where the outside world ceased to matter, or Devon at least.

There were friendly faces to join in the fun. I knew Dan as a cheerful local mountain leader, Ben and Tom had followed the journey on social media, and a chap called Toby, who wasn't well enough to join us for the walk, had still come all this way to shake my hand. Flattering. Antoinette, her friend Sandra, and son weren't walking with us either, but she had come simply for moral support and to ensure that only the proper Cornish pasties came my way.

The track over Rough Tor was untaxing and with a load of previous expeditions and challenges between the group, a Scottish Munro would have given a better test. The summit of Cornwall was decked by granite and a trig point, with panoramic views across Bodmin Moor and scattered county towns and villages, dulled by overcast skies. The inner child within had been ridiculously excited for six months to post about climbing a Brown Willy.

Having eight miles left was a relief, but the race was still on. Cornwall was a place of winding lanes and hedgerows that left remorseless souvenirs on the shiniest panels of tourist cars. Boscastle was a tiny port village hidden away like a pearl down the hillside. The youth hostel was a little stone cottage tucked away from the outside world (and phone signal). Oli had left a message with the manager to join them for dinner at the local pub before 8.30pm. I downed my tools and hurried over. Oli had told his parents I needed feeding, and they generously treated me to dinner in a gourmet pub. They were hopefully used to sons coming back hungry from expeditions with Oli and his brother Toby off exploring far-flung places, so I felt less of a disappointment turning up in such a scruffy state. They must have wondered where Oli had found me. Adventure clearly ran through the family blood, and their travels made fascinating stories over the local seafood.

I was just in time to catch the last of the sunset on a walk to the lip of the harbour. The hillside dropped into the turquoise waters gently sploshing below, and the sea breeze tickled the grasses. The sky burned with a final blade of fire across the sea. A couple sat admiring the romantic scene from a bench nearby. I was falling more deeply in love with my own country as it kept wooing me with these love notes of nature in unforeseen places. As far as county tops went, Brown Willy would be a hard one to beat.

CHAPTER 29

It was a punishing climb out of Boscastle and onto the Atlantic Highway. Widemouth Bay was the typical surfers' playground with dark cliffs lurching into the waves.

My mood was darkening too. There was less to look forward to than on the day before, so I had to create something myself. The local seafood caught my eye and inspired a big lunch stop in Bideford and more time to sort things out. On 80-mile days in the placid Exmoor loneliness, the isolation was bleak; the landscape was sparse.

I pulled into a layby for an interview with *The Oxfordshire Guardian*. Her last question hung on my mind:

'Has doing this helped your mental health?'

I had been so busy that it was the first time I had reflected on my own mental health. Undeniably, the curiosity had opened a can of worms by digging up the troubles that I was happily able to forget in the outdoors but running away from them would never solve the problem. The episodes of binge eating hadn't kicked the bucket, though I saw them for the need they were trying to fill.

I knew I would have to cycle a very long way to come back cured. But I was learning to see things in a way I had never seen them before. Each day put new pages in the scrapbook, as puzzle pieces slotted in to place and experiences were stored as a reference for future struggles.

Nothing moved quickly here except for unspoilt rivers cutting deep valleys, and an exhilarating downhill to Exford at nearly 40 miles an hour. The sleepy village was the perfect setting and almost reclaimed by the countryside. The quietness of YHA Exford, a grand old building, didn't help the insular feeling. I was forgetting the friends who were only a Wi-Fi connection and a few taps of a keyboard away for some moral support. When they checked in as usual every day, and asked if I was okay, it was easier to just dismiss it with the universal cliché: 'I'm fine,' than to explain something that couldn't really be changed. Of course, I wasn't "fine", but I was still moving forwards, and that was a kind of "fine". I wasn't sure how okay I could expect to be on something like this.

But everyone who had taken part stayed in touch – and that meant the world. Maybe they were hanging on with popcorn to see if the underdog could make it. If they'd put a gamble on me reaching the finish line, considering my physical state and various mishaps, we could have topped the fundraising target 10 times over.

Exford village never really woke up. There was barely a whisper on the climb up to Dunkery Beacon. It was a five-kilometre jaunt, to a cairn of stones and the county summit of Somerset. Exmoor passed the baton to the Quantock Hills. The first target was reaching Cheddar for lunch. With another 60 miles alone, there wasn't much else to aim for between the deep oak woodlands and combes, but these basic creature comforts opened the possibility of enjoying something new. After realising the road was heading straight over the top of the sheer green hills ahead, I was immensely grateful to notice that the angry knee was keeping quiet. But I wasn't about to push my luck, and pedalled the hills as slowly as I could get away with.

At least the rain was warm. It eased for a while towards the limestone ridge of the Mendip Hills and Cheddar Gorge in the distance. Time pressure nearly took me through without stopping, but after the low ebb of the day before, I stuck to the plan. It was the perfect spot for a cheddar cheese toastie to sustain the climb through Cheddar Gorge. The thought had been an obsession for most of the morning. The overhanging limestone cliffs of the gorge were the most dramatic of the journey; these neck-craning walls faded into Yoxter, the brilliantly named Chew Magna, and the flatter farmland towards Bristol.

A bridleway climbed a grassy hillside looking across the tower blocks of Bristol and over barbed wire into a sloping field with the county boundary of Bristol cutting across. It was unusual that the city was itself a ceremonial county. I much preferred the gnarly beasts of Scottish mountains than trying to find the highest spot of an unmarked boundary line in a field, especially with a phone so wet that the screen was almost unusable. It was just four miles of cycling to the waterfront and the youth hostel where I spent the night preparing in vain for the talk the following day. My business suit had gone walkabouts from the luggage room. Rehearsing for the talk didn't come easily with two more tops and 80 miles in the legs although the key message was clear enough: it was 60 days in the making.

A delayed 5.30am train, a missed connection, and a frantic £60 taxi ride to Alderman Peel High School in Norfolk got me to the sports hall, just in time for an assembly to around 350 students. Luckily my memory hadn't completely gone to toast. There was less margin for error at the annual awards that evening. Being the guest of honour was no paper errand to be taken lightly, and I owed it to the students' achievements to do a good job. The venue, Holkham Hall, was an extravagant place with deer in the grounds. Seeing my name on posters in the corridor and pop-up banners was terrifying; I didn't feel good enough for any of it. They'd had Olympians speak in previous years. This was a big deal – I couldn't mess up. But the circumstances had taken that control away from me and put me out of my comfort zone. It was the first time I had felt genuine fear since I'd been bordering on hypothermia in Scotland.

I descended on the canapés like a hawk; grabbing as much protein as I could get for recovery, while trying to comfort myself from thoughts of the task ahead. Someone commented on my appetite. Hopefully after the talk he would understand. For once I was learning to accept the net gain of calories on rest days was essential if I was to maintain my weight, and felt too done-in to care about what bulimia thought about it.

It was nearly time ... the lavish hall was filled with nearly 600 people ... I told myself I knew the components of a good talk, and I looked for something inside to draw upon. I gave it everything I had, and all things considered, I was pleased with my performance.

Like so many things in life, talks usually did turn out better than feared, and the typical relief that surged in afterwards took over anyway. Smiling on stage, shaking the award winners' hands one by one was more exhausting than cycling all day, as my legs began to jitter through exhaustion. I just hoped they would hold me up. For a moment it dawned how significant it was to be here, presenting awards to remarkable young people, when only 22 years old myself. After closing remarks, the head boy and girl invited me back on stage to present a souvenir photo of Norfolk and a cheque. The students who climbed Beacon Hill had raised an astonishing £850 for Young Minds. For the first time all night, and perhaps the whole challenge, I was truly lost for words at what this had all become.

Afterwards, the head boy, Alex, approached me quietly to ask all about Everest and said how much it had inspired him, presumably to achieve even bigger goals. There was no better feedback than from the students themselves. The PE teacher, Scott, offered a lift to Norwich and the pre-booked Travelodge where my booking didn't exist.

It turns out there were two Travelodge hotels in Norwich, and the other was a mile walk across the city at nearly midnight. Despite the exhaustion, I was beaming; it was done. Now I had a clear run to the finish – and nothing was going to stop me. There was a hell of a lot to share over the next few days and it felt like the last chance to get the message out. I still had the small matter of raising over £5,000 to hit the target.

That was all going to be a lot easier in damp cycling gear, and I happily stuffed the smart shoes and business suit, creases galore, into a cardboard box for the final time.

*

After catching the first train back to Bristol, I was happy to be back on the bike where I felt at home. Reaching Bath would get some progress under the belt. The honey-coloured Georgian architecture made for nice riding, but finding lunch was a giant faff. On these bigger days I had managed to divorce myself from the idea of perfectionism in favour of grabbing whatever I felt like.

Sometimes things were simpler with time pressure, because the usual obligations to fully experience places on the route were dismissed for the bigger priority of arriving on time. A photographer from *The Wiltshire Gazette* was coming to meet me at Pewsey Downs, and my legs weren't going to work any wonders to arrive at the promised time. I tried anyway. The devious climbs were subtle, but enough to steal the pace and mess up calculations.

Framed perfectly behind tractor tracks in the golden fields, the Pewsey Downs popped out of nowhere a few miles after Devizes and into the rural fringes of the county. After the blandness of towns and cities, there was a much bigger appreciation for the minute changes in the landscape that normally wouldn't have bothered a blink. Vicky, the photographer, waited at the car park and scribbled a few quotes about mental health as news of Climb The UK spread into the county of Wiltshire. Talking about the challenge was naturally getting easier with repetition, however hard I tried to offer something original each time. My reflections were changing as each day passed. Unlike Bristol, the signpost suggested there was something worth walking towards.

The county top of Milk Hill was somewhere in a field of broad beans at 295 metres elevation. Only the spot height of 294 metres was marked on the map and so I began a treasure hunt for a tiny cairn among rows of shin-high crops while on the phone to BBC Radio Wiltshire. The Downs were secluded enough to lose phone signal entirely mid-interview. Mum told me afterwards that she had heard my short-tempered swearing while I was still live on air. (It turned out she was winding me up.)

The stress of the afternoon was intensified by the heat, and my legs were completely beat. A friend, Becca, was waiting near the town of Hungerford to walk the next two counties, I was determined to be on time; fed up with my perpetual failure to meet promises, and blaming only myself. The satisfaction and achievement of finishing each day was continually muddied by arriving late.

I can see you! Becca texted; watching the speck on the road far below the outcrop. 'Oh no you can't!' came to mind. The tension was probably printed clearly enough on my face as I waged fury against one final hill and arrived at the car park where Becca and her spaniel, Holly, were waiting with a hug and a smile.

People bringing supplies sometimes interfered with my routine and my temperamental appetite, but Becca had nailed it with a slab of dark chocolate that popped my eyes out of my head.

Walbury Hill, an Iron Age hill fort, was a mere lump off a long ridge with a trig point in a field marking the highest point of Berkshire. A friendly local chap, Andy, had called earlier in the day to arrange meeting up. His mum, Kate Smith, had been an avid follower of my Everest expeditions and he handed me a £5 note as beer money on her orders.

A lonely trig point stood off the footpath and into a ploughed field. It didn't matter to us and we made a moment of reaching a trig point that on my own would have just been touched, ticked and mostly forgotten about before focusing on the next, but neither Andy nor Becca had climbed Pilot Hill before. The sunset matched the mood of celebration with the trees breaking the dancing clouds like black soldiers in receding daylight.

It was long-past kitchen closing time when I got to my snug hotel in Burghclere, and I was happily ready to admit defeat and hit the sack, head throbbing, and chest still racing from the calorie deficit. But, as an ultra-runner, Becca knew better. Without refuelling properly after 17 hours on the go, I would be setting off on the wrong foot tomorrow. She drove me to Tesco in nearby Newbury to wander the aisles in a hi-vis jacket for something more substantial than complimentary biscuits in the hotel room. Becca had saved the day. Back at the hotel, I fell asleep halfway through recording a voice diary. It was all beginning to feel like a dream.

CHAPTER 30

I had never felt so rough getting on my bike in the morning. The heart rate monitor wasn't lying. For a moment I had questioned my ability to make it when feeling worse than the day before, but I'd done it so many times before. There were still three counties to tick off, more miles to cycle, and I was physically weaker. But I kept bouncing back in this game of tit-for-tat: I was stronger in mind, it was flatter, and there was company to look forward to.

One hundred miles felt daunting. Sleep deficit was kicking in, hard. Four hours' sleep was not nearly enough – by this point, nothing probably would have been. The encouraging messages of *keep going* contradicted the soothing messages of *take it easy* – but that wasn't an option. Although well intended, they started to feel irritating and unhelpful when people had no idea just how I felt. The stress of the daily routine put me on the defensive, always on the lookout for somewhere to offload. Biting heads was all too easy when someone told us what we already knew, but we were either powerless, or unwilling, to change. I called home from the roadside. Mum was troubled now, too. There was no point in fretting, I told her; there was nothing she could do. My friends and family were taking the brunt of my fatigue and didn't deserve it. I vowed not to snap back and to pause before anything blurted out.

*

Whitehorse Hill was the high point of Oxfordshire in the ancient rolling downlands, with yet another white horse figure on the upper slopes. The Uffington White Horse was the oldest of the lot, and over 3,000 years old. I held out hope that a county might paint a giant white squirrel or something more original. Nearby was the site of Uffington Castle, another Iron Age hill fort, and the trig point beyond.

Stopping to inflate my tyres had made a dramatic difference; the bike felt in collaboration with the road, rather than scraping against it. Remembering to do this the day before would have saved a lot of effort. Struggling bred resilience and this made us more willing to accept it and push through, but not all struggles were useful. Some were just an inconvenience that stopped us dealing with more meaningful challenges. If there was an easier way to achieve the same objective, then it was usually a safe bet.

I was pushing hard to reach Cirencester before 1.00pm where a friend, Christina, worked at a high school, and we had arranged a flying visit. Time had slipped already, and I was in no state to push hard, having paid the price from the day before. Pulling the heart rate monitor belt off entirely had removed another worry. But in my tiredness, the slightest incline was over-exaggerated, while on the flat plains, the wind appeared to double. Everything had a knock-on effect. Stopping would mean being late for everyone joining me that afternoon, arriving late at the youth hostel, and getting behind on sleep before the 100-mile ride the following day. Something had to give. There was no more time for heroics – I was knackered. Missing an opportunity to inspire wasn't easily forgiven. Christina understood entirely that I had to take care of myself. I felt much better instantly; the maddening hills miraculously vanished; the headwinds were unavailable for comment. Positive replacement thoughts were close at hand as I looked forward to the company that afternoon, stopped fighting the surroundings, and connected to them instead.

The terrain of the Cotswolds was flourishing with dip-slope valleys, farmland, and escarpments.

Cirencester was quickly a vague memory as Tony appeared on the other side of the road a few miles later, smiling and waving, quickly turning around and riding by my side. It was fantastic to see him. He had taken time off to show me around his home county of Gloucestershire. Miles passed as we chatted side-by-side when the roads allowed, exchanging chocolate and stories of Scotland where we had first met weeks earlier at Durness Youth Hostel. We skirted Cheltenham and began the climb up Cleeve Hill. It gave a much bigger sense of achievement than the county top itself. Fortunately, he had noticed the route online had missed the true county high point by a quarter of a mile, about five metres off the fence near a trig point.

The trig point was underwhelming, but the sun lit the wide-open grassland of Cleeve Common. The toposcope had much better views, where Tony pointed out Cheltenham Racecourse, and the Malvern Hills for the following day. We dropped downhill into Winchcombe like bolting horses on the track before Tony sent me on my way with a handshake.

Broadway was a picture-perfect village of cobbled streets and golden-stone buildings, mostly unchanged by the past centuries and like stepping into a film set. The shortcut quickly backfired when I ended up climbing Fish Hill instead. I reached for the now-melted Oreo biscuits from my jersey pockets; carelessly smearing chocolate crumbs onto my face like Bruce Bogtrotter while the jar of peanut butter was out of reach ...

All the tourists had gone home as I pulled into the gravel driveway of Hidcote Manor. Tony, Nick, and Helen clapped and cheered nonetheless, probably anticipating that I was going to declare something more meaningful than: 'I'm buggered!'

Ebrington Hill was another county summit that could have been ticked from the roadside with your engine still running. That didn't give much chance to walk and talk considering friends were coming along, so we planned a two-kilometre stroll from Hidcote, and tried to condense 63 days of travelling into 10 minutes up the rough track. We checked out the nearby 261m spot height on the map just in case, but the summit of Warwickshire was a sorry old trig point, abandoned on the corner of a barley field. The fading daylight caught my attention, but a whiff of coffee and Helen's homemade flapjack made a fitting celebration: something I often failed to acknowledge when alone. Tony waved me off with his own London 2012 Olympic torch, and I headed off to another round of clapping and cheering with just eight miles downhill.

Crossing the bridge into Stratford-upon-Avon signalled the end of 103 miles and three county tops. The Shakespeare town of wonky timber-framed Tudor buildings was packed at 10.00pm on a Friday night. I resisted the urge to upload any Shakespearean-inspired prose to social media; I needed this time for me. There was a good technique I'd been taught in these cases when I felt like I was getting drawn into the pressures of social media. I could use an item – my phone, in this case – and focus on the sensation of touching it to bring me back into the present moment – and it felt liberating to take back control.

*

Waking up with the same fatigue was a worry, but I left on time; give or take 10 minutes.

The next stage in this episode of spinning legs was longer still. A saturating lashing of rain was not the most encouraging start. I shrugged it off. Masochistically, the more suffering, the more I would enjoy the finish, and it was now close enough to believe. Once the end of a struggle felt almost certain, we were willing to push that bit further. The sense of control that gave was even more enjoyable for the exhilarating and overwhelming feeling of relief to follow. Without the struggle there was no contrast: every peak needed the trough to rise clear of the base level.

Nick and Helen had come out for another instalment a few miles out of Warwickshire, and met me in the brilliantly named village of Flyford Flavell. Nick shook things up a little and was waiting on his ElliptiGo – an over-sized red elliptical bike that certainly grabbed attention. The lanes led to the centre of Worcester where it got much busier. Helen was on standby with supplies and met us at the north quarry car park with their friend Kiri. My usual hastiness to stick to the schedule had us rushing off, drinking tea from flasks in transit, and marching briskly up the path, with Nick practically throwing flapjacks at me for self-maintenance.

There was no prize for guessing which county was topped by Worcestershire Beacon, a prominent hill fringed by dense woodland and butterfly meadows between a hectic criss-cross of paths. From the receding hairline of green, the summit cleared to a dramatic viewing platform and a panorama of 13 counties that was well worth the effort. Along the way, we exchanged stories of our own personal peaks and troughs. I was glad for the chance to hear Kiri's story as we leapt down the track. Kiri was a few years older, a fast marathon runner, and her natural enthusiasm for adventure gave no inkling of the challenges she had overcome, including running injuries and disordered eating that I knew only too well. Finding kindred spirits who understood such an insular battle was a step closer to understanding ourselves. I felt as if we had set off as a group of friends enjoying a weekend walk and had left connected on a new level. Climb The UK had been the catalyst for all sorts of deeper conversations and that felt like an incredibly powerful thing.

On to the Midlands, and the bumpy roads of the Black Country. A track off the road near Dudley Golf Club led towards an unsightly communications tower on Turner's Hill. Hopefully the *Anti-Social Behaviour Area* sign wasn't referring to hill baggers. Luckily the gate was open and the highest point of the West Midlands was marked, not by a trig point, but a radioactivity warning sign on the barbed metal fence.

The final target – the finish – was as simple as spinning. The booked accommodation at Wilderhope Manor was out in the sticks of rural Shropshire, and I was too goosed to be dealing with avoidable surprises. Ringing ahead to check the food serving times seemed a lot of effort but it was just another way of mentally inflating the tyres.

Shropshire was a county of tamed wilderness and farmland that felt a little unfinished. It was getting dark by now and I felt the relief when Wilderhope Manor appeared at just before 10.00pm. This Elizabeth manor-turned-youth-hostel brought a childhood fantasy of Harry Potter to life, with the restored dark-oak doors, wrought-iron chandeliers and oak spiral staircases inside reminding me of Hogwarts. There was no room key – everything was open for all – one of the little touches that made each youth hostel so unique. I was too late to explore this one properly and it was gone midnight as I posted social media updates from my bed.

CHAPTER 31

In the light I could truly appreciate Shropshire and its whaleback hills. Brown Clee Hill itself was dressed in woodland and slippers of early mist that leached the colours to green. I met Brucie in a layby near Cleobury North. Brucie had followed the journey on social media and made the trip from nearby Kidderminster to take part himself. We were soon on our way, following quiet tracks from the country estate into unkempt plantation forest with stillness hanging in the trees; even the birds seemed conscripted to this silence. I was pretty good at filling it. Listening to Bruce, who had a 17-year-old daughter struggling with mental ill health, was eye-opening. The parents' perspective was one that I could probably least relate to myself. Mum had always told me that it was hard to help, or even know what to say, and I had never understood why.

Sufferers were often so overwhelmed by their own challenges to even appreciate that those around them were inevitably dragged along for the ride by commitment to their loved ones. This sense of burden must only have made the person in question feel worse or even like it was their fault. In most cases, parents felt simply duty-bound: this was their job. Hearing it from Bruce, someone who wasn't my family, helped me to see it from both sides. My expectation of Mum to understand – just because she was my mum – surely added to her own pain of feeling unable to fulfil that role.

It seemed the solace of endurance cycling wasn't just helpful for those suffering directly with mental health, but their support teams too, as Bruce spoke modestly about his cycling challenges and the familiar delights of pedalling until breaking point.

Out of the treetops appeared an ugly scalp, littered by crumbling quarry works of times gone by, and a microwave relay station. The track skirted a jumbled mess of grassy spoil heaps to reach the highest of the hills' two summits – Abdon Burf – the highest point of Shropshire. Overcast skies didn't do any favours for the views across to Titterstone Clee Hill before we headed down in a loop and I managed to get us briefly lost.

Back on the road, Brucie drove past like the team car, snapping photos and willing me on towards the next county. Mum had noticed the map and texted: *Ludlow is a lovely town, I love it there!* The walk had taken longer than expected, and I would have to push hard to make time for a visit. A bustling café among the shop fronts was the quickest choice to refuel rider and his gadgets for the day ahead. It was tempting to just power through on empty, but I reminded myself for the umpteenth time that I was still in this game for another week yet.

*

Great Rhos was one of the more inconspicuous county summits, but a colleague from Westgrove Group, Laurie, was keen for a challenge and made the three-hour drive with her partner to join me. In perfectly synchronised fashion, the heavens opened within metres of the *Welcome to Wales* sign near Presteigne. The historic counties of Wales were more ambiguous, and the first, Radnorshire, was mostly contained within the mountains. I was 15 minutes away when Laurie texted that they were going to start walking slowly to let her dogs cool off in the waterfalls just off the route.

I hurried up the path excited to see them. A short while later there was no sign of either. Following the forest would soon give a line of sight up the matted slopes ahead. Knowing that

Laurie was bringing supplies, I had skipped the shops in Ludlow, which was another school-adventurer error that left me with only a couple of mouthfuls of water on this broiling summer afternoon. But there was no sign of them, and in these wild corners of Wales there was more chance of connecting with aliens than finding phone signal.

Frustration had me analysing everything and trying to work out what had gone wrong – naturally turning the blame on myself. I felt so grateful that she had gone to such effort to support me and raise £125 for Young Minds, and I felt so guilty for disappointing them. But there was a considerable walk still to go, and reluctantly, I decided to head onwards.

Around the corner the bulk of Great Rhos glowed like embers in the late sun. A lone trig point stood in the centre of its broad heathery plateau with more sheep skeletons than there were people. Red flags fenced the edges of the slopes before they dropped into the weapon and explosives testing range in Harvey Dingle. Fron Hill stretched like a tongue, with square patches shaved in the grass like specks of salt, which hopefully wasn't the result of sheep becoming target practice victims. Tufty slopes dropped into a narrow pasture along Black Brook towards the mouth of the valley.

Later, I found out that Laurie had been on the opposite side of the valley altogether. But before making the long summit-less journey back, she had kindly left a stash of supplies and water on the bike, which quickly revived me into a recognisable lifeform. Cruising the final few miles brought the town of Kington, a popular watering hole that surpassed the remote outpost I had expected. A man greeted me outside the youth hostel, a grand Victorian cottage, before I had even unclipped from the bike, and introduced himself as Duncan. He would become one of the most memorable people I met along the way, for all the right reasons. He had read all about the challenge and couldn't do more to help. He was a volunteer spending the summer touring and working at hostels as a perfect way to combine his passions. I took liberty of his encyclopaedic knowledge for the final week since he knew pretty much every hill and every shop on the route. He had also followed the Scottish endurance cyclist Mark Beaumont on his world-record cycle around the world in 78 days that summer, saying that I was "very quickly following in his footsteps". I laughed – Mark was a huge personal inspiration: my challenges were a newspaper round by comparison. But it dared me to dream of what my future self could look like. This was how our idols came to be.

A gent who was travelling the UK by motorbike asked why I had set myself such a big challenge to start with. Everyone made these journeys for their own reasons, but we all had the common connection of going out into the unknown; challenging ourselves to find what we were looking for.

Hay-on-Wye was home to more second-hand bookshops than any town in the world; like a giant library. A road sign warned that the eight miles to Capel-y-Ffin over Gospel Pass, the highest road pass in Wales, was unsuitable for coaches. It was a slow wobble through the Black Mountains; a formidable wall of defence along the England and Wales border. Coasting down the other side was the consolation. The Llanthony valley emerged from the tunnel of trees, a sanctuary sunken beneath the hills; the sort of place where time stopped, and you would run away to be a hermit. There was little more than a phone box, an ancient chapel and a couple of houses.

Confusing footpath diversions didn't seem to lead anywhere except further from where I wanted to be, before giving up entirely, a gate appeared and revealed the path just five easy metres away. An eroded path met a sharp incline and the land pushed back for the first time since Scotland. Doing the full circle brought us back to the real mountains again, without doubt. It levelled out onto the characteristic table-top ridge where the famous Offa's Dyke Path ran straight across on a paved footpath through the minute wildflowers and heather.

The last English county of Herefordshire wasn't entitled to a ridge of its own and the highest point of Black Mountain was a piddly pile of stones in the heather beside the path, over the county boundary line. It had been slightly pimped up with the addition of scraggily elegant wild ponies. The good thing about ridges was that once up, they usually stayed up – except this was just the first. Uncomfortably far across the valley was the long ridge from Rhos Dirion and the Welsh county top of Monmouthshire. My heart sank to the floor – this was going to take a while. All I could think was that the longest walk remaining would soon be over with. The ridge continued to Hay Bluff before dropping to the pass and back up once again, climbing over the wonderfully named Lord Hereford's Knob – another strong contender in the weirdest names for peaks and places.

Chwarel y Fan had a trig point to mark the summit of Monmouthshire and the gap in the valley seemed to close in, while the peaks continued throwing insults across at each other like deep-seated rugby rivalry. These blackened scarps had never looked brighter against distilled blue skies. After thinking it was going to be unachievable, both tops were ticked. This shouldn't have come as a surprise by now. This simple joy of hillwalking represented life on so many levels: travelling to a brighter place and looking back at the darkness you had left behind, if life didn't move too quickly for us to overlook it completely.

Dropping steeply off the side through the bracken led to an old monastery, then a house offering the temptation of cold drinks. Holding out until Abergavenny would keep the momentum going. Playing games with my fuel tank seemed risky with rusting old cars reclaimed by the undergrowth serving as a warning that if you broke down here you would probably never leave. The roads were as unforgiving as Scotland, as I reached the top of another twenty-percent gradient to find a chap sitting on a bank by the roadside next to his mountain bike, coughing loudly.

'All okay, mate?' I called over.

'I'm fine boyo ... just bloody knackered!' he laughed. The musical Welsh accent made everything sound cheerful.

Riding into the Brecon Beacons National Park, I swapped green patchwork quilt for beautiful bleakness. Even in the spirit of adventure, there was something comforting in the peaks that we had climbed before. YHA Brecon Beacons was a microcosm of cosiness, brimming with outdoor folk and boots drying by the fire. Finding a phone signal involved a walk up the lane in the dark at the speed of two midge bites per hour. The hostel staff had reheated some dinner while I listened resentfully to a group of walkers agreeing on a leisurely 8.30am alarm for the following morning; making a mental note that in a week's time I'd appreciate it a whole lot more. Sleep was to be short-lived anyway when the fire alarm had everyone bolting outside after midnight.

My good friend Jeff Smith, and his daughter, Chloe, had made an ungodly early start from Cardiff to come along with me for a little stretch the next day. He had recently returned from a successful expedition to climb Mount Everest, and his selflessness to come all this way to show support humbled me. The last time we had climbed Pen-y-Fan was two years earlier after Everest 2015, when Jeff had invited me down to help get my head around what had just happened. Jeff had been my inspiration and had been the spark behind Walk For Nepal. Our journeys had evolved – Climb The UK became my new Everest, but I was chuffed to shake his hand as an Everest summiteer; it meant so much that he could be part of this, too.

After they headed for home to give a talk at a primary school that morning, I carried on, grateful for the kick of motivation. Sunrise in the mountains was reviving enough to lighten any mood but today it was a silvery glare of zebra-striped clouds across the sky, and arctic winds rattled the heather underfoot. The Brecons were renowned for their volatile weather. This half-hearted effort of light only deepened the cracks in the cliffs, corrugated like cardboard, and ridges that could only be described as moonscape. A group on a Duke of Edinburgh's award training expedition took my photo on Pen-y-Fan's distinct summit mound which doubled as the top of the mountainous historic county of Breconshire.

I knew that people wanted to see the highs and lows, physically and mentally alike, so a sheltered seat behind Corn Ddu gave me the chance to film a video blog and spill my feelings on camera. It might have been hard for people to understand how I could be so negative in this hauntingly beautiful place, but my mood had sunk like a popped balloon since crossing the border into Wales. This latest low ebb was because I knew the challenge was almost done – I was going to make it – but it still wasn't finished until the final peak, and I just had to keep going. It was like trying to be surprised on Christmas morning when you knew what was in the box. Partly, it was tied up in regret, berating myself for my mistakes and wishing I had done things better. Regretting what we didn't do stung longer than what we did, but my mentor, Steve, had assured me that, for going in blind what I'd achieved was "unbelievable".

*

I was desperate enough for warmth to break my burger van virginity at the car park.

'Where have you come from then?' the owner asked curiously.

Two miles from the hostel earned no kudos, but he was taken aback when he heard I'd cycled nearly 4,000 miles for one of his burgers! Ian, I discovered, had posters inside his van advertising his own charity fundraising efforts. An older workman pulled up for breakfast and Climb The UK became the focus of gossip over their morning brews. Ian poured another hot chocolate, on the house, and warned about thunderstorms and weather warnings ahead. I left with the warmth of hot chocolate and generosity.

The wind worked with me until the climb from Rhigos village slithered towards Craig-y-Llyn.

Craig-y-Llyn itself was a cinch: nothing more than a three-mile trek through forest to the county summit of Glamorgan. Bizarrely, a trig point was hiding in the vegetation off the path, as if to spare itself the embarrassment, and probably had more dogs cocking their leg up on it than it did hill baggers. Having two tops done by midday was unusual. There was time to stop for a hearty lunch in Glynneath; a meagre £6.50 provided almost two days of calories and set me up for the afternoon.

The Black Mountain range was a separate part of the Brecon Beacons National Park, and one of the wildest yet. This sense of mystery was what I loved about Wales. The withdrawn villages had the same remoteness of Scotland's Wester Ross, where you would probably starve without road transport. The unimaginatively named Mountain Road was a grim toil with the winds and thirteen-hundred feet of ascent until probably the fastest downhill of the challenge yet, swooping along river valleys and unclassified roads. YHA Llandeusant clung defiantly to the spirit of youth hostelling: a memento for what it used to be. It was one of the most remote youth hostels in the UK and the nearest shop was eight miles away. It was nearing 6.00pm and the threat of thunderstorms hung in the air. It didn't take long to realise that I would have to stretch the goalposts and complete another county top that night. I visualised the late-night feeling of triumph from Carn a'ghille-Chearr in the Cairngorms, and Bidean Nam Bian in Glencoe, to prove to myself that it could be done – now I needed momentum, and accountability.

The hostel was fully booked by a Duke of Edinburgh's award group but the YHA ambassador privilege had sneaked me in. The teachers of the group were more than welcoming, especially once they heard what I was doing and duly shamed the students for complaining about three days of effort. Health and safety alarms must have rung in a frenzy once they heard I was heading out again; now I had accountability. They kindly offered to save me dinner if I made it back in time, which changed dinner plans for the better, though their concerned faces clearly didn't bet much that I would make it back at all.

The rain was due at 9.00pm, so I quickly pitched the tent, refilled my water, and powered off up the valley. Now I had the momentum, and just needed the afterburner to kick in. The Beacons Way opened into a valley of wild horses, dominated by the grooved cliffs and bulging outcrops of typical Brecon Beacon proportions behind. Too far, too big, too late; my target seemed smaller with every step forwards. Picws Du stole the limelight. Fan Foel hid behind. I was too focused to even notice the exposure to the left of this rabbit-width path, hugging the sandstone shins of the hill. The windswept ridge smoothed into a plateau where a rock protruding through wiry cottongrass marked the summit of historic Carmarthenshire. Pushing the comfort zone had brought the reward as ever. It felt like one big secret that the Duke of Edinburgh group wasn't going to believe. Giddy relief washed over. I would be back in time for dinner. Singing Tom Jones aloud didn't pack the same punch as The Proclaimers. It came out as a slurred mess.

Most of all, I could stop feeling guilty about people trying to help. Generosity had a way of coming back to us, in the most surprising of places.

CHAPTER 32

Wales did thunderstorms big and proper, and entertained the students more than board games could. I was just relieved for last night's spontaneous effort. There was no chance of an updated forecast, but the hostel warden, Steve, suggested waiting a while as the lightning cracked against the hills like a sparking fuse. I had to get moving soon with 74 miles across Pembrokeshire hitting every hill along the way.

The deluge eased enough to make a push for the coast. It rained foxes here instead of cats and dogs, as cubs ran across the road. The oldest town of Wales, Carmarthen, was the last bet on the map to refuel and confuse the shopkeeper with a combination of typical cycling fuel and tinned vegetables for dinner in the basket. I couldn't remember much afterwards besides up, down, up, and down again, that made it nearly impossible to maintain pace. The downhills came too quickly to enjoy for long, though the struggles didn't drag on too long either. Lush countryside reclaimed the land and had clearly run out of every colour except green. It was called the Garden of Wales for good reason. A scanty tin bus shelter was the only hope of staying dry for an interview with Radio Cardiff.

Dotted within the Preseli Hills was the tiny village of Rosebush and its eccentric pub, Tafarn Sinc, with pink metal walls like an upscaled Ikea project full of the usual paraphernalia. The landlord kindly agreed to host the bike while I headed off up Foel Cwmcerwyn. Pembrokeshire was known for its sunny golden beaches and coastal paths that were, unknowingly, only 10 kilometres away through a stubborn layer of mist that made the skeletons of stunted trees in Pantmaenog Forest even more atmospheric.

A quick courtesy visit in the pub for pork scratchings dragged on, as curious locals quizzed me and likened me to Tour De France cyclist, Chris Froome. I got a deserved piss-taking for my pronunciation of Foel Cwmcerwyn.

I was eager to push on and get to Pwll Deri before dark since it was so remote that I might otherwise never find it. Miles of stone-walled lanes were led by the percussion of beating waves and a whiff of brine. The land dropped off into an endless expanse of blue. A white clifftop cottage appeared tucked beneath yellow gorse hedgerows and cowered from the frigid coastal breeze. YHA Pwll Deri was the perfect bolt-hole on the Pembrokeshire Coastal Path for slamming the doors shut for the day. Terrace windows opened straight out across the bay for a brew with a view. This bolt-hole was secretive enough that the trusty postie had failed to deliver the final parcel of Mountain Fuel supplies. It didn't matter so much now that my body was rejecting sugar for savoury, and chunks from a wedge of salty cheddar cheese were the best thing since sliced bread.

Being on the home straight encouraged a bit of risk and testing myself by eating whatever I wanted. What was the point of porridge and bananas for breakfast when I'd be back in the usual routine at home in a week? A 90-mile day seemed the perfect opportunity to experiment. I rationed a bag of giant cookies at the rate of one per 10 miles. I was past the point of getting away with almost anything I put in and proving for myself that willpower really wasn't the issue behind my bulimia.

I set off strong on a morning fling with the Pembrokeshire coast and the rows of multi-coloured cottages of Fishguard and

Newport. Their harbours came alive with cackling seagulls and morning life moving in sync with gently bobbing waves. The busy traffic of the A487 kept me busy as it meandered up and down the coast besides beaches of sand and green fields.

The only road to Eisteddfa Gurig car park skirted the "desert of Wales", a stretch of barren moorland to the south. My focus was distracted to the other side where mournful black clouds gathered above Plynlimon. Having company that night meant the county top was just an inconvenience; a testing shift at work before getting home to recharge the batteries. Phil was going to meet me afterwards. Maybe he'd had a premonition that torrential rain would pound the tarmac and send me bolting under a wooden shed.

The farm here probably lived off the extortionate car parking charges. Rustic hand-painted signs directed walkers around to a service track, then into an upland valley towards an old mine and the summit. Also known as Pen Pumlumon Fawr, Plynlimon was a modest peak with magnificent views on all sides. Overcast skies leeched the colour into dark shadows with only the glistening white of Nant-y-moch reservoir breaking through below. A fence line guided me down Pen y Drawsallt and out of the wind, scuttling down a pale brown track. Stones rolled loose as I ran down free, hoping to avoid rolling an ankle instead. Phil was waiting below. We had met for the first time at his brother Richard's wedding nearly two weeks earlier. He had come straight from work to fulfil his promise of treating me to dinner in his neck of the woods. I stopped my watch only 90 minutes after setting off and barely stopped for long before 15 miles back to the campsite in Llanidloes, throwing up the tent in record time.

Quickly settling on the local Indian restaurant for dinner was welcome news after 93 miles solo and 7,000 feet of climbing on the bike alone. Sharing our mountain adventures and stories was the perfect way to unwind. But the next day's weather forecast brought me back to reality. Heavy rain, from start to finish. As if riding 120 miles wasn't enough to deal with already. Each course now felt like the Last Supper. When it was all over, I was back in my tent and alone again.

With or without checking the forecast, I would have woken up to face the same situation, so I had to be grateful for the chance to prepare accordingly. Not only did it give the chance to minimise the risk, but also a sense of potential relief when the situation turned out better than expected. Overcoming the struggles so far had got me into this current position, just days away from realising my vision. There was no picking or choosing battles. I had found peace with the truth that we had so little control. And I had faith that the rest would come together. I hunkered inside my tent for the final time and sank into the mattress of grass for all the sleep I could get. The discomfort of the outdoors demonstrated that I had the choice over adversity, I had the tools to overcome it because as each day got harder, I did too.

Leaving at 5.00am was ambitious when nodding off just sending WhatsApp messages to friends. I'd already given myself the pep talk: *Alex you can't give up now, you're so close*. There was nothing much that friends could do for me either: not here, nor on the eve of Cho Oyu summit night the year before. Simply putting feelings in word format made them real and portioned the problem out into manageable bites.

Lashing rain and booming wind bullied the tent into a corner. I was starving, and my body couldn't catch up with the constant deficit. Getting breakfast was the priority. Stripping everything back to these basic human needs was sometimes the only thing that could guarantee progress. Motivation didn't always need the bells and whistles, or the life coaching to ignite from within. It came from simple time pressure: each minute in the tent was another in the dark that evening. I peeled myself outside and told myself that it couldn't possibly rain for the whole day ...

The first incentive was simply to get warmer, and the petrol station in Llanidloes was the first chance to warm up. Such targets were not particularly exciting, but they pulled me through. In periods of depression the challenge was finding a sense of achievement in getting to somewhere even more unextraordinary, where reaching the end of the day often felt like a distant but unlikely possibility. Setting intentions reduced procrastination, and even the smallest of tasks, from showering, eating or even turning up for work were little self-control wins to fuel us. Showing up was half the battle.

Climbing out of the village above Llyn Clywedog left the low ebb slightly behind with a quiet ride through upland valleys that crept around the mountains on roads so isolated that some were unmarked on the map. At the head of Cwm Cywarch stood three ugly towers of coal-black rock that quickly set the tone for the day. Aran Fawddwy, the county top of Merionethshire, was the only peak outside of Snowdonia National Park that reached over 900 metres high. A path pulled through the gap beneath imposing crags and splashed through swollen streams. The path eased over the crest to a wide boggy area with wooden planks and a fence giving the only hope of crossing. Even these were submerged under inches of water. The wood was glazed like grease and threw me off with a thigh-deep splash into thick mud. A barrage of furious cursing hung on my tongue until realising it was pointless; there was nobody around to hear it; the wood wasn't going to offer the satisfaction of arguing back. I was anxious not to spend the day cycling caked in bog buttercream, though the rain washed it straight off. Eventually, the rain eased off a little, but I stayed saturated.

Aran Fawddwy looked far ahead in the clouds. My spare phone had stopped working so there wasn't even music to fill this silence, until a rocky summit plateau appeared with howling winds buffeting my hood. It was mid-morning, but the greyness granted zero perception of time. Descending the same way didn't appeal much, and I stuck to the original plan. After leaving the trig point there was no hope of finding the route without a map

– the rocky ground and gullies didn't match up. It was a relief to eventually find an obvious track to run free and closer to safety. I felt strong as the track hugged the foundations of Pen yr Allt Uchaf, snaking not only down, but sideways. The mountain tripped me up, I was airborne. My head hit the grass with a whack! Fortunately, the patch was clear of rocks, and sheep shit. Still it left me dazed and shocked for a moment. It was a sudden wake-up call that this wasn't the time to be taking risks and getting injured so close to the finish, and the jogging turned to a careful shuffle.

I was frozen. Bwlch y Groes, or Hellfire Pass, generated heat from the strain while cars struggled past. The downhill lost the usual thrill as the chill penetrated every layer. The nearest town of Bala couldn't come quickly enough and I dived into the first café that came. Three coffees and toasted teacakes were the only hope of thawing out when too late for cooked food, sitting furthest from the door and nearest a radiator that wasn't even on; I pretended otherwise; hunched over to take a call from ITV News.

I bought myself a reasonable new jacket and relished the extra dry layer. There were two counties left to climb. Fortunately, the Berwyn Hills were a stone's throw from the town as I climbed the mountain road towards these unloved moorland offshoots, much softer than their brash siblings, and the eight-mile walk was mostly flat with the occasional bump. Locking the bike to the Denbighshire county sign assured me that I had at least found the right spot.

It was a grim affair of relentless wetness. My new coat was soon soaked through; I should have bought three! Every direction looked the same in the clag as the wooden boardwalk guided me across the scabby grass into snarling winds. I hunched down and hurried on. Tolerating it was about focusing on a certain end point. I was late enough to know that making the hostel for closing time at 10.00pm wasn't going to happen. Using everything I had left to arrive at a locked door in the middle of nowhere was not an option. It was too wet and cold to camp. There was still no sign of any summit and it would probably only appear in the last few metres. Moisture on the phone screen made it impossible to use beyond a few seconds to look for alternative accommodation. In desperation, I rang Mum. I asked her to look for alternatives back in Bala, or Beddgelert which was slightly further, and enough to keep me on schedule for tomorrow.

The text came back: *I'm sorry Alex but you're going to have to push on.*

Eventually, the Prince Llewellyn hotel in Beddgelert came to the rescue. The helpful landlord offered a room at half-price, would ask the chef to save me dinner, and was happy to hang around till midnight to let me in. For 30 minutes there was a solution and I was laughing through chattered teeth.

The summit cairn of Moel Sych was the first to reveal itself from the murk. With historic Montgomeryshire ticked, Denbighshire was only 10 minutes further along the rugged ridge on Cadair Berwyn. The obvious trig point tried to tip me off the scent of the true county high point on a vague rocky outcrop that was three metres higher and perilously close to the cliffs on one side. I was disorientated; no better than blind. Time irrespective, I visited both spots to be as certain as I could be. There was no chance of coming back. The summit photos were a blurry mess of monochrome film quality. I didn't care. Cold had set in when weight loss struggled to keep warmth in. The internal checklist went off the scale. Time was fading quickly. Up here there were only two colours: grey or black. Even getting to Beddgelert was becoming doubtful.

Google Maps says it's only three hours forty to Beddgelert Mum texted.

Fuck Google Maps! was my curt reply.

I wondered whether the support of my friend Chris might make it achievable, or whether moving further into the night with no facilities, on the edge of hypothermia, felt too risky when movement was the only heater. Mum had come back to tell me she had found a bed for me in Bala. I jogged onwards in giddy relief again. I was so near the end now – there was now a plan B for catching up the following day.

A van sat waiting by the road. Chris had waited regardless, ready to cycle with me for the final few hours. He was with Bill, a bike mechanic, who had driven over to help when Chris told him how late I was going to be. They had rocked up in what felt like Scooby Doo's Mystery Machine and serviced a sorry-looking bike at the roadside while waiting. I emerged in the guise of a drowned rat; barely able to speak. They threw a towel around me and dragged me inside. 'You're staying in Bala?' Chris asked, surprised. I nodded, feeling like the party pooper. After all this waiting, Chris would only get to cycle nine miles back to where he started. In the warmth of Bill's van, I quickly questioned the decision, but I had made the decision based on what I knew of the situation at the time, and I was sticking to it. Chris agreed it was the best move. Their banter and high spirits lifted mine over a late-night pizza in town.

The backpackers hostel became an adopted home with the bike locked to a piano in the hallway and gear strewn over the drying room. Falling 40 miles short demanded a 3.30am alarm to help me play catch-up. I always wanted challenges to end with an epic – a moment of drama where I broke down, made the biggest self-discoveries and gained the stories that had audiences grimacing in contemplation. I wasn't going to have to fake it. I had a very real epic to deal with: and I was playing the starring role.

CHAPTER 33

Stretching the muscles of resilience would craft a life-changing weapon for the future: if I could drag myself out of bed to face it, then depression was never going to keep me down for long. My GP had once described my depression as "highly functioning" because I was still able to operate well when feeling hopeless. I had the outdoors to thank for this. I was awake before the alarm went. I hadn't really slept anyway. At least waking up earlier gave me a good chance of leaving on time to tackle 108 miles, 11,000 feet of ascent on two wheels alone, and two mountains – including the highest in Wales. All of this was inconsequential. I was beyond scraping the barrel, I was feasting on it.

Neither mind nor body knew who was in charge now. My heart was on overtime. Reverting to a trusty fish-bowl pot of porridge knocked me sick with pizza still lingering from a few hours earlier. The town was silent and strangely bright against a metallic blue sky. Any doubt of making the finish was left behind at the hostel once a mile had clocked: I was already making progress into Snowdonia National Park, with sheep's eyes reflected in the headtorch across the fields and the occasional crowing of a rooster. Relentless forwards motion had kept things moving so quickly that the inner critic had taken a wrong turn and was probably scratching his head in a field somewhere, before skulking off to pick on someone else instead. I was just grateful not to have climbed this high mountain road the previous night as planned. The pearly morning glow had a winter clarity that I wanted to imagine frost on the branches. Rugged peaks were lit like matches by the sunrise, and the deep forests on both sides seemed much friendlier in the light. It was a sight for bloodshot eyes.

*

The best downhill had been saved till the end; plunging into the Vale of Ffestiniog towards the Isle of Anglesey and a majestic wall of Snowdonia mountains shadowing the forests filling every roll of land, capturing the showreel of Wales in one frame. Waterfalls tumbled to the roadside as I freewheeled faster than the water towards Llan Ffestiniog village where the first rays of sunlight took the bite of the chill from the air. The spectacular Pass of Aberglaslyn cut me off from the world. Crooked trees kept me under wraps like witches' fingers closing in on both sides. Cycling through it in the dark would have scared the pants off me. Nant y Betws opened wide as the Snowdon range and Nantlle ridge took a step back, but close enough to keep the valley and Llyn Cwellyn in silence. It also kept the signal out and with BBC Wales due to call for a radio interview, I was rushing to Snowdon Ranger hostel, where I had planned to stay the night before, to find a payphone. I was too late. Either way, the lady behind the counter offered my second breakfast of the day which would fill the tank to push to Holyhead without stopping. A parcel had been waiting for me. My flapjack stalker, Hannah, had been hot in pursuit for a flapjack top-up. Sugar mostly turned my stomach, so she had sent a hefty wedge of Scottish Kintyre cheddar, oatcakes, and another envelope to be opened on the final peak.

Ten minutes later, I was moving again through Nantgwynant and Waunfawr as walkers emerged from their tents, vans, and bunkhouses to hit the hills on a bright summer morning. Mum had barely got out of bed before I had crossed the blue-green of the Menai Strait and the iconic bridge onto the Isle of Anglesey to the cackle of gulls. She couldn't believe the progress. Stopping for some electrolyte drink eased the headachy sickness as I celebrated the JustGiving total exceeding £16,000.

Taking the direct line down, the A5 road fleeted between the island villages, weathered gracefully by salty air. I hadn't expected that my cyclist friend, Mick, would still be keen to come after the delays. There was no mistaking the green Vegan jersey cruising in the opposite direction. In good timing Mick was on holiday with his family on Anglesey at the time, and I was made up to see him, especially today. Mick had been the support crew for my "Everesting" cycling challenge two years earlier, so had seen me in this state before.

Holyhead Mountain, the crowning glory of the island which was also a historic county and current principal area, didn't seem to be getting much closer. Its small stature defined a hill rather than a mountain above 608 metres, but a five-minute stroll to reach the summit was ambitious. My local radio station had been calling for an interview but there was no time to stop on the steep town roads through Holyhead. It was the sort of day where everything else went out the window.

Breakwater Country Park was surrounded by cliffs and old quarries reclaimed by nature. The planned route went to the foot of a cliff with no way up. We found our own way up the myriad of tracks over rock-strewn heather that was scorched in the sun. People gathered on the summit cairn like stick figures as the slopes dropped down to the Irish Sea and ferries chugged across the blue expanse. South Stack lighthouse and Holyhead Harbour broke through the warm haze.

Mick was the perfect cycling companion, and happy to skip the obligatory coffee stop in favour of catching up with time. He willingly took the lead as a pacer and we cruised at nearly 16mph towards Snowdonia; the bold outlines stood high and proud though brooding dark clouds didn't inspire as much confidence. Swearing at the rain was normally enough to make it disappear. I hardly noticed the showers, or anything, in this trance of pushing

277

pedals. We were soon 10 miles away and I texted Steve with an updated ETA, continually fretting about keeping them waiting any longer.

'Stop panicking!' Mick told me eventually. He was right, everybody would understand.

Friends including Steve and Jenny, two Westgrove colleagues – Tony and Phil, and Mick, cheered me up the driveway of the Royal Victoria hotel in Llanberis. I kept my head down, shy of the attention. However hard I tried to keep up the positive persona, there was no use hiding the stress on my face. Steve reached out to steady the bike and I lost balance, hitting the floor in a heap. The look of relief was clear when they had arranged a room at the hotel and spared cycling another fifteen miles over Pen-y-Pass to a friend's house in Betws-y-Coed. Having the day shortened slightly was surprisingly invigorating, as if my body could consciously plan for what was coming and release a few extra reserves.

Mick pulled up alongside modestly. If not for him pulling me along they would have been waiting a while longer. He would join us for the second county of the day notwithstanding the long ride back in the dark. I was perpetually worried about daylight hours and darkness, and my responsibilities to get everyone down safely. Steve and the team were experienced walkers, relaxed and well-equipped, and we had enough time. The Llanberis track was 10 miles out and back, and had been chosen for the logistical ease of starting in Llanberis village. It was also a bit of a slog. On the steepest early section of tarmac, I was unknowingly puppet-marching on the spot, without moving forwards while Jenny coaxed me upwards with flasks of coffee and sandwiches. By the halfway house every step was getting heavier, weaker, and more lethargic.

The mud-brown cliffs of Clogwyn Du'r Arddu loomed ahead before we ascended into the curtain of cloud 30 minutes from the top. Steve and Jenny had supported my challenges from afar, and now they were seeing them in their authentically unglamorous, glory. They had never quite witnessed digging deep to this level before. Friends probably questioned their duty of care by helping this challenge to succeed and seeing me in such a state; though willingly self-inflicted.

I dashed straight for the summit café before an announcement over the tannoy warned that it would be closing imminently – getting locked in the bog at the highest point of Wales on the penultimate day of the challenge would have topped everything off quite majestically. The spiral stone steps of the summit were taken literally one at a time; more a victory crawl than a walk; with everyone waiting at the top. Sun broke through grey-black cumulus like a nod from higher places to reveal the grandeur of this mountain throne. Glaslyn and Llyn Llydaw plunged to turquoise puddles thousands of feet below and orange-tinged dusk spread like wildfire over the desolate land. The moment unfolded perfectly. I had climbed Snowdon more times than I could remember though having the top of Wales mostly to ourselves was a rare treat. Getting to see something further than the rocks beneath your feet was even better. The group was giddy with their luck and happily gathered for photos.

I was slowing the group down on the shale and slabs. Even talking was tiring – luckily for them! The combination of sleep deprivation, stress, and endurance left me a little dead inside, but subconsciously awake. I had felt like this only once before, when descending Cho Oyu at over 7,000 metres' altitude, puking in the snow every few steps. My mind was clearly drawing on something deeper than experience. It was worse than any fatigue that depression had ever inflicted. The saving grace was having a clear reason to urge each foot forwards. It was not excitement, but a certain finish line. These struggles would always end – but all felt equal in this state of exhaustion. The Llanberis track met a tarmac road where a shout came from the café. Nick and Helen appeared, beaming. They'd been too late to walk with us but waited to cheer us down. Nick had volunteered his birthday weekend to come to North Wales for the big finale. My words came almost slurred as I tried to thank them. The surprises didn't stop there with Mike, Sonia, and Dan waiting even further down.

'Long time, no see!' I cheered, introducing the group. The tracker had run dead and they had nearly walked up the mountain to find us. We walked back to the hotel, chatting and making plans for the big finale in the morning. Until then I was little good for anything but sleep.

My gate-crashing of the hotel toilets with scraggy helmet hair and the offending shorts left wedding reception guests less than pleased. I couldn't stomach anything for dinner besides a leftover bag of cashew nuts. I only wondered whether room service could help with the seemingly impossible task of sorting my kit for the following morning. I just had to keep moving forwards now. And that had worked a charm so far.

CHAPTER 34

Day 72: summit day.

A summer sunrise lit the room. I could only watch helplessly as it dragged me confidently into the day I had dreamt about for months. Dark chocolate and coffee for breakfast knocked me sick. I didn't really need to eat; I just needed to make it. But I knew taking on fuel was a necessity.

After being late near enough every day of the challenge it seemed safer to leave Llanberis late, too. There was no traffic to blame at dawn. My legs didn't ache; they were just empty on the slow and steady crawl up the Pen-y-Pass road I knew well. The 46 miles could have been 130. Miles were irrelevant when the process was the same and summit fever had settled in. This sleepy Sunday morning held all the ingredients for a perfect finale, and even the warm air was blowing behind rather than against me for once.

There was little energy to give, besides pushing pedals and holding the two wheels straight as if staggering back from the pub. The irony of collapsing now was not lost. As time passed and energy faded, style and precision were harder to keep up, leaving just the basic components needed to complete the challenge; like your body shutting down unnecessary body functions to reserve enough energy to reach a marathon finish line. By this point it was being dragged along bruised and battered.

For the first time, I might finally achieve something that I had set out towards. This epiphany was a new experience that I didn't really know how to experience. Truthfully, many moments in life failed to match up. Unrealistic high expectations could quickly become disappointments, or an internal battle against ourselves that we could never win.

It was the perfect opportunity for reflection. The early days felt so long gone that they were a different experience altogether. It wouldn't be long until someone would ask me what the next challenge could be. I had become hypervigilant, eavesdropping on the imaginary arguments in my head, gathering a series of answers on standby. 'Rest' was the first. I didn't want to think of any discomfort, for weeks, months, maybe more. I was looking forward to doing whatever I felt like doing, even if that was nothing, before life dragged me back in again.

Besides this relief and guiltless indulgence, I was confident of finding peace within myself for a while longer: to feel worthy, content, and capable of so much more. It was a pretty good indication that I had stretched myself to the absolute limit. To think that all of this had positively impacted the lives of other people was the purpose above all. Even more magical was the full extent of the impact was still to be revealed. It only took one experience to change a mindset, and this could change a life. I was nothing special; a brick in the wall; and it had worked for me.

My own mental toolkit had got a whole lot bigger and sharper. Questions were answered, and new ones emerged. We only stopped growing when we stopped asking questions. The tools were not to fix things but maintain ourselves along the natural peaks and troughs of life that I now understood.

My anxiety had one more trick in store, and I worried about the logistics for the final peak, Moel Famau. It worried about everything that needed to be done, in which perfect order, about what I would say, and whether I would actually make it on time for once. I fretted how I was going to raise the final couple of thousand pounds needed to hit the fundraising target, and how I might cope with an overwhelming crowd of 50 or 60 people that were expected to come along.

Bulimia worried about all the food instead – how I'd cope or refrain from the cake and buffet that Mum had put on – maybe to make sure someone saved it a piece. Without doubt, this toxicity had been somewhere in the panniers all the way, but had failed to weigh me down.

At 20 miles to go, the A5 rolled smoothly between the trees, blossom hedgerows and fringes of farmland that were slightly dull, but only in comparison to everything else over the last 72 days. It was important not to let comparison stop us appreciating the individual beauty of things.

I tried not to stop for long – to redeem the chronic lateness once and for all. Each time it was difficult not to get carried away. An Instagram message from a teenager at one of the school talks said he couldn't believe how this had come together and how much it inspired him to see someone doing so much; so far; day after day. One lady was going to be waving at me from her garden – and to this day I never found out where, but it was a lovely day to be out. There were heaps more, and I couldn't keep up. Donations came in faster than ever on the final push, and mostly from people I didn't know. Nick and Helen drove past, tooting and waving out of the window, reminding me to push on. I would meet them soon.

Eventually, the horizon went up once more. A niggle of excitement was hard to ignore. The rolling heather-clad Clwydian Hills were a mosaic of green and burgundy; their colours tempered in weary eyes; the final barrier to home. Moel Famau took the podium. The nobble of Jubilee Tower was clear to see on its polished bald head. Everything suddenly seemed as certain as it could comfortably be.

The shopfronts of Ruthin were the last sign of life before a final two miles of climbing on maxed-out gears. This quad-smouldering beast had been saved to the very end. Bikey McBikeface was loyal in duty until she was signed off for the day. The curve of the peak was nearing in every sense and it had little left to do but enjoy the descent at 40 miles per hour down to the lower car park where Mike waved me in, and everyone was waiting.

Mum didn't let me unclip from the bike before rushing for a hug and dropped me to the gravel like a domino. She started crying. I had no idea what was going on. Words failed me. It was guilt and gratitude in equal measure.

She didn't have me back just yet. We weren't out of the woods until we left the shade of trees above the car park and climbed to the top of the final county. Mike and Sonia had pitched a gazebo laden with banners and decked with cake. The sun was shining. Stepdad Chris was nearly dragged across the car park as Hector pulled for me with the force of a Rottweiler. He didn't give a damn about how many counties I had climbed – he just wanted his human home. I was positively overwhelmed by the number of people who had turned out already. It was the first time seeing my PR agent, Mick Ord, after badgering him via telephone for the last two months. His photographer friend, Jonathan, had been drafted in to get the "money shots" and busily worked his way around the growing crowd taking photos. Friends, followers, supporters, and friends of friends had travelled from as far as Liverpool, the Midlands, and the Lake District. Others had followed the journey on social media and wanted to bring the journey from phone screens to real life. I was made up to see Dad, step-mum Debbie, step-brother Jake, and step-brother-in-law Ally, walking towards me. A cohort of Westgrove Group colleagues had come from afar. The gathering came over to chat and I was giddy like a kid at his birthday party.

Collectively, we truly had the young, the wise, and those who hadn't yet tried. Getting everyone up the hill was a little like herding cats, and everything went over my head. Mike had become my logistics man and we hatched a plan. Rupert Bonington ran into the car park and said hello, grabbing some gear to operate his drone before turning to run back up into position apparently effortlessly. I gave some form of a thank-you speech, probably forgetting everything important, and the group started making their way up in two waves, with Mick shaking a bucket for donations.

Moel Famau was a gentle giant of proportion that was slightly short of official mountain classification, but it had everything and more. A running friend, Andy, took the opportunity for a hill session and ran to catch us halfway. Brigadier John Thomson was strolling further up and insisted that I shouldn't wait for him. There was no chance of going to the top without him when he had coached me up and over so many mountains in my work and challenges so far. In the same military etiquette, we remained a team. Steve was on the phone to Lucy Meacock, the presenter of our local ITV News channel, Granada Reports, who had unwittingly found her own route from the higher car park, without phone signal, and was rushing up to meet us in true breaking news urgency.

Everyone had gone ahead, and I was worried about keeping them waiting for too long. The summit remained, hidden in suspense behind the stiff upper lip of the hill. David Henderson and Mike stood looking down, in the same pose at the Shining Tor car park on day one.

Steve patted me on the back before hurrying to prime everyone.

'Take this in, mate. Take in every moment; you've bloody earnt it,' he said.

I walked the final 100 metres on my own, but far short of alone. I wanted to rehearse the moment after waiting so long but knew I never could. This was it: elation, nerves, relief. No more suffering; no more exhaustion. This was it. I was only looking forwards now.

It seemed everyone on Moel Famau and perhaps the Clwydian Hills had joined the party, invading the stone square of Jubilee Tower. The banner was stretched out, reading:

Mental illness isn't a weakness: together we can overcome ANY mountain.

The statement was truer than ever today. I reached for the envelope from Hannah in my jersey pocket from the day before. Rather than a gold-encrusted flapjack, it was a khata scarf, a traditional offering of goodwill in Tibetan Buddhism. I later found out this one had been given by the Dalai Lama himself.

A hill of noise approached, picking faces out of the crowd as I weaved through the hill, taking those final stone steps of Jubilee Tower, giving Mum a dumbfounded look in the eye. The flat metal plaque on top was the highest we would be, and a platform for the final step. I stood at the edge, the Union Jack came to my shoulders and I thrust it into the air. It was done.

For a moment there was nothing but blue potential above, just how I had imagined Everest would be. It was like my Everest summit day, only better, with warmth and sun raining down. I turned at the edge of the wall as the crowd cheered again; a silent wind clapped my back. The skies had dropped their weapons and opened across the Clwydian Hills for miles and miles with nothing to blot the landscape. The curvature of the earth was not impossible to imagine in the elation.

My eyes welled up through the smile; not for pain, but the chance it could all be real; the epiphany in my mind months earlier. It hadn't sunk in. Fortunately, Mike and Jonathan took the role of chief herders for the group photo. It didn't feel right to be above the crowd, and I skipped down to lie in front of the banner. Steve seized the perfect moment to step forwards. The group fell silent as he explained they had a bit of a surprise for me; slowly unrolling a giant paper cheque of £3,808 to Young Minds UK. The total had just passed £20,000!

Everyone cheered in surprise. The realisation hit me seconds after. I was close to tears; ecstatic. I had doubted this target only hours earlier, and now it had been doubled. The generosity and initiative of the public had come together wonderfully to send out a message loud and clear. In doing so, they had invested their faith in me reaching this final summit, and I was humbled to have delivered. If there was ever a moment for making an ad-hoc thank-you speech, this was it: I had plenty of experience of winging it.

'It's clear to see what this means to so many people, and I can't tell you how much that means to me,' I began. I can't remember the rest, but afterwards, everyone cheered.

The historic county of Flintshire was lost for being the final one and it was Dad who pointed out the lonely trig point about 20 metres from the tower. The trig point wasn't the true top, but I was taking no chances now. I messed about; standing on top, balancing on one leg. 'Don't break yourself now!' people said nervously.

'It doesn't matter if I break myself now!' I laughed.

Jordi, a Catalan filmmaker from Veracity Digital, came over to film an interview. The Everest documentary that they had first intended three years earlier had now taken on a very different story. We let the hill rest in peace and gradually strolled back down to the car park. Like a wedding day obligation, everyone insisted I should cut the cake first, considering it had a map of all the counties printed in icing. The second speech was hardly better and inevitably missed most of the acknowledgements I needed to give. Regrets jumped at their chance to shine – and were stopped in their tracks.

The cake did the rounds as people lapped up the sun and tested my new-found encyclopaedic knowledge of county tops. Lucy Meacock had been taken by the experience and chatted happily to Mum as they teased my sun-bleached blonde hair.

Mick and Jon made a quick getaway to get the photos sent to the media. Rupert rushed back to the Lake District for his wife's birthday. I was forever indebted. The crowd gradually dispersed with farewells, handshakes, and photos. A nervous-looking girl, Jess, seized a quiet moment to come over. She was a similar age, a novice walker, and avid mental health advocate. She wanted to express her thanks. Having asthma and her own mental health challenges had left the familiar anxieties of whether she could make it. This had proved otherwise. It was the springboard for more. I saw her getting emotional and we hugged. Moments like these were the proof of the pudding.

Mike and Sonia were the last ones standing there as we returned to the car park and took our memories safely away. It seemed appropriate considering they had been there from start to finish. It had been everything we had imagined at that Sunday roast dinner months earlier.

'You should be incredibly proud of yourself, mate,' Mike said. He was proud as heck and I couldn't thank them enough.

There was nothing left but to get in the car. 'I've just climbed the UK!' I croaked. Mum kept looking back, beaming. I sat taking in the simple pleasure of gazing out of the window, with the sun's rays warming my face. Less than a decade earlier I had looked out at the hills of Scotland in similar awe, inspired by possibilities and a genuine sense of "what if?" that had led me outside to the world's highest peaks to find an answer. I had practised my art through the outdoors and now I knew what these hills were for. The view had been there all along, much closer to home than expected. We cruised down the A55 as 'Don't Stop Believin'' blasted out of the radio. The next track of 'Every Breath You Take' sank the mood. I grinned. We attached our own meaning to these things.

I might have run out of candidates for the worst day of my life, but there was only one best day. Over my short life so far, I had spent enough time in those peaks and troughs of life to know that they made each other worthwhile. By getting outside and choosing my peaks more literally, I grew better at taking the first step out of darkness. Life in black and white was boring when we could live in technicolour. We were born HD-ready. The peaks and troughs of life were inevitable. Choosing to fight was optional. I had chosen to fight my mental demons. And I had won.

But what was I going to do next?

PART THREE

THE REAL EVEREST

"After climbing a great hill, one only finds that there are many more hills to climb" - Nelson Mandela

Something was missing.

However much it might have been earned, the liberty of doing nothing quickly got boring. Weeks of frustrating lethargy had me falling asleep at four in the afternoon, like Grandma in her slippers. After teaching my legs to run again, I was supposedly done with adventure for the year. I caught up with the back end of summer to plod around the forest trails and pick blackberries.

It took various health check-ups before I felt remotely normal again. Switching out of challenge mode took a while when the switch was broken, and the momentum continued rolling with weeks of admin, media articles, donations to organise, and sponsors to follow up with.

I had been away from home for two months without being truly far away. A chance meeting with Barry Evans, the founder of the Eifion Trust, a charity based in nearby Tarporley but working to support people in Nepal, brought a fantastic opportunity to light. Barry and his wife, Ann, needed someone to visit and report on their projects in Nepal. Few people had the health, youth or willingness to spend days travelling off-piste in a Jeep around comparatively inaccessible areas. To me, it seemed like an adventure, and the perfect opportunity to see the real Nepal that had been worst affected by the earthquake. I had been looking for the chance to return, and been waiting for a more compelling reason to justify the time or expense than rocking up with a rucksack and going for a trek. Barry's offer had tied everything together perfectly. There was no question, I simply had to go: and there was no greater way to reflect at the end of such a life-changing year.

I flew out to Kathmandu on the 1st of December with a packed three-week agenda. But this trip to Nepal had a very different mission.

Kathmandu was a city where spiritual heritage and poverty met in the same place. Not much had changed as the sun hammered the labyrinth of bustling brick streets, decked by an electrician's nightmare of wiring and tooting taxis. Rickshaws rattled past the shopfronts of wool, ornaments, and tea, as locals haggled for better prices. A chest full of dirty fumes was not so good for my health, but it was good to be back, nonetheless.

The trip gave me the opportunity to fulfil a variety of personal errands. First, I went to meet Bandi Lopchan Sherpa, the widow of Lakpa Thundu, my friend from the Cho Oyu expedition, who had been tragically killed on Ama Dablam the year before. At the time, followers and supporters from as far as New Zealand had responded to a blog post and generously pledged cash to support the family of this wonderful mountain man. It felt important to deliver these donations in person, and now I finally had the chance. I felt anxious as Bandi appeared, arriving shyly in the hotel lobby with their two young boys. The spitting resemblance to Thundu choked me a little. Finding the words was difficult. The eldest, a young teenager, translated through her broken English. She kept saying 'thank you' as I handed a few hundred dollars over, and a few Cadbury chocolate selection boxes from Mum. It was a small gesture, barely worthy of such a man, but I hoped the funds would help them along now Thundu, their breadwinner, had gone.

Sadly, I hadn't time to take up their offer of Dahl Bhat for lunch, as a taxi took me to the PHASE Worldwide offices to meet the team carrying out the work that we had funded from the two Walk For Nepal events. Everyone was crammed into a tiny office and began introducing themselves in turn. Meeting the people working on the ground day by day was a humbling reminder that made the fundraising part seem easy. Coincidentally, the expedition leader from both Everest attempts, Tim Mosedale, was back in Kathmandu following an expedition to climb the peak, Ama Dablam, itself. With so much to catch up on, we arranged to meet at Himalayan Java in Thamel, the same popular coffee outlet in which we had killed time waiting almost a week to fly home after the initial expedition went down the gutter. The dynamic had completely changed. I was no longer a client, but here on my own accord and leading myself. Tim was pleased to see me back and doing my own thing.

We were reflective. Our three teammates were close in our minds. He understood as I explained how my passion and drive for the mountain had changed since those fateful early rock climbs together in the Lake District. It felt like I meant it and the lack of stammering suggested the same. 'Sometimes we keep hanging at something and keep trying, then realise it's not for us,' he said, 'but that's the only way we can find out.'

Tim was full of praise for "smashing it" with Climb The UK, where I had finally been able to prove my capabilities. It meant a lot to win approval from the first mentor I'd had, beyond the mountain itself.

*

The extravagant Dwarika's Hotel hosted me for a few days to visit their impressive Dream Village project, a huge undertaking to rebuild 230 homes in villages destroyed by the earthquake. Barry had expressed an interest in the project and wanted me to be the eyes and ears. Before expeditions it was standard practice to wrap ourselves in cotton wool, especially in one of the most polluted cities in the world. Clinging for dear life on the back of a motorbike felt somewhat rebellious as I went to visit Hope Camp, a shelter complex that housed the village's children while their homes were rebuilt.

One of the Portuguese volunteers, João, showed me around. They were a lively, happy bunch. I left a copy of my book, *Icefall*, which one girl hurried off to read while the boys logged on to YouTube. I got to know João and Catarina over breakfast. Catarina was an architect who felt she had more to give and searched for a way to use her skills more meaningfully. João had a youthful glint in his eye that belied his bushy greying hair, and insisted that he felt young, too. His life was simple, he explained: he wanted to give back more than he took. Their life outlook was inspiring and left me pondering my own purpose for the remainder of the trip.

Since the challenge, I had been eagerly returning to running and recovering fitness that had been replaced by the slow endurance efforts of Climb The UK. The next morning, fuelled by the calories of an unlimited breakfast buffet, or just the freedom to explore, I ran amid the organised chaos of Kathmandu. "Riverside Walk" conjured images of paradise, but was more like a neglected maze of half-finished streets, waste, and wild monkeys cackling abuse as the cloud of dust kicked up behind me.

The fever set in a few hours later. My legs ached, and I was shivering despite the balmy heat of the hotel courtyard. There followed a grim, sleepless affair of clock-watching, chills, and burning up through the night. I was going nowhere. I spent two days bed-bound, and a doctor diagnosed a respiratory infection.

There were certainly worse places to be ill than the Dwarika. The suite had more grandeur than my friend Richard's car had offered when shivering at the foot of Ben Lawers with a chest infection during Climb The UK. Just as he had supplied hot chocolate on the camp stove, the hotel staff nursed me with hot lemon and fresh fruit on room service, and I was too weak to refuse. The doctor suggested it was most likely triggered by running in the pollution. Spluttering like a Benson and Hedges-sponsored athlete, I was beyond angry at myself when knowing I should have rested. And why did I run? Because I didn't want to gain weight.

*

Barry was keen that I met the remarkable Sangita and her mother Ambica, the owners of the hotel and visionaries of the Dream Village project. Ambica was in the sunny courtyard the next afternoon, reading a newspaper with the focus of someone busy who clearly got things done, and a slightly intimidating aura that sent my stammer running a mile. My confidence had been wiped out along with my immune system, and I spent the best part of 20 minutes trying to summon the courage to approach her. The prospect of missing opportunities never sat lightly, especially equipped with the Starfish Project technique. Taking a few costal breaths and seizing the moment was the only way.

The conversation didn't get off to the best start as she handed me a pack of tissues for my streaming nose. I persevered, and her serious face began to glow as she spoke about her passion for the projects. The kids at Hope Camp were like an extended family to her, and she wanted to make it possible for them to become whatever they wanted to be: lawyers and doctors and more. Dream Village lived up to its name.

*

I needed to visit Bhim, the cook from our expedition. Bhim had broken his arm in the avalanche at Base Camp and been out of work for months. I wanted to know he was alright.

I flagged down a taxi to their flat and he happily ran over with arms fixed and outspread. His famous chips were as good at home as they were 5,000 metres higher at Base Camp. It was great to catch up and reminisce as old friends, and fascinating to see how he lived in between expeditions. Bhim had come home safe from Everest to his wife, son, and daughter. I couldn't help but look around the four walls of this comfortably modern flat in a quiet suburb and think of Bandi and the three others whose fates had been decided on the other side of the coin.

The next part of the trip was led under the watchful eye of the Rotary Club of the Himalayan Gurkhas. We joined the hum of traffic and psychedelically painted buses on the highway in a cloud of fumes that stung my eyes red-raw. Being stuffed in a Jeep for five days with four former Gurkhas was hardly conducive to recovering but if I could climb Scottish Munros in a similar state, anything else felt uncomfortably like an excuse. For the next few days we spent long hours visiting project sites, truly out in the sticks, where the remoteness was also the reason they were so necessary. We left the city for the foothills on high mountainous roads, with my first glance of the "real" Nepal that I had never seen.

Looking out, we saw how the other half lived. Men hauled bamboo up the mud roads, farmers tended to their fields and young brothers walked to school, holding hands. The homes were rudimentary to say the least. Roadside eateries caught my attention through the scratched window, and I pondered how filthy they looked.

I was glad to experience these new places, though it was disheartening to see the scale of such poverty and feel powerless to even scratch the surface. We arrived at a lush farming village of white-thatched huts. A feast of fried goat arrived at the table with rice and vegetable curry. I had stopped eating meat (apart from fish) earlier in the summer, and was never so pleased to see a spoon arrive to eat my curry, while the others had to get their hands stuck in.

Restricting my diet was risky when it had been the precursor to the eating disorder in the first place, but my biggest motivation for becoming pescatarian was a bid for taking more control when my usual routine and meal-planning efforts were side-lined by Mum's home cooking. 'Pretend I'm away on expeditions,' I had told her in vain.

Afterwards, we toured around the new classrooms that had been rebuilt after the earthquake, and I felt pride in seeing my home county of Cheshire marked on a commemorative plaque on the wall. The Gurkhas took honour in completing these projects with military thoroughness and in upholding their world-class reputation, too.

These Gurkhas might have softened around the edges but were quick to notice me turning up two minutes late for dinner! A plate of vegetable Momo dumplings arrived, quickly followed by another. 'One is not enough, if not full up to here, not enough!' Naryan chuckled, gesturing to the neck. It was stressful but I had accepted my lack of control for the next few days and reframed the situation as a one-off chance to taste proper Nepali life. A sewage drain flooded the dining-room floor brown, and a man was arm-deep in the drain trying to clear it before going back into the kitchen.

The journey was an experience to say the least. High roads teetered above massive drop-offs and the threat of landslides was always close in mind. As the expression went, 'If he's not afraid of death, he's either lying, or he's a Gurkha.' Estimations of distance were useless on the cratered mud roads, recently repaired from the monsoon, and I was amused to have cycled 100 miles across Norfolk faster than we had driven 50, jostled around in the back like nodding dogs on a rollercoaster. The ViewRanger app that guided me around the UK was the only hope of visualising progress. The idea of reading or writing was futile for the sake of travel sickness. I resorted instead to the liberty of nothingness and zoning out completely. We stopped for tea regularly and I watched in amusement as a tea-shop owner returned promptly with a bucket of milk fresh from their very own buffalo. I didn't bother asking for sugar.

We visited another secluded village and a school, and we were greeted with an entourage of flower necklaces and a slapping of face paints. They showed off their new toilet block with pride. A meeting was called in the staff room and a young teacher sat next to me typing things into Google Translate.

'Where do they come from?' I asked the principal outside, puzzled by the lack of homes among the terraced farmland. He pointed to the crest of the hill. Simultaneously, a barrage of children ran past excitedly and through the gates, like indigenous fell-runners, on what would easily suffice as a training run back home. Major Bhim told me that people here had a great life – it's just education and healthcare that are the problems. In the clean air, looking around at the flourishing palettes of green and harmony of nature flanked by a backdrop of the outlying Annapurna range, it was hard to disagree.

Major Gopal led us down to the rice paddies of Khusi Khola village. At the high school, an overwhelming guard of honour and effusive clapping welcomed us into the playground, serenaded by flower chain necklaces. Three-hundred-and-fifty students watched in fascination at the table, wondering how the chief guest was going to act. Nodding in agreement would hopefully avoid offence. For nearly two weeks I had been an ambassador for the Eifion Trust and inadvertently pinched the credit for the goodwill of Barry and Ann, and the hard work of the Gurkhas, when I had done nothing but turn up and take photos. Still, they wanted me to carry their message of gratitude home.

I met Sanu early in the morning and we left again in a Land Rover for the three-hour drive towards the Dream Village project close to the Tibet border. I could soon see the fragmented foundations of villages scattered up the hillside and a road zig-zagged to the top. Little remained upright except the monastery which bulged outwards as if whacked by a giant mallet. I nervously followed Sanu inside to find shattered glass and shrines. At the top of the hill was a scorched football field with cracks in the dirt where the ground had gaped open. If not for the patter of hammers in the village below, the hillside would have been as silent as nature intended.

'This is my second house!' Sanu laughed. He pointed out the rubble where his old house used to be. We went inside the tin-walled shelter for Dahl Bhat. Sanu polished his shoes for a meeting in Kathmandu the next day; his wife curiously watched the strange English bloke cross-legged on their floor.

Sanu used to be a farmer but had lost his crops too. This elementary way of living was a testament to their fortitude. His wife came to offer more rice. Their willingness to share the little they had was a moral compass we could all aspire towards.

Back in Kathmandu, it was straight to work in an internet café to prepare for a high school talk the following day and the thought terrified me. So it was no wonder the comfort of food started calling me instead. I had segmented these daunting commitments into tick boxes, day by day, knowing the satisfaction I could derive from ticking them off, one by one.

I met Major Lilbahadur Gurung MBE in the morning; a highly revered Gurkha major and a veteran of the 1971 International Everest expedition, which made for interesting conversation. Our next visit had a very special meaning. "Charlotte's Haven on Earth" was an orphanage founded by Lilbahadur and Krishna, funded by Barry and Ann in memory of their daughter Charlotte, an ex-pupil of my high school, Tarporley High.

The children had never met someone from the school thousands of miles across the world that had become part of their second chance at life. They were lined up outside on the courtyard, excited and eager to welcome me into their home like a brother. It was hard to believe the stories of hardship that came from this family unit, as the boys and girls burst happily into dance and songs in each room we entered. I left feeling deeply moved by the experience.

Barry had asked me to speak at Valley Public Secondary School. This was a whole new experience considering I didn't speak a word of Nepalese, but Lilbahadur assured me their quality of English would put many Britons to shame. We were led through a dark corridor and the entrance to a packed assembly hall, ushered in like VIPs as the room fell silent with 300 students turning to stare. We were led to a sofa with flowers. There were three dances and musical ensembles to welcome the special guest – I hadn't registered this was me.

Crunch time came, and it went surprisingly well, besides promptly whacking my head on the low Nepali ceiling to their great amusement. New reserves of confidence came through the crackling microphone. In the question and answer session, one boy posed the question of how many countries I had visited, and which was my favourite. Saying anything besides Nepal would likely have sent books and pencils airborne towards me. I had never expected to be sharing the story to a global audience. I had never expected any of it: and this made the next step exciting.

I was relieved to have fulfilled my duties, and Major Lilbahadur wished me well, with an extended, firm handshake that expressed his gratitude; it meant a lot to be acknowledged by such a man.

I was exhausted, too. There was, however, one final mission to complete.

It was a 4.45am start to catch the flight to Lukla, the infamous mountain airstrip that served as gateway to the Everest trail. Lukla was the homecoming; a comforting landmark as you neared home after a long journey. After sobbing like a toddler in fear on my first flight to the acclaimed "world's most dangerous airport" years earlier, I barely flinched this time. I knew how little we controlled in the grand scheme of things.

We touched down with a deep breath of the invigorating mountain air that welcomed me back to my spiritual home. My lungs were glad for the rest. The barbed snow peaks were tinged orange as the sunrise heaved itself over their walls to burn off the frosty shadows below. It was both déjà vu and a world apart. The trails were the same, but no longer led the path to achieving a goal: only finding the goal. Everything felt familiar, right down to Mum's anxious questions about acclimatisation, having been at the receiving end of my various high-altitude illnesses. Only the popular landmark of "YakDonalds" and the imitation Starbucks Coffee were no longer to be found.

A week didn't give me much time to go far or climb high, and a carefully planned itinerary would make the most of it. Immediately I felt capable and confident, free to go when, where, and how I wanted, safely. The pure air was the first opportunity to truly dig deeper and think. Being here independently seemed perfectly in tune with how it had all started: stripped back to the lone boy heading off into the mountains to discover himself by challenging his challenges outright.

Most trekkers were coming down rather than up. I went at my own speed, as fast as the thinner air would allow; meandering along the teahouses, Mani stones, and rhododendron forests that commanded their own time. Rags of Khata scarves flapped from the suspension bridges spanning dizzying river gorges. The sense of awe in the environment was never lost. I spent the first night at a teahouse in Phakding – rudimentary but comfortable wooden lodges for trekkers – run by the local Sherpa. I tucked into the teahouse staples of garlic soup, and Tuna Momo dumplings, which an expedition teammate had once likened to slugs. It would be interesting to see how I responded to food on a budget, alone, without the excuse of an 8,000-metre peak for bulimia to get excited about. Food became fuel – the surroundings took care of the emotions instead.

December was quiet season and the lodge was empty. There was nobody with whom to play cards or share perspective of the day. My thoughts had nowhere to go. Sadly, the lodge had fallen victim to Wi-Fi. I came across an article online listing the 101 most inspiring UK adventurers, and was slightly miffed to have been completely overlooked. For a moment, it hit where it hurt; a public rejection of what I wanted to be and feel. My usual reactive response would be heading to the cupboards.

Something deeper caught me. I had already concluded that the Sergeant Major voice and my rational voice came from the same place. What was a list worth? It didn't diminish the feedback that people sent me about how I had inspired them. I had compiled my own list of these comments and emails over the years, to read in the moments when I lost meaning, and that list was priceless.

Seeking recognition was usually scorned as a self-fulfilling prophecy, but in the right places, being recognised could reassure us that we had our ladder up the right tree. The need for approval was much deeper and went right back to the school playground, where I lost any reason to accept myself. Completing outdoor challenges made up for this shortfall and opened the window to the warming internal glow of approval. But approval had a hitch – we were forever at the mercy of other people giving us permission to feel good about ourselves. And I knew that approval from others was useless without learning to approve ourselves first. For example, Barry and Ann wanted and claimed no recognition for their efforts here in Nepal, yet were the most generous of the generous. They had created the most incredible legacy, something that I aspired to, myself.

The hill to Namche Bazaar wasn't the unforgiving dusty slog I remembered vividly, now the weight of the task ahead was hoisted from my shoulders. The chocolate cake at Everest Bakery had not lost its touch either. Namche Bazaar was a bowl-shaped village and the closest thing to civilisation after Lukla: a hub of hotels, shops, bakeries, bank, and the cleverly named Hotel HillTen, that made it a popular port of call for trekkers to refresh their palates with pizza and beer. I had almost forgotten the concept of Christmas until the decorated tinsel tree in the window of Café 8848 brought the reminder of going home. I carried on to the next hamlet of Kyangjuma with apprehension. A matter of days before leaving, news broke that my friends Tashi and Lakpa had lost their popular teahouse in a freak fire. They were safe, first and foremost. I had been due to stay with them and couldn't help but think disaster seemed to follow me here.

This was the sort of reactive language that anxiety would use. In the strangest of ways, the timing with my trip gave a platform to share their plight and rally some help, with an envelope of donations from friends, family, and followers back home to help them rebuild their teahouse, home, and livelihood.

There was a lingering whiff of smoke. Lots of people had gathered outside the shell of a smouldering teahouse, with little standing but charred foundations and a couple of wall pillars that stood as a memento. It was a heartbreaking sight. A big clear-up was underway. Ama Dablam Lodge had been built by Lakpa himself decades earlier and was beloved by the passing trekkers who stayed and slept there, like we always had – Tim brought all his expedition teams here in the knowledge they would be looked after like at Grandmas' house. It held a lot of memories for so many people and the Everest trail would never be quite the same without it. Lakpa came over first with his usual bear hug. Tashi barely moved from her chair; the toil apparent on her face as the young kitchen girl rubbed the tension from her neck. Lakpa, a former climbing Sherpa, was more optimistic inspecting the damage. 'Our old one was rubbish anyway,' he said. 'We're going to make the new one much better and make money again!' He cheered stoically, pointing to the new rock he had gathered on the platform below. Tashi was lifted by this promise but kept muttering how amazing her prayer room had been, now reduced to embers. She recalled how 400 people, friends and family, had run from the nearby villages to help as the news spread quicker than the fire, which had taken hold in a chimney. There was of course no fire brigade and the nearest road was days away. They had thrown mud, sand, and buckets of water in vain. I walked around while a team of 30-plus men continued shifting rubble and tarred-rock.

Lakpa called from the bakery: a smaller adjacent building that had miraculously survived. They were serving lunch for the team of hungry labourers in the dining room and Tashi brought a large bowl of pasta and vegetable soup straight over. I felt a little embarrassed having done nothing except turn up on a leisurely trek. Tashi showed the drawing of the new teahouse building she planned. 'Dreaming, dreaming,' she chuckled. Shortly after, a young girl ran into the room.

'Look.' Tashi beamed. It was Jyoti, the seven-year-old girl who my family had sponsored for the last two years. Tashi and Lakpa were well-off by Sherpa standards, and had a persuasive knack of finding sponsors for poorer local families who needed help. The agreed sponsorship paid her lodging to live with family in Khumjung so she could attend school. Jyoti was more interested in her bowl of soup than the strange man sitting next to her. It was enough to finally meet her and feel we had played a small part in giving her the chance that she deserved. 'Thank you,' she chirped sweetly before running off with a Snickers bar.

Tashi had her deep faith restored by the donations and kindness of people around the world. It clearly bothered her to be in this position of needing help herself, when she prided helping others. The support from others had clearly been their pillar of strength among the crumbling pillars of their home and joy. It was a testament to the fact that giving help to others in the trough only came back around when we fell in, but we had to get ourselves to land first.

I already knew the Himalayas could bring devastation and beauty together in the same place. The sunrise view from Ama Dablam Lodge was as transcendent as ever, with the sweet steam of milk tea warming my fingers through the metal cup. Day broke and it was time to pack.

'No, no – you are family, you don't pay,' Tashi insisted, refusing rupees for the hospitality that came intrinsically to the Sherpas and Nepalis. I eventually gave it to Lakpa under the guise of a Christmas present; his arm was easier to pull.

*

After Climb The UK, I had been short-listed for the prestigious *Pride of Britain* award in the category of: Regional Fundraiser of the Year. It was an annual highlight of British TV screens for tickling the heartstrings. I was even more amazed that Mum had kept the secret long enough to lure me into a café where the ITV News reporter pounced to present the award.

Being in that room, let alone a finalist, was the greatest recognition. Prince William walking behind us elicited a double take, and Jeremy Corbyn even quizzed me about the county top of Shropshire. I would never forget meeting Jake Coates, the regional winner from London. He had raised £140,000 for the hospital that treated his wife, Emmy, who sadly lost her battle with terminal cancer. Jake was the most humbling person in the room. He was quick to step over his own achievements to learn about everybody else. His words have never left me. 'It's not about the amount you raise, it's the difference you make.' Later that evening, Jake took the overall award, and every dry eye in the room went with him.

Over the last few weeks I had realised that beautiful truth for myself ...

With each visit to Nepal my heart was pulled further towards causes and pleas for help that far outstripped the resources – problems so big that we might never truly get on top of them. Truly, the sum of money might not have been huge, but the difference it made to the people in Nepal felt massive. I started to feel that my work there was done, and I had fulfilled the promise to myself after the earthquake in 2015, and Camp Two on Cho Oyu.

*

The mud trails, still layered with ice at over 3,000 metres' altitude, were enchanting in the morning dusk. The panoramic view from the famous Tengboche monastery was always the best: it usually offered the first proper glimpse of Everest. Today, it was hidden in the cloud and waiting until the time was right. I chose a busy lodge for lunch in hope of striking up conversation with fellow trekkers. The lack of human interaction had bothered me more than expected as I failed to defy the evolutionary need for socialising. Chatting to others was as uplifting here as chats at home, for allowing us to share our feelings with others in the same position, and conversations were the start of exciting possibilities.

We had all milked the kudos of Everest, but nowadays, I had a knack to get around mentioning it, though it was more difficult when asked what I did for a living. We liked to put labels on things to make sense of them. But I was no climber: that was a title I didn't own. I was a runner because I loved running outright. I didn't come to the mountains for a love of climbing; I came to find answers by climbing mountains.

The trails plunged steeply to the placid farming village of Phortse, where apart from four Japanese trekkers, characteristically cocooned in scarves and slurping soup, the room was even more silent. Life became beautifully simple. I had little to decide besides what to have for dinner and the familiar obsessive planning of routine. It could seem boring without Wi-Fi; we were programmed to share our experiences with others and get our fix of dopamine highs from every "like". It was a startling realisation – just how different these experiences felt without needing approval from Instagram; they were ours to enjoy alone.

There was nobody on the woodland trails, decorated by frozen waterfalls and primitive stupa relics, besides occasional trains of grunting Yaks that moved aside for nobody. It was a happy time to be alive. Machhermo village was covertly tucked inside a valley. The Peaceful Lodge was ironically full of Americans and I found somewhere else to stay, exercising the freedom of choice to socialise when it was needed. The vulnerability of being alone was clear when a sudden throbbing headache and weakness set in. I was concerned, without an expedition leader to reassure me.

Copious amounts of tea didn't do much. The risk of going too high too fast had me worried, despite checking the itinerary with others beforehand. Anxiety was guided by the horror stories of deteriorating in the night with altitude sickness. It was a sleepless and restless night, not helped by the sound of a scuttling rat that had me launching my bag across the room towards it and retreating every inch of exposed skin inside the sleeping bag.

With early altitude sickness it was too risky to visit another friend, Tenzing, in the next village of Gokyo at 4,750 metres. I hated letting him down. Climb The UK raised the mirror and urged me onwards. I knew when to listen: two weeks of project visits had taken it out of me more than an expedition, emotionally and physically. I had seen nearly everyone that had been realistically possible, and cramming anything else in would have achieved nothing useful.

I was forever battling the expectation of more, driven by the vision of how quickly life flashed by; forever trying to get ahead of something over which I had no control. Racing through life missed out on all the fun. Nobody could expect to keep pushing the barrier every time just because we could: that inner reserve was best saved for special occasions.

My body had already proved that it wasn't much good in the high mountains, but it had done a fine job of the highest counties. Resolved by common sense, I dropped down to the lower altitude of Dole village with the dome of Cho Oyu knocking this dilemma out of proportion behind me. I guess it meant I would have to come back one day. The skyline inspired more questions: Who am I? What's my main effort? What drives me?

Killing time was wonderfully productive as I climbed to a high ridge above the village to catch the Himalayas falling to sleep. I longed to bring others here to share the same vista and get assurance that it was real. On the other hand, maybe it was something to cherish in my own meaning and leave imagination unbounded. Every corner brought another photo opportunity.

At this rate it would be dark before arriving in Namche Bazaar. At least I had a DSLR camera to do them justice, having carried the regret of missed opportunities during Climb The UK, for the sake of sparing the few grams of a real camera. Learning from these gripes was often the only way to put them right in our minds. Tashi was pleased to see me again on the descent. I had barely settled before a cheese toastie arrived from their makeshift kitchen, like the apple pie that arrived as we had come down from Everest after the earthquake; despite the cracks in the walls that sent them sleeping outside in fear of after-shocks. This was one place I could count family, and that was something else Tim hadn't included in the price of our last expeditions.

They had lost so much in material goods but had hope, resilience, and support to get by for the next few months; they would be alright. I hurried after her cousin, a young guide, who led the way back to Khumjung at Sherpa-speed, and showed me the lodge where Jyoti lived. She was playing outside and watched us arrive, pressing her hands with a squeak of 'Namaste'. I waved goodbye and strolled up the high street of stone steps along lines of sacred Mani walls and the bizarre sight of streetlights behind. Khumjung was the Sherpa capital, and home to the purported "Yeti scalp" that had conned tourists in a place so extraordinary that anything could pass as believable. A ghostly fog tickled the guarding hills and distant ridgelines of silhouetted trees. I turned the corner as the trail clutched the steep lips of the valley, filled with a celestial cloud inversion; seducing me to swim across to enlightenment.

A Japanese trekker jumped excitedly as I appeared around the next corner; this lone contemplative trekker had inadvertently framed the landscape perfectly, before I stepped into shot. He giggled, and shook my hand, then set about snapping away again. I gave him my business card to email the photo in return.

The broad earthy plateau dropped off into the sky as the hill-top neared; a pinnacle of its own kingdom, amid the silhouette of smoky ridgelines in the distance, detached from earth below. Ambient winds broke the silence of nobody else around. The plateau was humbled by the grandeur of its surroundings, radiant orange in the smouldering dusk. I was in heaven.

To the north-east, Everest and Lhotse were suddenly unveiled from the white flag of the jet stream. I stood below, gazing at the frosted white lines and formidable faces of the peak with appreciation. Looking and dreaming was the start: doing was better. I was safe in the knowledge of taking that first step up the mountain already, and proving to myself that, eventually, I could achieve whatever I set my mind on. There was no excitement in reaching a certain outcome. There was nothing left to prove. In time, I had graduated from the actor playing out a script of my life, to the author; writing the next chapter. We could paint the picture how we liked. My eyes followed the ridge lines from the numb toes of contemplation, over the walls of uncertainty and frozen rocks of disappointment, to reach the pinnacle of glory.

At the top, my eyes could only go one way: down the other side into the trough of the valley, where the next climb began. The mountains clearly knew a thing or two about the peaks and troughs of life. The biggest risk was staying somewhere between for too long, in order to live longer as less than what we were capable of being. We couldn't change our challenges without replacing them with something on a higher level. Everest was only one summit on the journey of life, and the trick was leaving something bigger behind.

With my head above the clouds, everything became beautifully clear. This was my epiphany. It had been two and a half years since seeing her this close, and standing at the foot of her peak, moving through dark clouds to find hope in higher places. Truth is, I had never truly left.

ACKNOWLEDGEMENTS

Thanks to the team at Trigger Publishing for the opportunity to share my story and wholeheartedly believing in me from start to finish. Their dedication to mental wellbeing has ensured the story reaches those who need it most, while understanding my own mental wellbeing as an author too. I'm indebted to Nick Walters at David Luxton Associates for guiding me through the process, and Jonathan Legard for the introduction.

An important thanks goes to Elise Downing for the spark of inspiration behind Climb The UK, championing adventures on our home soil, and very kindly providing the foreword for *Another Peak*.

Whether on the world's highest peak or travelling the breadth of the UK, we need a solid base camp to celebrate the peaks and get a leg up during the troughs. They say we're the average of the closest people around us, and I must have chosen well.

The first thanks must go to my mum, Debbie, for being the resilient rock in my life who has selflessly supported my ultimately selfish pursuits that inflicted enough anxiety to open a cattery – maybe one day you really will break my legs (but that would only stop me for a few months). Thank you for letting me forge my own path in the world, teaching me to stand up for what's right, and giving me the best in life.

My dad, Pete, was my earliest role model in life. Thanks for encouraging me to achieve my best in everything that I do and supporting me to become the person I wanted to be. From the early days of fishing and mountain biking around the local forest, I owe him for passing on a curiosity towards life and adventure. The ability to fix my own bike is unfortunately yet to materialise, but at least the Staniforth marathon record time is safely mine.

My grandmas, Norma and Betty, gave me a colourful childhood of love and reassurance, and typically spoilt me rotten – thank you for so many happy memories, and my wider family and cousins, too.

Thanks also to my step-parents, Chris and Debbie, for being a pillar of strength to hold the fort for my parents when I was away on challenges.

It's dangerous territory to begin listing names when I'm lucky to count on such a wide support circle, but I want to make a special thanks to the following people:

A big thanks to Steve Fives for wearing the hat of mentor, sponsor and foremost of a friend through the peaks and the troughs to realise my potential. Thanks also to Jenny Fives for mirroring that support and warmly welcoming me into your family. An extended thanks to Simon Whittle, Claire McKinley-Smith and The Westgrove Group colleagues for their commitment through the journey as their brand ambassador, which has always been about more than just the summit.

Chris Spray was my first mentor and coach who challenged the barriers my childhood had put before my dreams and stretched me with the right questions to put the steps into action. I can't thank you enough for your relentless belief in me and using your talent to help others excel.

I'm also indebted to Brigadier John Thomson OBE QVRM TD MSC RCDS for continually giving his expertise and coaching to guide me through the transitions of the journey and stay aligned with my "main effort". I wish every young person could receive such a wealth of life experience and I can only promise to pass these lessons forward at any opportunity.

Thanks to Hems de Winter for his mentoring sessions that helped me pursue the all-important "why" to feel how I want to feel at the end of each day.

Richard Ellis has been a confidant and the company, morale support, photography, and suitable piss-taking during my challenges was often the difference between pushing on and calling it quits. Thanks for offering an honest ear to express myself (whinge) behind the scenes.

Even disasters bring blessings and it was Everest 2015 that led to meeting Mike Henshall. Thanks for being a great friend, sounding board, and spreading so much positivity in the world – and to Sonia and Dan for joining him. I look forward to future roast dinners to see what we come up with next.

Ste Rumbelow has been another close confidant I can count on for anything, and has provided the logic, confidence, and common sense behind many of my biggest decisions.

Friends are there when you need them – even when you can't see them – so I want to say hi to Paul Arnold, Rich Whitehouse, Andy Bell, Barbara Wilkie, Adam Rixon, Chris Pownell, Tom Pearson and Adam Rixon for finding the funny side when life gets too serious.

It's not "what you know but who you know" so I'd like to thank Lord Lieutenant David Briggs, Jim Clarke at the Apprentice Academy, Sarah Perris, Barry Heald, Mike Punter, Mark Powell, Diana Heywood, Rachel Llavin and Jane Harrad-Roberts.

Thanks to Rob Casserley, Marie-Kristelle Ross, Rolfe Oostra at 360 Expeditions, Henry Todd and Dan Wallace for an unforgettable adventure on Cho Oyu. And, of course, our superhuman Sherpa team; a great inspiration to us all.

Charity fundraising is never easy, and support from companies was instrumental in reaching the fundraising target during Climb

The UK. I'm massively grateful to the following businesses and individuals for their donations and sponsoring county tops in aid of Young Minds:

- Czarnikow Group – Greater London and City of London
- Mark Brocklehurst at Sharples Group – Lancashire
- Yorkshire Bank – North, West, South and East Riding of Yorkshire
- The Rotary Club of Bentley Cheshire – Cheshire
- Michael Constantine Wealth Management – Derbyshire
- Stu and Tracey at Breese Adventures – Denbighshire
- Jane Hart and Ruth Moran at Nudge Your People – Surrey
- Jacha Potgeiter at the Alpine Coffee Shop, Betws-y-Coed
- Carl Rogers and Tony Bowerman at Northern Eye Books

Thanks to Ellis Brigham Mountain Sports, Mountain Fuel Sports Nutrition (and whoever created Scottish Tablet) for fuelling my journey, Inov-8 and Marmot Europe for providing my footwear and clothing, and Bullitt Group for the rugged CAT S60 smartphone which was massively appreciated.

It's a privilege to be an ambassador for YHA England and Wales to help transform young lives through real adventure, and their support in providing hostel accommodation during Climb The UK and my training has been invaluable. Thanks also to Hostelling Scotland and Hostelling International Northern Ireland for providing accommodation with an equally warm welcome.

A special mention to Alastair Lawrie for his help providing a Genesis Tour De Fer bike for Climb The UK – it was the perfect machine for the job.

Thanks to Oli Reed and ViewRanger for quite literally putting Climb The UK on the map with a navigation system where even I failed to get spectacularly lost. Mike's quick solutions and saintly patience were especially appreciated.

Managing the media interest for a bloke on a bike racing through four countries with sporadic phone signal and two headline news events was never going to be easy – so a big thanks to Mick Ord for getting the Climb The UK message far and wide. And thanks to Jonathan Davies for capturing the "money shot" on Moel Famau and photos that will be treasured forever.

A big shout to Tackt-Isle Adventures who made the idea of kayaking to the Isle of Wight achievable with true outdoor grit. And thanks to Andy Porter, Sarah Swanston, and Jordi at Veracity Digital for donating their services to tell the story, despite the blockbuster taking a very different twist!

Thanks to Barry and Ann Evans for their support and facilitating the opportunity to visit Nepal in 2017 on behalf of the Eifion Trust and Willington Evans Foundation. Thanks for all that you do in aid of a place so close to my heart. I'm incredibly grateful to everyone who supported the Walk For Nepal events, and the PHASE Worldwide team for ensuring its success – I'm very proud to be an ambassador for the charity to empower people in rural Nepal.

It was thanks to the bravery of Tom Fairbrother publicly sharing his own battles with eating disorders as an athlete that put the pieces of the jigsaw together. His openness inspired the courage to share my story in hope of inspiring others. By empowering others, we empower ourselves too.

The greatest success of Climb The UK was sharing the journey with so many people. The generosity, kindness, and hospitality received was a humbling reminder of everything positive in society that made me proud to be British.

This list is by no means exhaustive but I couldn't forget the everyday heroes who joined me, challenged themselves, and offered hospitality along the way:

- David Henderson, Chris Welton, Amy Morley, Michael Constantine and Elaine Retallic
- Steph Jones, Fiona and Mandy Callaghan-Staples (and the famous Audrey!)

- Rupert Bonington and James Appleton
- Jim Davies Physiotherapy
- David and Sonya Coulter for a warm welcome to Northern Ireland (and the custard creams)
- Ian Ellis
- Louise Mclelland (and Pollaidh)
- Robin Scott
- Hannah Jones – the flapjack stalker!
- Fraser Brown
- Rose Marie Armour
- Ron, Ros and Jenny Anderson
- Nick and Marie Cragg
- Ellis Stewart
- Ste Rumbelow and family
- Dr Ash Routen
- Kirsty Hardman and the Alderman Peel High School students on Beacon Hill
- Rob Mack at Young Minds UK
- Kim Wilton-Woodhouse
- Dan and Rachel Pidcock
- Holly Worthington, Dan Turbutt, Leah Western and Will Robinson
- Roger Fidler and Ruth
- The Black Down team – Becca Humphreys, Annick Hollins, Jenna Hollins, Karinna Hollins, Dave Bateman, Clair Wadey, Andy Wareham, Tom Brampton and Lorraine Herring
- Rebecca Stephens and Jovan
- Andy Munnings and all at Townhill Junior School, Southampton
- Simon Lewis at SVL Adventures
- Sophie Wade-Smith and all at Gurnard Primary School
- Gerry Proctor for arranging the talk at De La Salle Academy
- Richard and Katharine Mostyn (and their wedding guests)
- Ben James, Tom Ferguson, Daniel Jones, Toby Treacher and Antoinette Costin in Cornwall

- Oli Broadhead and family for welcoming me to the Cornwall coast
- Andy Smith
- Sarah Galvin
- Christina See
- Tony Payne
- Nick and Helen Oakes, and Kiri Stone
- Tony Worth
- Bruce Stokes
- Laurie Barton-Wright
- Jeff and Chloe Smith
- Phil Mostyn
- Bill Tinsley
- Mick Walker
- Phil Tomlinson, Tony Page and Mick

And everyone who made the finale on Moel Famau exactly how I'd imagined, including, but not limited to: Lucy Meacock from ITV Granada Reports, Rick Parry, Dale and Jayne Mullane, Jessica Wren, Chris Barber, Mike Shaw, John and Alison Thomson, Jordi Vidal Oliveras and Anna Kozdyrk, Ron and Sandra Rawlinson, Andy Carter, Dan Hadley and the Westgrove Group colleagues.

The team at Young Minds UK deserve a special thanks for the work they do for the mental wellbeing of children and young people; their faith and support during the challenges was hugely appreciated too. I'm proud to support your work, if only in a small way, so that every young person gets the best possible support to overcome their mental health challenges. Keep fighting.

A final but far-reaching thanks to everyone who donated to the fundraising target, followed on social media, and sent encouragement during the Climb The UK challenge. There are far too many to realistically include all, but every donation, comment, and interaction gave me a reason to spin, made a difference to the lives of young people, and reminded me why I'd started. Hopefully our paths will cross one day and I can hear about your challenges, too.

If you found this book interesting ... why not read these next?

Man Up Man Down

Standing up to Suicide

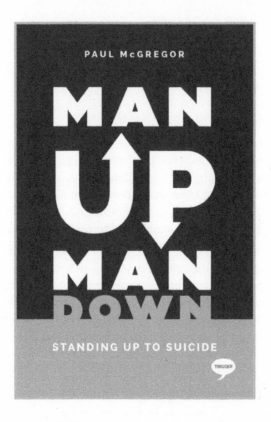

When his dad died suddenly by suicide, Paul was devastated. Now he's on a mission to change how we think about men's mental health and what it really means to "man up".

Must Try Harder

Adventures In Anxiety

After 30 years hiding in the shadows, beset by extreme social anxiety, Paula McGuire decided to change her worldview – one terrifying and exhilarating challenge at a time. In this book, Paula shares her extraordinary journey from recluse to adventurer.

Within The White Lines

How the Beautiful Game Saved My Life

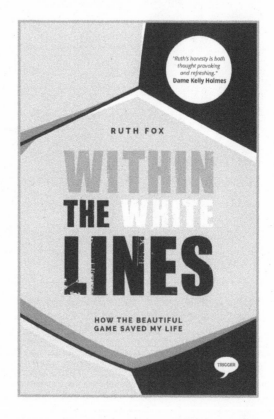

When she was 14, Ruth's perfect life began to crack. Now a campaigner for mental health awareness, she explains how football helped pull her back from the brink of suicide.